Church Leadership

Church Leadership

by
John MacArthur, Jr.

"GRACE TO YOU"
P.O. Box 4000
Panorama City, CA   91412

© 1989 by
JOHN F. MACARTHUR, JR.

All Scripture quotations, unless noted otherwise, are from the *New Scofield Reference Bible*, King James Version. Copyright © 1967 by Oxford University Press, Inc. Reprinted by permission.

ISBN: 0-8024-5384-8

1 2 3 4 5 6 Printing/LC/Year 93 92 91 90 89

Printed in the United States of America

Contents

These Bible studies are taken from messages delivered by Pastor-Teacher John MacArthur, Jr., at Grace Community Church in Panorama City, California. These messages have been combined into a 9-tape album entitled *Church Leadership*. You may purchase this series either in an attractive vinyl cassette album or as individual cassettes. To purchase these tapes, request the album *Church Leadership*, or ask for the tapes by their individual GC numbers. Please consult the current price list; then, send your order, making your check payable to:

The Master's Communication
P.O. Box 4000
Panorama City, CA 91412

Or call the following toll-free number:
1-800-55-GRACE

1
The Call to Lead the Church—Elders
Part 1

Outline

Introduction
A. The Excellence of Previous Leaders at Ephesus
B. The Problems with Current Leaders at Ephesus
   1. Some weren't qualified
   2. Some departed from God's Word
   3. Some were women
   4. Some were apostates
   5. Some weren't dealing with elders correctly

Lesson
I. An Important Calling (v. 1*a*)
   A. The Formula
   B. The Creeds
   C. The Contrast
      1. A sacred task
      2. A difficult task
      3. A strategic task
II. A Limited Calling (v. 1*b*)
   A. The Masculine Gender in the Text
   B. The Woman's Role in the Church
      1. Her limitations
      2. Her contributions
III. A Compelling Calling (v. 1*c*)
   A. Defined
   B. Described
      1. A godly passion
      2. A godly perspective

IV. A Responsible Calling (1d)
   A. Defined
   B. Delineated
      1. Leading the church (1 Tim. 5:17)
      2. Teaching the church (1 Tim. 5:17)
      3. Praying for the church (James 5:14)
      4. Caring for the church (1 Pet. 5:2)
      5. Setting church policy (Acts 15:6-29)
      6. Ordaining elders (1 Tim. 4:14)
 V. A Worthy Calling (v. 1e)
VI. A Demanding Calling (v. 1f)

Introduction

The character and effectiveness of any church is directly related to the quality of its leadership. That's why the Bible stresses the importance of qualified church leadership and delineates specific standards for evaluating those who would serve in a sacred position. Failure to adhere to biblical standards has caused many of the problems churches throughout the world currently face.

Lack of qualified leadership was the problem Timothy faced in Ephesus, so Paul gave him a detailed explanation of the prerequisites for elders (1 Tim. 3:1-7).

   A. The Excellence of Previous Leaders at Ephesus

   The Ephesian Christians were well acquainted with excellent leaders. Several years prior to writing 1 Timothy, Paul had started the church at Ephesus and had spent three years there training a group of godly men to serve as elders (Acts 18:19; 20:17, 31). Those men developed such a deep love for Paul that they openly displayed their affection and sadness when he told them they would not see him again (Acts 20:37-38). At that time the Ephesian church was a strategic church with solid leadership.

   B. The Problems with Current Leaders at Ephesus

   The last thing Paul said to the Ephesian elders was, "I know this, that after my departing shall grievous wolves enter in among you, not sparing the flock. Also of your own selves shall men arise, speaking perverse things, to draw away disciples after them" (Acts 20:29-30). Paul knew Satan would attack the church by sending false leaders to teach lies and heresies, and that is exactly what happened. Upon returning to Ephesus after his first Roman imprisonment, Paul decided to leave Timothy there to resolve the situation while he traveled on to Macedonia. He was not gone long before he wrote to Timothy with instructions regarding several issues in the Ephesian church.

1. Some weren't qualified

Unqualified leadership was the major issue confronting the Ephesian church. Apparently each of the qualifications Paul mentions in 1 Timothy 3:2-7 is in direct contrast to what that church was tolerating in their leadership. For example, in verses 2-3 he says that an elder must be "blameless, the husband of one wife, temperate, sober-minded, of good behavior, given to hospitality, apt to teach; not given to wine, not violent, not greedy of filthy lucre, but patient, not a brawler, not covetous." The implication is that some of the leaders at Ephesus lacked these Christian character traits.

2. Some departed from God's Word

Some of the leaders had departed from God's Word, and when that occurred, God's standards for leadership were set aside as well.

Paul said to Timothy, "I besought thee to abide still at Ephesus, when I went into Macedonia, that thou mightest charge some that they teach no other doctrine, neither give heed to fables and endless genealogies, which minister questions rather than godly edifying which is in faith. . . . From which some, having swerved, have turned aside unto vain jangling, desiring to be teachers of the law, understanding neither what they say, nor that about which they affirm" (1 Tim. 1:3-4, 6-7). Apparently some of the leaders were teaching false doctrines and had no understanding of the Old Testament law or the New Testament gospel (vv. 8-11).

First Timothy 6:3-5 says, "If any man teach otherwise, and consent not to wholesome words, even the words of our Lord Jesus Christ, and to the doctrine which is according to godliness, he is proud, knowing nothing, but doting about questions and disputes of words, of which cometh envy, strife, railings, evil suspicions, perverse disputings of men of corrupt minds, and destitute of the truth, supposing that gain is godliness." Their message and motives were perverse. They had "erred concerning the faith" (v. 21).

3. Some were women

Apparently some women had usurped the role of leadership in the church. In response Paul said, "I permit not a woman to teach, nor to usurp authority over the man, but to be in silence" (1 Tim. 2:12).

4. Some were apostates

First Timothy 4:1-3 says, "The Spirit speaketh expressly that, in the latter times, some shall depart from the faith, giving heed to seducing spirits, and doctrines of demons, speaking lies in hypocrisy, having their conscience seared with a hot iron, forbidding to marry, and commanding to abstain from foods, which God hath created to be received with thanksgiving by them who believe and know the truth." In contrast Paul said to Timothy, "[Be] nourished up in the words of faith and of good doctrine, unto which thou hast attained. But refuse profane and old wives' fables, and exercise thyself rather unto godliness. . . . Take heed unto thyself and unto the doctrine; continue in them" (vv. 6-7, 16a).

5. Some weren't dealing with elders correctly

First Timothy 5:19-20 says, "Against an elder receive not an accusation, but before two or three witnesses. Them that sin rebuke before all, that others also may fear." Apparently some of the elders were in need of public rebuke because of their sinfulness.

As a safeguard Paul warned Timothy not to ordain a man to the ministry too quickly. He was to be cautious about whom he placed into leadership (v. 22).

All the problems in the Ephesian church were related to the main issue of its spiritual leadership, so it was essential for Paul to give Timothy instruction and encouragement for dealing with the need for qualified leaders forthrightly.

Paul instructed Titus, a contemporary of Timothy ministering on the isle of Crete, to "ordain elders in every city" (Titus 1:5). That was necessary because the Cretian churches didn't have any elders at the time. But that was not the case at Ephesus. By the time Timothy began his Ephesian ministry, elders had been ministering there for several years (Acts 20:17, 31). Timothy's task was to insure that those elders met God's standards (1 Tim. 3:2-7).

The Importance of Godly Leadership

A church is only as godly as its leaders. A pastor once said to me, "I think I've discovered why my church is not as effective as I want it to be: half of the men on my elder board are unsaved!" That may seem like an extreme example, but many churches fail to uphold the biblical standard for spiritual leadership. Such failures always impact the quality and integrity of a church's ministry.

Quite often a church that is failing to impact the world or that is experiencing strife and conflict among its membership looks to new programming or other peripheral areas for answers, when the real problem may be that its leaders are spiritually unqualified for the task. That's the first place to check.

In his description of the qualifications for elders, Paul focused on the character rather than the function of an elder. A man is qualified because of what he is, not because of what he does. If he commits sin, he is subject to discipline in the presence of the whole congregation (1 Tim. 5:20). The church must carefully guard that sacred office.

Are You Called to the Ministry?

How do you know if you're called to the ministry? In the Old Testament God spoke out of heaven or sent angels to deliver His call, and in the New Testament the call often came directly from Jesus Christ. Today it is different. I believe that the call to the ministry now comes by the Holy Spirit's compelling a man's heart. Paul said, "This is a true saying, If a man *desire* the office of a bishop, he *desireth* a good work" (1 Tim. 3:1, emphasis added). If you sense a strong desire to participate full-time or extensively in ministry, that may be God's call to serve Him in that capacity.

Another key element of God's call is qualification. All who desire spiritual leadership must also meet the stipulations listed in 1 Timothy 3:2-7.

Lesson

In 1 Timothy 3:1 Paul delineates six facets of the call to spiritual leadership.

I. AN IMPORTANT CALLING (v. 1*a*)

"This is a true saying."

A. The Formula

Paul used the formula *This is a true saying* five times in his writings: 1 Timothy 1:15; 3:1; 4:9; 2 Timothy 2:11; and Titus 3:8. The formula indicates that the point being made is an axiomatic, believable, or obvious fact, and in each case it introduces something of great importance.

B. The Creeds

The formula is used only in the pastoral epistles, which means it didn't come into use until late in the ministry of Paul, after the churches had been well established.

It is apparent from its usage that the expression was a common way in the early church to introduce a very important fact or creed. For example in 1 Timothy 1:15 Paul says,

"This is a faithful saying, and worthy of all acceptance, that Christ Jesus came into the world to save sinners." That is the foundational truth of Christianity.

C. The Contrast

1. A sacred task

In 1 Timothy 3:1 Paul uses the formula to introduce the call to be an elder. The contrast between the work of Christ (1:15) and the work of leading the church (3:1) points out the importance that Paul and the early church placed on church leadership. It is a lofty and honorable calling—a sacred task.

2. A difficult task

Even though church leadership is a sacred task, some people enter the ministry with impure motives, such as a desire for money, job security, or prestige. There were a few people like that in the early church (1 Tim. 6:5; 1 Pet. 5:2-3), but I believe that the especially difficult nature of the ministry at that time discouraged many from assuming leadership for the wrong reasons. In those early years the church experienced much persecution. Its leaders were more apt to face great dangers and difficulties than they were to gain prominence or prestige.

The difficulty and sanctity of the ministry is probably what motivated the early church to develop the creed, "This is a true saying, If a man desire the office of a bishop, he desireth a good work" (1 Tim. 3:1). It exalts the role and encourages men who are called to it to think seriously about the ministry as a life career.

3. A strategic task

Church leaders have always been in strategic positions. That's why it is so important that they be called by God and qualified to serve.

Beginning in Acts 14 we see the rising profile of elders in the New Testament church.

a) Acts 14:23

On their first missionary journey, Paul and Barnabas appointed elders in every church.

An elder is a spiritually mature man who leads and teaches the church. Such a man is also referred to as a pastor, overseer, presbyter, shepherd, and bishop. "Elder" refers to the spiritual maturity of the individual; "bishop" and "overseer" refer to his leadership responsibility; and "shepherd" and "pastor" refer to his responsibility to nurture the flock. Each term describes a different facet of the same office (cf. Acts 20:28; Titus 1:5; 1 Pet. 5:1-2).

b) Acts 15:2, 4, 6, 22-23

These references illustrate the prominent role of the elders at the Jerusalem Council.

c) Acts 20:17-38

Paul admonished the Ephesian elders to guard their sacred responsibilities very carefully.

d) Philippians 1:1

Paul addressed his Philippian epistle to the overseers and deacons of the church at Philippi.

e) 1 Thessalonians 5:12-13

The Thessalonian elders had charge over the church and diligently labored on its behalf. Consequently, the believers there were to love and highly esteem their elders for their work.

f) Hebrews 13:17

Elders are held accountable to the Lord for their guardianship of the people entrusted to them, so the people were admonished to obey their leaders.

g) 1 Peter 5:1-4

Peter instructed the elders to shepherd the flock by providing a godly example and by exercising proper motives.

h) 1 Timothy 3:2-7; Titus 1:6-9

In these passages Paul listed the qualifications for elders.

The ministry is a worthy and important calling, and the sacred task of an elder requires that he be spiritually qualified.

II. A LIMITED CALLING (v. 1*b*)

"If a man."

The office of an elder is limited to men. That conclusion is supported by Paul's use of the masculine gender in this context and his instruction on the woman's role in the church.

A. The Masculine Gender in the Text

The pronoun translated "a man" (Gk., *tis*; lit. "anyone") is in the masculine form, thereby indicating that men are the subject here. In addition, each of the descriptive qualifications listed in verses 2-6 is in the masculine form, and thus refers to men. Furthermore, it is impossible for a woman to be "the husband of one wife" (v. 2). It's obvious that this calling is limited to men.

B. The Woman's Role in the Church

1. Her limitations

In 1 Timothy 2:11-14 Paul says, "Let the woman learn in silence with all subjection. But I permit not a woman to teach, nor to usurp authority over the man, but to be in silence. For Adam was first formed, then Eve. And Adam was not deceived, but the woman, being deceived, was in the transgression." A woman is not to teach men in church. Since elders are the teachers in the church, women are not allowed to be elders. Men and

15

women have equal spiritual privileges, capacities, blessings, and promises; but their roles within the church differ. God has ordained the principles of authority and submission to function within the church just as He has within society.

2. Her contributions

A woman has the wonderful privilege of teaching other women and children. She can also exercise her spiritual gifts through evangelism, counseling, helps, and other crucial ministries. But preaching in the church is reserved for men.

The balance comes in 1 Timothy 2:15, where Paul says, "[Women] shall be saved in childbearing, if they continue in faith and love and holiness with sobriety." For most women, their greatest impact on society is through raising godly children. If a women is godly and if God chooses to give her children whom she raises in the nurture and admonition of the Lord, she will have a profound influence on a new generation. Men may have the outward, overt leadership, but women may have just as great an influence indirectly.

III. A COMPELLING CALLING (v. 1c)

"Desire [Gk., *oregō*] . . . desireth [Gk., *epithumeō*]."

A. Defined

Oregō (lit. "to reach out," "stretch," or "grasp") refers to external movement. We can see that in the pursuit of the ministry by external means such as discipleship and schooling. *Epithumeō* (lit. "a passionate compulsion") refers to an internal drive or desire.

B. Described

1. A godly passion

A man who is called to the ministry has an internal desire so strong that it motivates him toward external pursuit of that goal. His desire to minister is so strong that

16

he doesn't have any other option—ministry is his consuming passion, and he pursues preparation and qualification for that task.

The man whom God calls does not have a passion for position or rank, but for the work of the ministry itself. Commentator Patrick Fairbairn said, "The seeking here intended . . . must be of the proper kind, not the prompting of a carnal ambition, but the aspiration of a heart which has itself experienced the grace of God, and which longs to see others coming to participate in the heavenly gift" (*Pastoral Epistles* [Minneapolis: James & Klock, 1976], p. 136). Some men seek the pastorate for financial gain (1 Pet. 5:2); others, like Diotrephes, love "to have the pre-eminence" (3 John 9). But those who are truly called have a God-given compulsion to serve the Lord. That compulsion may be stronger in some than others, but it is always present to some degree.

Biographer C. W. Hall quoted Salvation Army Commissioner Samuel Logan Brengle as saying, "The final estimate of men shows that history cares not for the rank or title a man has borne, or the office he has held, but only the quality of his deeds and the character of his mind and heart" (*Samuel Logan Brengle* [New York: The Salvation Army, 1933], p. 274). If a man has ambition for position or rank only, he is likely to be corrupted in his pursuits, but if he desires to serve God, that desire tends to purify his actions and guard his motives. Paul said, "Though I preach the gospel, I have nothing to glory of; for necessity is laid upon me; yea, woe is unto me, if I preach not the gospel!" (1 Cor. 9:16). Paul was a driven man: he was compelled to preach the gospel.

A Lesson from the Devil

Hugh Latimer, a popular preacher of the sixteenth century English Reformation who was martyred for his faith, couldn't restrain himself from preaching. The eternal plight of men and women and the emptiness of the clergy of his day compelled him to speak out.

His "Sermon of the Plow" was directed at preachers who lacked passion and used their pastoral office for promoting themselves rather than proclaiming God's truth. In it he said, "I would ask a strange question: who is the most [diligent] bishop and prelate in all England, that passeth all the rest in doing his office? I can tell, for I . . . know him well. But now I think I see you listening and hearkening that I should name him. . . . I will tell you: it is the devil.

"He is the most diligent preacher of all other; he is never out of his [diocese]; he is never from his [curate]; ye shall never find him unoccupied. . . . The diligentest preacher in all the realm; he is ever at his plough: no lording nor loitering can hinder him; he is ever applying his business, ye shall never find him idle, I warrant you. . . .

"Where the devil is resident, and hath his plough going, there away with books, and up with candles; away with bibles, and up with beads; away with the light of the gospel, and up with the light of candles, yea, at noon-days. . . . Up with man's traditions and his laws, down with God's traditions and his most holy word. . . .

"Oh that our prelates would be as diligent to sow the corn of good doctrine, as Satan is to sow cockle and darnel! . . . There was never such a preacher in England as he is. . . .

"The prelates . . . are lords, and no labourers: but the devil is diligent at his plough. He is no unpreaching prelate: he is no lordly loiterer from his [curate], but a busy ploughman. . . . Therefore, ye unpreaching prelates, learn of the devil: to be diligent in doing of your office, learn of the devil: and if you will not learn of God, nor good men, for shame learn of the devil" (*Sermons by Hugh Latimer*, edited by George Elwes Corrie [Cambridge: University Press, 1844], pp. 70-77).

Latimer was calling for passion in the ministry. The church needs leaders who are compelled to minister out of love for God's Word and a passion for lost souls. Do you have that kind of passion?

2. A godly perspective

A spiritual leader must have a heart for that which matters most to God.

a) 1 Samuel 13:14—Samuel told Saul, "The Lord hath sought him a man after his own heart." God wants men with submissive, obedient hearts.

b) Ezekiel 22:30—God said, "I sought for a man among them, that should make up the hedge, and stand in the gap before me for the land." God wants men who will represent Him—who will share His interests and passions.

God calls to the ministry the kind of person only He can produce. Bible schools and seminaries can help equip a man for ministry; church boards and pulpit committees can extend opportunities for him to serve; but only God can call a man and make him fit for the ministry.

The call to the ministry is not a matter of analyzing your talents and then selecting the best career option, or taking some kind of personality profile. It's a Spirit-generated compulsion to be a man of God and serve Him in the church.

Pastor J. Oswald Sanders wrote, "The real qualities of leadership are to be found in those who are willing to suffer for the sake of objectives great enough to demand their wholehearted obedience" (*Spiritual Leadership* [Chicago: Moody, 1967, 1980], p. 20).

Samuel Logan Brengle challenged the people of his day who wanted to go into ministry by outlining the road to spiritual leadership: "It is not won by promotion, but by many prayers and tears. It is attained by confessions of sin, and much heart-searching and humbling before God; by self-surrender, a courageous sacrifice of every idol, a bold, deathless, uncompromising and uncomplaining embracing of the cross, and by an eternal, unfaltering looking unto Jesus crucified.

"It is not gained by seeking great things for ourselves, but rather, like Paul, by counting those things that are gained to us as loss for Christ. That is a great price, but it must be unflinchingly paid by him who would be not merely a nominal but a real spiritual leader of men, a leader whose power is recognized and felt in heaven, on earth and in hell" (*The Soul-Winner's Secret*: [London: The Salvation Army, 1918], p. 22).

Sanders added, "That is the type of man God is searching for and on whose behalf he desires to show himself strong (2 Chron. 16:9)" (*Spiritual Leadership*, p. 20).

IV. A RESPONSIBLE CALLING (1d)

"The office of a bishop [Gk., *episkopos*]."

Oversight of the church is an enormous responsibility.

A. Defined

"Bishop" is an unfortunate translation of *episkopos* because it carries modern ecclesiastical implications that are not consistent with its biblical meaning. I prefer the translation "overseer" because it more accurately reflects the idea of a leader or ruler.

In the Greek culture an *episkopos* was a city administrator or finance manager. Some scholars believe that the New Testament usage of *episkopos* is based on that usage. But also there was a monastic group of Jews known as the Essenes or Qumran community who lived at that time near the Dead Sea. The men who preached, taught, and exercised care and authority were called *episkopoi*.

It is likely that the biblical meaning of *episkopos* got its definition from the Qumran community rather than the Greek culture, for in that community the word reflected a wide range of spiritual responsibilities, whereas in the Greek culture its definition was limited to a narrow administrative role (L. Coenen, "*Episkopos*," *The New International Dictionary of New Testament Theology*, ed. Colin Brown [Grand Rapids: Zondervan, 1979], I:189-90).

The biblical overseer had the responsibility of leading, instructing, and shepherding the people. He also received contributions from the people, heard and verified accusations against believers, and administered church discipline where appropriate.

Each pastor and elder still has those responsibilities, and he is directly accountable to God for the quality of his leadership (Heb. 13:17). James 3:1 says it well: "Let not many of you become teachers . . . knowing that as such we shall incur a stricter judgment" (NASB*).

B. Delineated

An elder's responsibilities are multifaceted.

1. Leading the church (1 Tim. 5:17)

   The Greek word translated "rule" (*proistēmi*) in this verse means "to be ranked first" or "to stand first." Christ gives elders the authority to rule on His behalf using His Word. The church is not to be ruled by its congregation, but by those whom God calls for that task.

2. Teaching the church (1 Tim. 5:17)

   Elders are to preach and teach—"labor in the word and doctrine."

3. Praying for the church (James 5:14)

   James instructed those in the church who were sick to call for the elders to pray for them.

4. Caring for the church (1 Pet. 5:2)

   Elders are to provide oversight and set a godly example.

5. Setting church policy (Acts 15:6-29)

   The elders at Jerusalem established important ministry policies for the early church.

6. Ordaining elders (1 Tim. 4:14)

   It was the presbytery or elders who ordained Timothy by laying their hands on him.

If you think you might be called to the ministry, remember that it is an important calling. Are you willing to do something that important? It is also a limited calling. Are you the right sex

* *New American Standard Bible.*

to serve in that capacity? It is a compelling calling. Do you feel a strong compulsion toward the ministry? And it is a responsible calling. You will be taking on a great responsibility. God will hold you accountable, and you will be publicly disciplined if you sin.

V. A WORTHY CALLING (v. 1e)

"A good work."

The Greek word translated "good" (*kalos*) refers to that which is noble, excellent, honorable, or of high quality. That is a high estimate of the pastorate. It is of great value, and in fact I believe it is the most worthy task in the world!

Pastor Martyn Lloyd-Jones said, "To me the work of preaching is the highest and the greatest and the most glorious calling to which anyone can ever be called" (*Preaching and Preachers* [London: Hodder and Stoughton, 1973], p. 9). Not every elder is the primary preacher or spokesman in a church, but whatever his role may be, it is the highest calling to which anyone can ever be called. It is indeed a worthy work.

VI. A DEMANDING CALLING (v. 1f)

"Work."

If you're faithful in the ministry, you will find it to be a difficult task. The Greek word translated "work" (*ergon*) implies an expenditure of energy, effort, and zeal. As used here it carries the idea of a lifetime commitment to a never-ending task. It's the same word Paul used to exhort Timothy in 2 Timothy 4:5: "Do the work of an evangelist." For Timothy that was not a temporary task—it was his life's work. That's why we are instructed to esteem those who oversee us (1 Thess. 5:12). They have committed themselves to a demanding task.

The ministry is not like an assembly line that stops and lets you walk away. So when you consider your own call to the ministry, you must ask yourself if you are willing to tackle such a lifelong occupation. Paul understood that kind of commitment, and he suffered greatly for his work (Acts 9:16). Men who sense that kind of calling must then be examined according to the qualifications listed in 1 Timothy 3:2-7.

Focusing on the Facts

1. _____ _____ was the major issue confronting the Ephesian church (see p. 9).
2. Why did Paul leave Timothy at Ephesus (1 Tim. 1:3-4; see p. 9)?
3. What instructions did Paul give Timothy to help him avoid the errors made by the false teachers (1 Tim. 4:6-7, 16; see p. 10)?
4. What is the proper way to deal with a sinning elder (1 Tim. 5:19-20; see p. 10)?
5. A church is only as godly as its _____ (see p. 11).
6. What are two elements of God's call to the ministry (see p. 12)?
7. What formula did Paul use to introduce important doctrines (see p. 12)?
8. What was especially difficult about pastoral ministry in the early church (see p. 13)?
9. What terms are synonyms for the word *elder* (see p. 14)?
10. To whom was the Philippian epistle addressed (Phil. 1:1; see p. 14)?
11. How did Paul support his position that the office of an elder is limited to men (1 Tim. 2:11-15; 3:1-2; see pp. 15-16)?
12. Explain the difference between the words translated "desire" and "desireth" in 1 Timothy 3:1 (see p. 16).
13. One whom God calls does not have a passion for _____ or _____ but for the work of the ministry itself (see p. 17).
14. How did Hugh Latimer portray Satan in his "Sermon of the Plow," and what was his point (see pp. 17-18)?
15. According to Samuel Logan Brengle, what is the road to spiritual leadership (see p. 19)?
16. Define "bishop" as used in 1 Timothy 3:1 (see p. 20).
17. What are the responsibilities of an elder (see p. 21)?
18. What was Martyn Lloyd-Jones's estimation of the ministry (see p. 22)?
19. Define "work" as used in 1 Timothy 3:1 (see p. 22).

Pondering the Principles

1. We have seen that church leadership is a sacred task requiring the highest level of spiritual credibility and maturity. Sadly, some people pursue church leadership for the wrong reasons, such as for money, job security, or prestige. If you are in a position of spiritual leadership, what are your motives? Peter said,

"Shepherd the flock of God among you, exercising oversight not under compulsion, but voluntarily, according to the will of God; and not for sordid gain, but with eagerness; nor yet as lording it over those allotted to your charge, but proving to be examples to the flock" (1 Pet. 5:2-3, NASB). Guard your motives carefully so that you will receive an "unfading crown of glory" (v. 4) when Jesus returns.

2. Diligent, qualified leaders are a precious commodity in any church. Paul said, "Let the elders who rule well be considered worthy of double honor, especially those who work hard at preaching and teaching" (1 Tim. 5:17, NASB). Hebrews 13:17 says, "Obey your leaders, and submit to them; for they keep watch over your souls, as those who will give an account. Let them do this with joy and not with grief, for this would be unprofitable for you" (NASB). Your leaders have a difficult task for which they are personally accountable to the Lord. Be sure to honor them by supplying their financial needs, and add joy to their ministry by submitting to their oversight. Pray for them and encourage them often. Take time to send them a note of encouragement.

3. Hugh Latimer vividly addressed the lack of passion among the ministers of his day (see pp. 17-18), and what he said is just as appropriate today as it was when he said it. No matter what area of ministry you serve in, the subtle threats of complacency or compromise are always present. Read 2 Timothy 1:6-14. How did Paul encourage Timothy when Timothy's zeal was apparently waning? How might you encourage others in that situation? If you are lacking passion for your ministry, fervently pray that God will give you a renewed sense of urgency and commitment to His work. Remember, "God has not given us a spirit of timidity, but of power and love and discipline" (2 Tim. 1:7, NASB).

2
The Call to Lead the Church—Elders
Part 2

Outline

Introduction
A. The False Leaders in Ephesus
B. The False Leaders in Israel
    1. Old Testament examples
    2. New Testament examples

Review
   I. An Important Calling (v. 1*a*)
  II. A Limited Calling (v. 1*b*)
 III. A Compelling Calling (v. 1*c*)
 IV. A Responsible Calling (v. 1*d*)
  V. A Worthy Calling (v. 1*e*)
    A. According to Cotton Mather
    B. According to Will Sangster
    C. According to John Wycliffe
 VI. A Demanding Calling (v. 1*f*)
    A. The Significance of Ordination
    B. The Sign of Ordination
    C. The Symbol of Ordination
    D. The Safeguards of Ordination
       1. Careful evaluation
       2. Prayerful consideration
    E. The Sequence of Ordination
    F. The Standard of Ordination

Lesson

Conclusion

Introduction

God has entrusted to spiritual leaders the sacred responsibility of caring for His people. Sadly, not all spiritual leaders are faithful to that task. The leaders at Ephesus and the leaders of Israel are examples of those who failed to lead in a godly way, and the results were tragic.

A. The False Leaders In Ephesus

When Paul left Ephesus for Macedonia, he left Timothy behind to deal with the various problems in the Ephesian church (1 Tim. 1:3)—problems that had been caused by the failures of its leadership. Some of its leaders were teaching false doctrine and other wrongful teachings that were not edifying (vv. 3-4). Some wanted to teach Jewish law, although they lacked adequate knowledge of its meaning (v. 7). Some women were trying to usurp the authority of the men (2:12). Some men were advocating celibacy and abstinence from certain foods (4:3). Some of the leaders were sinful and in need of public rebuke (5:20), and some sought leadership out of pride or a desire for financial gain (6:4-5).

Such problems illustrate the priority of selecting qualified leadership for the church. Whatever the leaders are, the people become. As Hosea said, "Like people, like priest"

(4:9). Jesus Himself said, "Everyone, after he has been fully trained, will be like his teacher" (Luke 6:40, NASB). Biblical history demonstrates that people will seldom rise above the spiritual level of their leadership.

B. The False Leaders in Israel

   1. Old Testament examples

   The Old Testament portrays Israel as an apostate nation. Israel's apostasy was directly related to the spiritual decline of its leadership.

   a) Jeremiah 2:8

   The Lord said, "The priests said not, Where is the Lord? And they that handle the law knew me not. The rulers also transgressed against me, and the prophets prophesied by Baal, and walked after things that do not profit."

   The priests, rulers, and prophets were corrupt, and the consequence was the apostasy of the entire nation.

   b) Jeremiah 5:30-31

   The Lord also said, "An appalling and horrible thing is committed in the land: the prophets prophesy falsely, and the priests bear rule by their means, and my people love to have it so; and what will ye do in the end of it all?" The people reveled in the deception and spiritual impotence of their leadership, but they reaped the inevitable judgment that follows such apostasy.

   c) Jeremiah 8:8-12

   Jeremiah said to the Jewish leaders, "How do ye say, We are wise, and the law of the Lord is with us? Lo, certainly in vain made he it; the pen of the scribes is in vain. The wise men are ashamed; they are dismayed and taken. Lo, they have rejected the word of the Lord; and what wisdom is in them?" (vv. 8-9). Although the leaders claimed wisdom and a commitment to the law of God, in reality the law was useless to them because they had rejected it.

The Lord then said, "Therefore will I give their wives unto others, and their fields to them that shall inherit them; for every one from the least even unto the greatest is given to covetousness, from the prophet even unto the priest every one dealeth falsely. For they have healed the hurt of the daughter of my people slightly, saying, Peace, peace; when there is no peace. Were they ashamed when they had committed abomination? Nay, they were not at all ashamed" (vv. 10-12). The prophets proclaimed a false peace but failed to proclaim obedience to God.

d) Jeremiah 10:21

Jeremiah said, "The shepherds are become stupid, and have not sought the Lord; therefore they shall not prosper, and all their flocks shall be scattered." The failure of Israel's leaders brought tragic judgment upon the people.

e) Jeremiah 12:10

Jeremiah also said, "Many shepherds have destroyed my vineyard, they have trampled my portion under foot, they have made my pleasant portion a desolate wilderness." God's people were victimized by false spiritual leaders.

f) Jeremiah 23:1-2, 4, 9, 11, 16

"Woe be unto the shepherds who destroy and scatter the sheep of my pasture! saith the Lord. Therefore, thus saith the Lord God of Israel against the shepherds who feed my people, Ye have scattered my flock, and driven them away, and have not visited them; behold, I will visit upon you the evil of your doings, saith the Lord. . . . I will set up shepherds over them who shall feed them. . . . Mine heart

28

within me is broken because of the prophets. . . .
Both prophet and priest are profane . . . . Hearken
not unto the words of the prophets that prophesy
unto you. They make you vain; they speak a vision of
their own heart, and not out of the mouth of the
Lord."

The failures of Israel's leadership had enormous implications for those who trusted and followed them.

2. New Testament examples

The Lord's indictment of Israel's leaders is not confined
to the Old Testament.

a) Matthew 23:13-33

Jesus said to the scribes and Pharisees, "Ye shut up
the kingdom of heaven against men; for ye neither go
in yourselves, neither permit them that are entering
to go in. Woe unto you, scribes and Pharisees, hypocrites! For ye devour widows' houses, and for a pre-
tense make long prayers; therefore, ye shall receive
the greater damnation. Woe unto you, scribes and
Pharisees, hypocrites! For ye compass sea and land
to make one proselyte, and when he is made, ye
make him twofold more the child of hell than
yourselves.

"Woe unto you, ye blind guides, who say, Whosoever shall swear by the temple, it is nothing; but whosoever shall swear by the gold of the temple, he is a
debtor! Ye fools and blind; for which is greater, the
gold, or the temple that sanctifieth the gold? And,
Whosoever shall swear by the altar, it is nothing; but
whosoever sweareth by the gift that is upon it, he is
bound. Ye fools and blind; for which is greater, the
gift, or the altar that sanctifieth the gift? Whosoever,
therefore, shall swear by the altar, sweareth by it,
and by all things on it. And whosoever shall swear
by the temple, sweareth by it, and by him that dwell-
eth in it. And he that shall swear by heaven, sweareth by the throne of God, and by him who sitteth on
it.

"Woe unto you, scribes and Pharisees, hypocrites! For ye pay tithe of mint and anise and cummin, and have omitted the weightier matters of the law, justice, mercy, and faith; these ought ye to have done, and not to leave the other undone. Ye blind guides, who strain at a gnat, and swallow a camel.

"Woe unto you, scribes and Pharisees, hypocrites! For ye make clean the outside of the cup and of the platter, but within they are full of extortion and excess. Thou blind Pharisee, cleanse first that which is within the cup and platter, that the outside of them may be clean also.

"Woe unto you, scribes and Pharisees, hypocrites! For ye are like whited sepulchers, which indeed appear beautiful outward, but are within full of dead men's bones, and of all uncleanness. Even so ye also outwardly appear righteous unto men, but within ye are full of hypocrisy and iniquity.

"Woe unto you, scribes and Pharisees, hypocrites! Because ye build the tombs of the prophets, and garnish the sepulchers of the righteous, and say, If we had been in the days of our fathers, we would not have been partakers with them in the blood of the prophets. Wherefore, ye are witnesses against yourselves, that ye are the sons of them who killed the prophets. Fill up, then, the measure of your fathers. Ye serpents, ye generation of vipers, how can ye escape the damnation of hell?"

b) Galatians 1:8-9

Paul pronounced a severe curse upon anyone who preached a false gospel.

c) Colossians 2:8, 18, 20-23

Paul warned his readers to avoid the false teachings of philosophy, mysticism, and asceticism.

d) 2 Peter 2:13, 17, 22

Peter described false teachers in graphic terms: as spots and blemishes (v. 13), wells without water (v. 17), dogs that return to their own vomit, and sows that return to wallow in the mire after being washed (v. 22; cf. Jude 12).

e) James 3:1

James warned of the serious retribution of God upon unfaithful teachers.

f) 1 John 2:18, 22

John referred to false teachers as "antichrists."

Spiritual leadership is a serious issue in the church. Those who betray that sacred trust incur severe judgment. Therefore, careful consideration must be given to the calling and qualifications of anyone who expresses a desire to lead the church.

Review

I. AN IMPORTANT CALLING (v. 1*a*; see pp. 12-15)

II. A LIMITED CALLING (v. 1*b*; see pp. 15-16)

III. A COMPELLING CALLING (v. 1*c*; see pp. 16-20)

IV. A RESPONSIBLE CALLING (v. 1*d*; see pp. 20-22)

V. A WORTHY CALLING (v. 1*e*; see p. 22)

A. According to Cotton Mather

The American Puritan minister Cotton Mather thought that the office of the Christian ministry, rightly understood, was the most honorable and important that any man could ever attain. To him one of the wonders of eternity would be reflecting on the wisdom and goodness of God in assigning that office to imperfect and guilty man (cf. *Selections from Cotton Mather*, Kenneth B. Murdock, ed. [N.Y.: Hafner, 1965], p. xi).

B. According to Will Sangster

Will Sangster, who preached in London's Westminster Hall during the time of World War II, wrote, "Called to preach! . . . Commissioned of God to teach the Word! A herald of the great King! A witness of the eternal gospel! Could any work be more high and holy? To this supreme task God sent His only begotten Son. In all the frustration and confusion of the times, is it possible to imagine a work comparable in importance with that of proclaiming the will of God to wayward men?" (*The Craft of Sermon Construction* [Philadelphia: Westminster, 1951], p. 24).

C. According to John Wycliffe

The fourteenth-century preacher John Wycliffe lived during a period in history when priests were the spiritual leaders; yet they did not allow God's Word to be preached by lesser priests. Wycliffe's indictment of such priests in his *Contra Fratres* reveals his passion for the sacred task of preaching. Like Cotton Mather, he believed that the highest service to which men may attain on earth is preaching the Word of God.

Those men understood the worthiness of the ministry; it is a high and holy calling.

VI. A DEMANDING CALLING (v. 1*f*; see p. 22)

Ordination of Church Leaders

Ordination is the act whereby a church officially acknowledges the calling and qualifications of a man for ministry. Scripture delineates several aspects of ordination.

A. The Significance of Ordination

The Greek word translated "ordain" (*kathistēmi*) is used many times in the New Testament. It means "to set aside" or "to appoint."

B. The Sign of Ordination

In the early church, the official sign of ordination was the laying on of hands. The apostles or others in spiritual leadership placed their hands upon the individual being set apart for ministry. By doing so they affirmed their union with him and in a sense transmitted their blessing to him. Timothy was ordained to the ministry by that process. Paul said to him, "Neglect not the gift that is in thee, which was given thee by prophecy, with the laying on of the hands of the presbytery" (1 Tim. 4:14).

C. The Symbol of Ordination

The laying on of hands comes from an Old Testament symbol. When a Jewish person offered an animal sacrifice, he placed his hands on that sacrifice as an act of identification or union (F. F. Bruce, *The New International Commentary on the New Testament: Acts* [Grand Rapids: Eerdmans, 1975], p. 130). The sacrifice was offered in his place—for his sins—so he identified with the offering in that way.

D. The Safeguards of Ordination

1. Careful evaluation

Paul warned Timothy, "Do not lay hands upon anyone too hastily and thus share responsibility for the sins of others" (1 Tim. 5:22, NASB). Ordination is a weighty responsibility. A habitually sinful man has no right to be in the pastorate. When church leaders affirm by ordination that a man is called and qualified for the ministry, they are identifying with him in such an intimate way that if he sins, they are associated with his sin. Therefore ordination is not something that the leadership can afford to take lightly.

2. Prayerful consideration

Acts 20:28 says that the Holy Spirit appoints overseers; the church simply affirms His choices. Therefore the early church sought the will of God through prayer and fasting before they ordained men for the ministry (cf. Acts 13:2-3; 14:23).

E. The Sequence of Ordination

Ordination was first done by the apostles (cf. Acts 14:23). As the church grew and the apostles began to pass from the scene, ordination was done by apostolic representatives, such as Titus (cf. Titus 1:5). As the church further developed, ordination then passed to the leadership of each local church. Today the privilege and responsibility of ordination still rests with local church pastors and elders.

F. The Standard of Ordination

The man who desires the office of an overseer desires a good work (1 Tim. 3:1), but the decision to place him into church leadership should never be based on his desire alone. It is the responsibility of the church to affirm his qualifications for ministry by measuring him against God's standard for leadership as outlined in 1 Timothy 3:2-7.

Lesson

The overarching characteristic of an elder is blamelessness.

I. THE PRIORITY OF BLAMELESSNESS

Paul said, "A bishop . . . must be blameless" (1 Tim. 3:2*a*). The Greek word translated "must" (*de*) emphasizes an absolute necessity: blamelessness is absolutely mandatory in an overseer. It is a basic, overall requirement. In fact, the other qualifications Paul lists in verses 2*b*-7 define and illustrate what he means by blamelessness.

II. THE PARAMETERS OF BLAMELESSNESS

The Greek text indicates that verse 2*a* refers to a present state of blamelessness. It doesn't refer to sins that the man committed before or after he became a Christian, unless such sins remain as a blight on his life. No one is blameless in that sense. The idea is that he has sustained a reputation for blamelessness.

III. THE DEFINITION OF BLAMELESSNESS

"Blameless" (v. 2) means "not able to be held." A blameless man cannot be taken hold of as if he were a criminal in need of detention for his actions. There's nothing to accuse him of. He is irreproachable.

IV. THE RATIONALE FOR BLAMELESSNESS

A. Modeling Christ's Character

A church leader's life must not be marred by sin or vice—be it an attitude, habit, or incident. That's not to say he must be perfect, but there must not be any obvious defect in his character. He must be a model of godliness so that he can legitimately call his congregation to follow his example (Phil. 3:17). They need to be confident that he won't lead them into sin.

A church leader becomes disqualified when there's a blight on his life that communicates the message that one can live in sin and still be a spiritual leader.

A Double Standard in the Ministry?

Spiritual leaders must be blameless because they set the example for the congregation to follow. That is a high standard, but it isn't a double standard. Since you are responsible to follow the example of your godly leaders (Heb. 13:7, 17), God requires blamelessness of you as well. The difference is that certain sins can disqualify men from being church leaders, whereas that's not necessarily true for less prominent roles in the church. Nevertheless, God requires blamelessness from all believers (cf. Eph. 1:4; 5:27; Phil. 1:10; 2:15; Col. 1:22; 2 Pet. 3:14; Jude 24).

What about you? Is your life a worthy example for other believers to follow? Is the pursuit of blamelessness a priority for you?

B. Guarding Christ's Reputation

There are always malicious people looking for ways to discredit the reputation of Christ and His church. A leader who is not blameless plays right into their hands, giving them unparalleled opportunity to justify their lack of belief.

The standard for church leadership is blamelessness, not sinless perfection. There must be no ongoing sin in a leader's life, for that would discredit his example and would create an opportunity for malicious people to undermine the credibility of Christianity.

Satan's Favorite Prey

It's not coincidental that many pastors fall into sin and disqualify themselves from ministry. Satan works very hard to undermine the integrity of spiritual leaders, for in so doing he destroys their ministries and brings reproach upon Christ. Therefore, spiritual leaders must guard their thoughts and actions carefully, and every congregation must pray earnestly for the strength of its leadership.

1. Spiritual leaders have a greater potential for temptation

    I believe the devil attacks spiritual leaders with more severe temptations than most Christians ever experience. It stands to reason that those who lead the forces of truth and light against the kingdom of darkness will experience the strongest opposition from the enemy.

    Satan directs the hottest attack toward those who hold fast to God's Word—those who preach and teach it boldly without compromise. Faithful leaders are targets of the most subtle insinuations, incessant solicitations, and violent assaults of the enemy. Yet the grace and strength God gives are sufficient for the task. Out of the conflict comes victory that encourages greater effort and increases spiritual strength.

2. Spiritual leaders have a greater potential to be maligned

    Although the fall of any Christian is tragic, the devastation resulting from the fall of a pastor carries enormous implications because of the scope of his ministry. Such a fall affects untold numbers of believers and nonbelievers and maligns the faith.

Some people maliciously look for the smallest fault in a leader so that they can discredit his ministry. Consequently, leaders must be careful to maintain blameless lives in order to prevent those who watch them from having the opportunity to make accusations.

3. Spiritual leaders have a greater potential for chastening

A spiritual leader who sins is anything but insulated from God's chastening. Since he knows more than the average lay person, he is held more accountable.

4. Spiritual leaders have a greater potential for hypocrisy

The sins of a spiritual leader are more hypocritical than the sins of others because it is his business to preach against sin.

There is a greater potential in the ministry to be tempted, maligned, chastened, and for hypocrisy. Consequently, spiritual leaders are likely to experience a higher level of spiritual conflict and may require greater accountability, grace, and strength than other men. God is aware of that need and is gracious in undergirding his servants. Often that undergirding comes through the faithful prayers of a congregation on behalf of its leadership. So be sure to pray for your leaders.

Are You a Stained-Glass Window?

An unholy pastor is like a stained-glass window: a religious symbol that keeps the light out. That's why the initial qualification for spiritual leadership is blamelessness.

The seventeenth century Puritan Richard Baxter wrote, "Take heed to yourselves, lest you live in those sins which you preach against in others, and lest you be guilty of that which daily you condemn. Will you make it your work to magnify God, and, when you have done, dishonour Him as much as others? Will you proclaim Christ's governing power, and yet condemn it, and rebel yourselves? Will you preach his laws, and willfully break them?

"If sin be evil, why do you live in it? if it be not, why do you dissuade men from it? If it be dangerous, how dare you venture on it?

if it be not, why do you tell men so? If God's threatenings be true, why do you not fear them? if they be false, why do you needlessly trouble men with them, and put them into such frights without a cause?

"Do you 'know the judgment of God, that they who commit such things are worthy of death;' and yet will you do them? 'Thou that teachest another, teachest thou not thyself? Thou that sayest a man should not commit adultery,' or be drunk, or covetous, art thou such thyself? 'Thou that makest thy boast of the law, through breaking the law dishonorest thou God?' What! shall the same tongue speak evil that speakest against evil? Shall those lips censure, and slander, and backbite your neighbour, that cry down these and the like things in others?

"Take heed to yourselves, lest you cry down sin, and yet do not overcome it; lest, while you seek to bring it down in others, you bow to it, and become its slave yourselves: 'For of whom a man is overcome, the same he is brought into bondage.' 'To whom ye yield yourselves servants to obey, his servants ye are whom you obey, whether of sin unto death, or of obedience unto righteousness.' O brethren! it is easier to chide at sin, than to overcome it" (*The Reformed Pastor* [Carlisle, Pa.: Banner of Truth, 1956], pp. 67-68).

That is a good reminder: we must live what we preach. That's why Paul told Timothy to be sure that the church leaders were blameless.

Baxter went on to say, "When your minds are in a holy heavenly frame, your people are likely to partake of the fruits of it. Your prayers and praises, and doctrine will be sweet and heavenly to them. They will likely feel when you have been much with God: that which is most on your hearts, is like to be most in their ears. . . .

"When I let my heart grow cold, my preaching is cold; and when it is confused, my preaching is confused; and so I can oft observe also in the best of my hearers, that when I have grown cold in preaching, they have grown cold too; and the next prayers which I have heard from them have been too like my preaching. . . .

"O brethren, watch therefore over your own hearts: keep out lusts and passions, and worldly inclinations: keep up the life of faith, and love, and zeal: be much at home, and be much with God . . . . Take heed to yourselves, lest your example contradict your doctrine . . . lest you unsay with your lives what you say with your tongues; and be the greatest hinderers of the success of your own labours. . . . One proud, surly, lordly word, one needless contention, one covetous action may cut the throat of many a sermon and blast the fruit of all that you have been doing" (pp. 61-63).

The ministry is a noble calling, but it will bring you into direct conflict with the enemy. Blamelessness is essential for spiritual credibility and victory.

V. THE GUARDIANS OF BLAMELESSNESS

How does a spiritual leader protect himself from the onslaughts of Satan? The answer is threefold: Scripture, prayer, and fellowship.

A. Scripture

The best way to be insulated from the attacks of the enemy is to be continually saturated with God's Word.

1. The purpose of studying Scripture

We must study God's Word with a pure heart so it can do its work in us. Only then will we be worthy vessels through whom the Spirit can minister.

David said, "Thy word have I hidden in mine heart, that I might not sin against thee" (Ps. 119:11). Being continuously exposed to the living Word guards us from sin and makes us pure (cf. John 15:3).

2. The peril of not studying Scripture

Tragically, many spiritual leaders allow themselves to be drawn away from God's Word. Perhaps the nature of their ministry doesn't require them to be studying the Word each day, so their lives aren't regularly exposed to its convicting truth. Or perhaps they have grown complacent in their commitment to the Word. If so, they have neglected the strength received as God's Spirit ministers through His Word, and they have created a serious weakness in their spiritual armor.

B. Prayer

Prayer acknowledges our dependency on God for spiritual strength and victory. It is an admission that we need help.

C. Fellowship

In my spiritual battles I draw great strength and encouragement from those around me who are engaged in the same struggles. I thank God for that fellowship.

Conclusion

Spiritual leadership is not for everyone. The church must carefully evaluate all prospective leaders and ordain only those who have a strong desire for ministry and who meet the qualification of blamelessness.

Focusing on the Facts

1. Why did Paul leave Timothy in Ephesus (1 Tim. 1:3; see p. 26)?
2. How do the words of Jesus in Luke 6:40 relate to the issue of qualified spiritual leadership (see p. 27)?
3. How does Jeremiah 10:21 describe false leaders, and how did God judge them (see p. 28)?
4. Upon whom does Jesus pronounce a series of woes in Matthew 23:13-33 and why (see pp. 29-30)?
5. How did Peter describe the false teachers of his day (2 Peter 2:13, 17, 22; see p. 31)?
6. What is ordination (see p. 32)?
7. What is the significance of the laying on of hands in the ordination ceremony (see pp. 32-33)?
8. How can a church safeguard itself from ordaining the wrong men (see p. 33)?
9. Who bears the responsibility for ordaining leadership in the church today (see p. 34)?
10. Define "blameless" (see p. 35).

11. Why must a church leader be a model of godliness (see p. 35)?
12. Is God's standard for blamelessness in spiritual leadership a double standard? Explain (see p. 35).
13. Why are spiritual leaders more likely to experience greater spiritual conflict than other believers (see pp. 36-37)?
14. How can a congregation help strengthen its leaders (see p. 37)?
15. What three things can a spiritual leader do to protect himself from Satan's attacks (see pp. 39-40)?

Pondering the Principles

1. We have seen the confusion and judgment that comes when people listen to false spiritual leaders. By way of contrast, read 1 Thessalonians 2:1-12, noting the commitment (vv. 1-2), character (vv. 3-8), conduct (vv. 9-11), and consuming passion (v. 12) of Paul and his associates. If you are a church leader, how does the quality of your ministry compare to theirs? Do your people sense in you a depth of commitment and compassion that is grounded in a deep love for God and His Word? Is it your goal to see your people living "in a manner worthy of the God who calls [them] into His own kingdom and glory" (v. 12, NASB)? Be diligent in the Word and in prayer so that your ministry will be consistent with God's priorities and your heart tender towards His people.

2. Paul thanked the Philippian church for their expressions of love and support (Phil. 1:3-4; 4:10, 16-18) and encouraged them to pray for him (Phil. 1:19). Such a congregation would be a source of strength and encouragement to any leader. Be faithful to "obey your leaders, and submit to them; for they keep watch over your souls, as those who will give an account. Let them do this with joy and not with grief, for this would be unprofitable for you" (Heb. 13:17, NASB). Take every opportunity to encourage those who minister to you, and pray for them daily.

3
The Call to Lead the Church—Elders
Part 3

Outline

Review

Lesson

I. An Elder Must Be Blameless in His Moral Character (vv. 2b-3)
  A. "The Husband of One Wife"—Sexually Pure (v. 2b)
    1. A preferred translation
    2. A prevalent temptation
    3. The proposed interpretations
      a) That an elder can't be a polygamist
        (1) Jewish intolerance of polygamy
        (2) Roman tolerance of promiscuity
      b) That an elder can't marry a second time
      c) That an elder can't be divorced
      d) That an elder can't be single
      e) That an elder must be devoted to only one woman
  B. "Temperate"—Not Given to Excess (v. 2c)
    1. Its definition
    2. Its twofold usage
      a) In the literal sense
      b) In the figurative sense

Review

In 1 Timothy 3:1-7 the apostle Paul describes the call and characteristics of elders in the church. We have seen that an elder must be
called by God (see pp. 12-22). That call is initiated by the Holy Spir-

it, who places within him a strong desire to serve God in the capacity of an elder (v. 1; see pp. 31-34).

In addition, we saw that an elder must be confirmed by the congregation as it examines the quality of his life. He must be blameless (v. 2a)—above reproach and an example of godliness against which his people can measure the quality of their own lives. Blamelessness is the overarching characteristic of an elder (see pp. 34-40).

Restoring Fallen Spiritual Leaders

Recently I was asked, "If a man sins when he's in the ministry and then repents, can he be forgiven and restored?" I replied, "Yes, of course God will forgive that person. He forgives every penitent sinner." However, God's forgiveness does not necessarily include restoring a fallen pastor to his former position of ministry.

Every time a fallen leader is placed back in his ministry, the standard of virtue for spiritual leadership is lowered a little bit. That leads to a higher level of toleration for sinfulness in leaders. As people begin to perceive a lower standard of holiness in their leaders, they will probably lower the standard for their own lives as well.

Today, the church in America is seeing an unprecedented volume of fallen pastors who are restored to their ministries. I believe that phenomenon has produced a corresponding decline in our perception of what it means to be a godly leader.

While I rejoice to see a fallen brother restored to the love and fellowship of the church, I am deeply concerned about the current trend toward a greater toleration of the sins of spiritual leaders. God's standard for leadership is under attack, so we cannot forget that the life of a spiritual leader must be blameless and worthy of imitation.

Lesson

In 1 Timothy 3:2b-7 Paul delineates four areas of life in which an elder must be blameless: moral character, home life, spiritual maturity, and public reputation.

Paul describes each of those characteristics in the present tense. They must be present in the life of every elder, yet they're also to reflect his past life. There must be no sin in his recent past that diminishes his present leadership example. Those who know him must perceive him as blameless in character.

That is a high standard, but that's because God calls all believers to be holy like Him (1 Pet. 1:16). Therefore, those who lead His people must maintain the highest possible standard for the sake of their example to the church. And the church must never compromise its standard of leadership.

I. AN ELDER MUST BE BLAMELESS IN HIS MORAL CHARACTER (vv. 2b-3)

"A bishop then must be blameless, the husband of one wife, temperate, sober-minded, of good behavior, given to hospitality, apt to teach; not given to wine, not violent, not greedy of filthy lucre, but patient, not a brawler, not covetous."

A. "The Husband of One Wife"—Sexually Pure (v. 2b)

1. A preferred translation

"The husband of one wife" is not the best rendering according to my studies of the Greek text. I believe the words translated "wife" (*gunaikos*) and "husband" (*anēr*) are better translated "woman" and "man."

The Greek construction places emphasis on the word "one," thereby communicating the idea of a one-woman man. Additionally, the absence of a definite article ("*The* husband of one wife") stresses character, not marital circumstances; thus the character of an elder must reflect fidelity to one woman.

2. A prevalent temptation

It is appropriate that sexual fidelity is first on Paul's list of moral qualifications because that seems to be the area that most often disqualifies a man from ministry. It is therefore a matter of grave concern.

45

3. The proposed interpretations

   a) That an elder can't be a polygamist

   The view that an elder can't have more than one wife at a time has been the traditional understanding of the English phrase "the husband of one wife," but the religious and cultural climate of Paul's day make it unlikely that he was referring to polygamy.

   (1) Jewish intolerance of polygamy

   Although some Jewish people practiced polygamy (William Barclay, *The Letters to Timothy, Titus and Philemon* [Philadelphia: Westminster, 1975], p. 76), it was forbidden by Jewish law and was not a major issue in first-century Judaism.

   (2) Roman tolerance of promiscuity

   Polygamy wasn't a major issue among the Romans. Divorce, concubines, and prostitutes were so prevalent that they didn't bother with polygamist marriages.

   Divorce was so rampant that it wasn't unheard of for a woman to get married for the twenty-seventh time and be the twenty-sixth wife of her husband-to-be! The first-century Roman satirical poet Juvenal ridiculed women for wearing out their bridal veils in so many weddings (*Woman: A Satire* [N.Y.: Rarity Press, 1932]).

   Thus elements in both the Roman and the Jewish cultures make it unlikely that Paul had polygamy in mind in this passage.

   b) That an elder can't marry a second time

   Some people say that "a one woman man" means that a man can't be an elder if he has remarried for any reason. But even if we use the translation "the husband of one wife," Paul can't be referring to remarriage, because God permits remarriage under certain conditions.

(1) 1 Timothy 5:9-15—"Let not a widow be taken into the number under sixty years old, having been the wife of one man, well reported of for good works, if she hath brought up children, if she hath lodged strangers, if she hath washed the saints' feet, if she hath relieved the afflicted, if she hath diligently followed every good work. But the younger widows refuse; for when they have begun to grow wanton against Christ, they will marry, having condemnation, because they have cast off their first faith."

"The number" refers to a select group of godly, virtuous widows over sixty years of age who had made a vow of consecration to a specific aspect of ministry. Apparently it required them to remain single in order to focus all their energies on that ministry. In return, they were cared for by the church.

Younger widows were prohibited from joining that group for fear that their natural desire for a husband might cause them to break their vow, thereby incurring judgment. Verse 15 says that some of those young women had "already turned aside after Satan"—apparently by committing sexual sins.

Paul commanded those younger widows to "marry, bear children, [and] rule the house" (v. 14). God honors a second marriage in the case of young widows.

(2) Romans 7:2-3—"The woman who hath an husband is bound by the law to her husband as long as he liveth; but if the husband be dead, she is loosed from the law [that bound her to] her husband. So, then if, while her husband liveth, she be married to another man, she shall be called an adulteress; but if her husband be dead, she is free from that law, so that she is no adulteress, though she be married to another man."

With the death of a marriage partner, the surviving partner is free to remarry. In fact, it's a wonderful option.

(3) 1 Corinthians 7:39—"The wife is bound by the law as long as her husband liveth; but if her husband be dead, she is at liberty to be married to whom she will, only in the Lord." The only qualifier given for the remarriage of a widow is that she marry a Christian. Although Paul used widows for his illustration, the same principle applies to widowers.

Since God honors remarriage after the death of a spouse, Paul could not have been prohibiting all remarried men from serving as elders.

c) That an elder can't be divorced

Some people say that Paul was prohibiting divorced men from serving as elders. But if Paul were referring to divorce, he could have clarified the issue by saying, "An elder must be a man who has never been divorced." But that statement would have posed problems, because the Bible teaches that remarriage after a divorce is within God's will under two circumstances.

(1) Divorce is acceptable when one partner commits continuous sexual sin.

Jesus said to some of the leaders, "It hath been said [by your rabbinical tradition], Whosoever shall [divorce] his wife, let him give her a writing of divorcement" (Matt. 5:31). Many Jewish men were divorcing their wives for insignificant reasons, and the only obligation they were being required to complete was the necessary paperwork.

But Jesus said, "Whosoever shall [divorce] his wife, except for the cause of fornication, causeth her to commit adultery [when she remarries]; and whosoever shall marry her that is divorced committeth adultery" (Matt. 5:32). His statement implies that those who divorce their spouses for reasons other than fornication are themselves adul-

48

terers and their new wives adulteresses. I believe that the "fornication" mentioned in this context refers to extreme situations of unrelenting and unrepentant sexual sin. God graciously permits the innocent party to be free from bondage to such an evil partner. With that freedom comes the freedom to remarry a believer.

Under Old Testament law, if a marriage partner committed adultery, he or she could be stoned to death. That would release the other partner from the marriage and free him or her to remarry. Although God no longer demands the death of an unfaithful spouse, the sin of adultery is regarded no less severely. Should God's grace in sparing the life of the adulterer penalize the innocent party by demanding lifelong singleness? I don't think so. The grace that spares the adulterer's life also frees the innocent party to remarry.

(2) Divorce is acceptable when an unbelieving partner leaves.

In 1 Corinthians 7:15 Paul says, "If the unbelieving depart, let him depart. A brother or a sister is not under bondage in such cases; but God hath called us to peace." If an unbelieving partner wants out of the marriage, the believer is free to let him or her go. God doesn't require you to live in a state of war with such a partner.

God hates divorce (Mal. 2:16) but is gracious to the innocent party when one partner commits continuous sexual sin or when an unbelieving partner leaves. In either case the innocent party is free to remarry.

Who Can Remarry?

Some people believe that remarriage under practically any circumstance is sinful, but that is not what the Bible teaches. Paul gives additional insight into that issue in 1 Corinthians 7, where he delineates three groups of single people.

1. Virgins (vv. 25, 28, 34, 36-37)

   A virgin is a single person who has never married or had a sexual relationship. Such a person is free to marry a believer whenever he or she chooses.

2. Widows (vv. 8-9)

   A widow is a formerly married person who has been left single by the death of a spouse. As we have seen, such a person is free to remarry (see pp. 47-48).

3. The unmarried (vv. 8, 11, 32, 34)

   - Their identity

     The identity of the "unmarried" group is an important issue with regard to Paul's teaching on remarriage.

     In verse 34 Paul makes a distinction between the "unmarried" and the "virgins": "The woman who is unmarried, and the virgin, is concerned about the things of the Lord" (NASB). In verse 8 Paul makes a distinction between the "unmarried" and the "widows": "I say, therefore, to the unmarried and widows." In verses 10-11 Paul says, "Unto the married I command, yet not I, but the Lord, Let not the wife depart from her husband; but and if she depart, let her remain *unmarried*" (emphasis added). The unmarried, therefore are those who were formerly married but are now single by divorce.

   - Their right to remarry

     Paul said, "It is good for them [virgins, widows, and divorced people] if they abide even as I" (v. 8). It's good to stay single, for as a single person you can give your undivided attention to pleasing the Lord (vv. 32-33). However, in verse 9 Paul says, "If they cannot have self-control, let them marry; for it is better to marry than to burn." If you're a virgin, a widow, or a formerly married person now divorced, it is better to remarry than to endure the constant desire for a mate.

Remarriage is clearly not a sin when it occurs within specific biblical parameters. We have seen that those parameters involve the person who has been widowed, the innocent victim of an unrepentant adulterer, or someone who's been abandoned by an unbelieving spouse.

d) That an elder can't be single

Some people say 1 Timothy 3:2 prohibits single men from serving as elders. But that position is refuted by the fact that Paul, who was an elder (1 Tim. 4:14; 2 Tim. 1:6), was himself single (1 Cor. 7:7-9).

e) That an elder must be devoted to only one woman

Paul was not referring to an elder's marital status, because that is not a moral qualification for spiritual leadership. However, if the elder is married, he is to be a one-woman man.

Unfortunately it's possible to be married to one woman yet not be a one-woman man. Jesus said, "Whosoever looketh on a woman to lust after her hath committed adultery with her already in his heart" (Matt. 5:28). A married—or unmarried—man who lusts after many women is unfit for the ministry. An elder must love, desire, and think only of the wife God has given him.

Sexual purity is a major issue in the ministry. That's why Paul placed it at the top of his list.

B. "Temperate"—Not Given to Excess (v. 2*c*)

1. Its definition

The Greek word translated "temperate" (*nēphalios*) means "without wine" or "unmixed with wine." It speaks of sobriety—the opposite of intoxication (P. J. Budd, *"nēphalios," The New International Dictionary of New Testament Theology*, ed. Colin Brown [Grand Rapids: Zondervan, 1979], I:514-15).

2. Its twofold usage

Its verb form (Gk., *nēphō*) was used in a literal and figurative sense in both Hellenistic and New Testament Greek.

a) In the literal sense

If Paul had the literal sense of *nēphō* in mind, he was requiring elders to abstain from any form of intoxication. Drunkenness was a serious problem in Ephesus, which is where Timothy was having problems with the elders. That was due in part to the drunken orgies associated with the pagan religious practices at the temple of Diana. The elders were to remain separate from such evil influences and set an example of sobriety for others to follow (Eph. 5:18).

The Mockery of Strong Drink

Wine was a common drink in biblical times. Because Palestine was so hot and dry, it was often necessary to consume a large volume of wine to replenish body fluids lost in the heat. To help avoid drunkenness, wine was normally mixed with large amounts of water. Even so, the lack of refrigeration and the fermentative properties of wine made intoxication a problem.

Even though wine can cheer a person's heart (Judg. 9:13) and was beneficial for medicinal purposes, such as relieving a stomach ailment (1 Tim. 5:23) or easing the pain of those near death (Prov. 31:6), its abuse was common. That's why Proverbs 20:1 says, "Wine is a mocker, strong drink is raging, and whosoever is deceived thereby is not wise."

1. According to Proverbs 23

Verses 29-35 of Proverbs 23 say, "Who hath woe? Who hath sorrow? Who hath contentions? Who hath babbling? Who hath wounds without cause? Who hath redness of eyes? They that tarry long at the wine; they that go to seek mixed wine. Look not thou upon the wine when it is red, when it giveth its color in the cup, when it moveth itself aright. At the last it biteth like a serpent, and stingeth like an adder. Thine eyes shall behold strange things, and thine heart shall utter perverse things. Yea, thou shalt be as he that lieth down in the midst of the sea, or as he that lieth upon the top of a mast. They have stricken me, shalt thou say, and I was not sick; they have beaten me, and I felt it not. When shall I awake? I will seek it yet again."

2. According to Genesis 9

Verses 20-23 of Genesis 9 record an example of the mocking effect of wine. Noah planted a vineyard, made wine, and became drunk. While he was drunk "he was uncovered within his tent" (v. 21). The Hebrew text implies some kind of sexual evil. Ham, one of his sons, saw him in that state and mocked him. His two other sons entered the tent backwards to cover him up because they were ashamed of his sinfulness.

3. According to 2 Samuel 13

Verses 28-29 of 2 Samuel 13 tell us that David's son Absalom had Amnon, his half-brother, slain while Amnon was "merry with wine."

Because of their position, example, and influence certain Jewish leaders abstained from wine. Priests could not enter God's house while under its influence (Lev. 10:9). Kings were also advised not to consume wine because it could hinder their judgment (Prov. 31:4-5). The Nazarite vow, the highest vow of spiritual commitment in the Old Testament, forbade its participants to drink wine (Num. 6:3).

In the same way, spiritual leaders today must avoid intoxication so that they might exercise responsible judgment and set an example of Spirit-controlled behavior.

b) In the figurative sense

It's likely that Paul's usage of *nēphō* went beyond the literal sense of avoiding intoxication to the figurative sense of being alert and watchful. An elder must deny any excess in life that diminishes clear thinking and sound judgment.

Commentator William Hendriksen said, "Such a person lives deeply. His pleasures are not primarily those of the senses, like the pleasures of a drunkard for instance, but those of the soul. He is filled with spiritual and moral earnestness. He is not given to excess (in the use of wine, etc.), but [is] moderate, well-balanced, calm, careful, steady, and sane. This pertains to his physical, moral, and mental tastes and habits" (*Exposition of the Pastoral Epistles* [Grand Rapids: Baker, 1981], p. 122).

Drinking is only one area in which excess can occur. Overeating has been called the preacher's sin, and often that's a just criticism. But spiritual leaders are to be moderate and balanced in *every* area of life.

The first moral characteristic God requires of an elder is sexual purity, most frequently displayed by devotion to one woman. That's a mark of true virtue, especially in a society where pornography and other forms of sexual promiscuity are proliferated through books, magazines, television, movies, and music. Second, God requires an elder to be clearheaded, which means avoiding the many excesses of our society. He must maintain a balanced, alert, and watchful life.

When a church considers a young man for the ministry, it must avoid the temptation to focus on his personality and speaking ability while neglecting the weightier matters of his calling and character. God's standards for spiritual leaders are high; if the church dismisses or lowers those standards, it will suffer, for its people will settle on a lower standard for their own lives as well.

Rather than lowering the standard, I pray that God will raise up leaders of godly character that His church might be all He wants it to be for His glory.

Focusing on the Facts

1. Don't forget that the life of a spiritual leader must be _____ and worthy of _____ (see p. 44).
2. In what four areas of life is an elder to be blameless (see p. 44)?

3. What is a preferred translation of the phrase "the husband of one wife" (v. 2b; see p. 45)?
4. Why is sexual purity first on Paul's list of elder qualifications (see p. 45)?
5. Why is it unlikely that Paul has polygamy in mind in 1 Timothy 2b (see p. 46)?
6. What are five interpretive options for the phrase "the husband of one wife" (v. 2b; see pp. 46-51)?
7. How did Jewish law view polygamy (see p. 46)?
8. What elements in Roman culture overshadowed polygamy (see p. 46)?
9. What does "the number" refer to in 1 Timothy 5:9 (see p. 47)?
10. What is Paul's command to younger widows in 1 Timothy 5:14 and why (see p. 47)?
11. Under what conditions does God permit the remarriage of a divorced person (see pp. 48-49)?
12. Who are the "unmarried" in 1 Corinthians 7:8, 11, 32, 34 (see p. 50)?
13. How do we know that Paul didn't prohibit single men from serving as elders (see p. 51)?
14. Is it possible to be married to one woman for life yet not be a one-woman man? Explain (see p. 51).
15. Define "temperate" (v. 2c; see p. 51).
16. Explain the literal sense in which "temperate" was used (see p. 52).
17. How does Proverbs 23:29-35 characterize one who is addicted to wine (see pp. 52-53)?
18. Explain the figurative sense in which "temperate" was used (see pp. 53-54).

Pondering the Principles

1. Review the section entitled "Restoring Fallen Spiritual Leaders" (see p. 44). Perhaps you or someone you know has experienced the confusion and disillusionment that results from the fall of a spiritual leader. What should your attitude be toward that leader (see Gal. 6:1)? Even though many have failed God's standard for leaders, never use such failures to justify lowering your standard of obedience. You must continue to obey the Lord, knowing that He will purge and refine His leaders.

2. What has this chapter taught you about the importance of fidelity within a marriage relationship? How can you maintain purity in that area when our society is so unrelenting in its attacks against biblical standards of morality? Read Psalm 119:9-16, 97-105. How did the psalmist keep his heart pure? From those passages make a list of things you can do to guard your heart from impurity, and prayerfully begin to put them into practice.

3. The Bible has much to say about the destructive nature of excessive wine, but what about drinking in moderation? Scripture is silent on the matter, so you need to answer that question for yourself. To help you think through the issue, reflect on your answers to these questions:

- Why do I want to drink wine (or any alcoholic beverage)?
- Is drinking wine necessary?
- Is drinking wine the best choice?
- Is drinking wine habit-forming?
- Is drinking wine potentially destructive?
- Is my drinking wine offensive to other Christians?
- Will drinking wine harm my Christian testimony?
- Am I absolutely certain drinking wine is right?
- Do I want others to follow my example?

4
The Call to Lead the Church—Elders
Part 4

Outline

Introduction
A. The Need for Spiritual Leadership
B. The Potential for Spiritual Leadership
   1. The place of human potential
      a) From a military leader's perspective
      b) From an educator's perspective
      c) From a pastor's perspective
   2. The priority of divine power
C. The Characteristics of Spiritual Leadership
   1. In general
   2. In specific

Review
I. An Elder Must Be Blameless in His Moral Character (vv. 2*b*-3)
  A. "The Husband of One Wife"—Sexually Pure (v. 2*b*)
  B. "Temperate"—Not Given to Excess (v. 2*c*)

Lesson
  C. "Sober-Minded"—Self-Disciplined (v. 2*d*)
    1. Its definition
    2. Its application
      a) Regarding humor
      b) Regarding good judgment
      c) Regarding right thinking
  D. "Good Behavior"—Well-Organized (v. 2*e*)
    1. Its definition
    2. Its application

E. "Given to Hospitality"—Hospitable (v. 2f)
   1. Its definition
   2. Its application
      a) To the early church
      b) To the pastor and elder
      c) To all Christians
F. "Apt to Teach"—Skilled in Teaching (v. 2g)
   1. Its definition
   2. Its delineation
   3. Its limitation

Conclusion

Introduction

A. The Need for Spiritual Leadership

There is a tremendous need today for church leaders who are authoritative, sacrificial, Spirit-filled, dependent on God, and characterized by integrity. Paul discusses the qualifications for such leaders in 1 Timothy 3:2-7.

B. The Potential for Spiritual Leadership

   1. The place of human potential

   Before considering those qualifications, it will be helpful to identify personality traits and natural characteristics that indicate leadership potential on the human level.

   Although natural aptitude for leadership should never be confused with a spiritual calling, all leadership demands some innate capabilities. Just as you can't effectively minister for the Lord through singing unless God gave you a pleasant voice, we must assume that God grants some basic characteristics to all potential leaders. When those innate capabilities are refined and empowered by God's Spirit, they become important ingredients for church leadership.

a) From a military leader's perspective

Field-Marshal Montgomery enunciated several ingredients necessary in a leader in war: (1) He should be able to avoid getting immersed in details. (2) He must not be petty. (3) He must be a good selector of men. (4) He should trust those under him and let them get on with their jobs without interference. (5) He must have the power of clear decision. (6) He should inspire confidence. (7) He must have a proper sense of religious truth and acknowledge it to his troops (Bernard L. Montgomery, *Memoirs of Field-Marshal Montgomery* [Cleveland: World, 1958], pp. 74-83).

b) From an educator's perspective

These are some of the issues that John R. Mott, a world leader in student circles at the early part of this century, considered in determining a person's leadership potential: (1) Does he do little things well? (2) Has he learned the meaning of priorities? (3) How does he use his leisure? (4) Has he intensity? (5) Has he learned to take advantage of momentum? (6) Has he the power of growth? (7) What is his attitude toward discouragements? (8) How does he face impossible situations? (9) What are his weakest points? (Basil Mathews, *John R. Mott: World Citizen* [N.Y.: Harper & Brothers, 1934], pp. 332-98).

c) From a pastor's perspective

In his book *Spiritual Leadership* ([Chicago: Moody, 1967, 1980] pp. 44-47), J. Oswald Sanders lists these questions and comments for determining whether someone has leadership potential:

- Have you ever broken yourself of a bad habit? To lead others, one must be master of oneself.
- Do you retain control of yourself when things go wrong? The leader who loses self-control in testing circumstances forfeits respect and loses influence. He must be calm in crisis and resilient in adversity and disappointment.

- Do you think independently? While using to the full the thought of others, the leader cannot afford to let others do his thinking or make his decisions for him.
- Can you handle criticism objectively and remain unmoved by it? Do you turn it to good account? The humble man can derive benefit from petty and even malicious criticism.
- Can you use disappointments creatively?
- Do you readily secure the cooperation and win the respect and confidence of others?
- Do you possess the ability to secure discipline without having to resort to a show of authority? True leadership is an internal quality of the spirit and requires no external show of force.
- Have you qualified for the beatitude pronounced on the peacemaker? It is much easier to keep the peace than to make peace where it has been shattered. An important function in leadership is conciliation—the ability to discover common ground between opposing viewpoints and then induce both parties to accept it.
- Are you entrusted with the handling of difficult and delicate situations?
- Can you induce people to do happily some legitimate task that they would not normally wish to do?
- Can you accept opposition to your viewpoint or decision without considering it a personal affront and reacting accordingly? Leaders must expect opposition and should not be offended by it.
- Do you find it easy to make and keep friends? Your circle of loyal friends is an index of the quality and extent of your leadership.
- Are you unduly dependent on the praise or approval of others? Can you hold a steady course in the face of disapproval and even temporary loss of confidence?
- Are you at ease in the presence of your superiors or strangers?
- Do your subordinates appear at ease in your presence? A leader should give an impression of sympathetic understanding and friendliness that will put others at ease.
- Are you really interested in people? In people of all types and all races? Or do you entertain respect of

persons? Is there hidden racial prejudice? An anti-social person is unlikely to make a good leader.

- Do you possess tact? Can you anticipate the likely effect of a statement before you make it?
- Do you possess a strong and steady will? A leader will not long retain his position if he is vacillating.
- Do you nurse resentments, or do you readily forgive injuries done to you?
- Are you reasonably optimistic? Pessimism is no asset to a leader.
- Are you in the grip of a master passion such as that of Paul, who said, "This one thing I do"? Such a singleness of motive will focus all one's energies and powers on the desired objective.
- Do you welcome responsibility?

Those are provocative questions for determining natural leadership potential; God's Spirit will refine, empower, and add specific gifts to an individual's innate abilities in order to produce an effective spiritual leader. The process begins with a God-given potential that is evident even before a man's calling, giftedness, or preparation for ministry.

2. The priority of divine power

Although innate leadership potential is an important ingredient in prospective leaders, we must not confuse potential for natural leadership with qualification for spiritual leadership. I have seen that principle illustrated in my own life as God has graciously and patiently prepared me for leadership in His church.

When I was in high school, some people thought I should run for student body president, so they entered my name into the straw vote they were taking to determine the candidates for that office. All prospective candidates had to be approved by the school's administrators, so one day I was called into the principal's office. He said, "It's come to our attention that you might run for student body president. Furthermore, the straw vote indicates that you might win. To prevent that from happening, we are withdrawing your name from the ballot." And that's exactly what they did! Although I had demonstrated some capacity for leadership, the school administration knew I wasn't mature enough to act as a responsible leader.

During my college years I came home one summer to work. The YMCA was hiring young people to oversee recreational activities at various elementary schools in our area. They wanted young men to open the gate, set up the ping-pong and pool tables, supervise the kids until five o'clock, then put everything away and lock the gate. I applied for the job and had to fill out a rather lengthy application. They wanted to know everything possible about me. After submitting my application I received a phone call informing me of an interview with the panel of people who were evaluating the applicants.

I went to the local City Hall and sat before a panel of five people who quizzed me for nearly one hour. At the end of that time I was rejected as unsuitable for that position of leadership. I was devastated. That was a traumatic experience for me.

In my senior year in college I was very active in church ministry and sports. It was suggested that I run for student body vice-president. I declined the invitation, but a dear friend of mine said he was going to take it upon himself to put my name in the running anyway. I thought he was kidding and that nothing would come of it, but he followed through on his promise.

On election day the various candidates were permitted to post banners and signs around the campus, and when I arrived on campus I was shocked to see that my signs outnumbered the others ten to one! But there was something unusual about those signs. My friend, who was so gracious and so concerned to see me run, had a reading disorder—a form of dyslexia—that impaired his ability to spell. And as a result, my name was spelled wrong on every poster! Not only that, it was spelled differently on every poster. Because it was so funny, I won the election.

So the only place my natural talents ever got me in leadership was student body vice-president because of a joke! I should add that I had the privilege of serving in a leadership role in seminary, but that was only after the Lord had graciously begun to blend the power of His Spirit with any natural abilities I may have had. That's always the point at which true spiritual leadership begins to develop.

So there are characteristics indicative of potential leaders, but they alone don't qualify a man for spiritual leadership. God's servants must be refined and specially gifted by His Spirit. Church leadership cannot be determined by human potential but by spiritual qualifications.

C. The Characteristics of Spiritual Leadership

1. In general

The New Testament tells us that spiritual leaders must be motivated by love—not constraint. They are to be gentle —not harsh or abusive in exercising their authority. They are to be humble, and they must be disciplined in the use of their time and resources. They must have a vision for God's redemptive plan, wisdom in God's Word, and un-compromising obedience to God's will.

They must also be willing to accept loneliness, failure, sacrifice, weariness, criticism, rejection, pressure, disap-pointment, and self-sacrifice. And they must avoid com-paring themselves to others, because that can lead to pride or jealousy.

2. In specific

First Timothy 3:2-7 is a list of specific characteristics and qualifications for church leaders. We have already seen that the overarching qualification for an elder is blame-lessness: his life must be above accusation (v. 2*a*; see pp. 34-40).

Review

An elder must be blameless in his moral character, home life, spiri-tual maturity, and public reputation.

63

I. AN ELDER MUST BE BLAMELESS IN HIS MORAL CHARAC-
TER (vv. 2b-3; see pp. 45-54)

A. "The Husband of One Wife"—Sexually Pure (v. 2b; see pp. 45-51)

B. "Temperate"—Not Given to Excess (v. 2c; see pp. 51-54)

Lesson

C. "Sober-Minded"—Self-Disciplined (v. 2d)

1. Its definition

The Greek word translated "sober-minded" is *sōphrōn*, and it refers to discipline or self-control. It's the result of being temperate (v. 2c). The temperate man avoids excess, so he can see things clearly; that clarity of thought leads to an orderly, disciplined life. He knows how to order his priorities.

The ancient Jewish scholar Philo defined *sōphrōn* as "a certain limiting and ordering of the desires, which eliminates those which are external and excessive, and which adorns those which are necessary with timeliness and moderation" (cited by William Barclay, *The Letters to Timothy, Titus, and Philemon* [Philadelphia: Westminster, 1975], p. 80).

Self-discipline is also required of older men (Titus 2:2) and of women who serve as deaconesses in the church (1 Tim. 3:11).

2. Its application

a) Regarding humor

Sōphrōn also indicates a person who is serious about spiritual things. Such a man doesn't have the reputation of a clown. However, that doesn't mean he avoids humor—any good leader is able to use and enjoy humor. But he appreciates that which really matters in life.

Some young men have a frivolous mentality, but the longer they serve Christ and observe life, the more they are able to see things from God's perspective. As time passes, their frivolity is tempered by their increased understanding that man is lost and disobedient toward God, and that hell is inevitable. That's part of being a sober-minded person. That doesn't mean there's no joy or laughter in their lives, but it's accompanied by an acute awareness of the seriousness of life and ministry.

b) Regarding good judgment

In a broad sense, *sōphrōn* speaks of a person with a sure and steady mind. Such a person is not rash but thoughtful, earnest, and cautious in the judgments he or she makes.

c) Regarding right thinking

A disciplined life is the product of a disciplined mind. This kind of person thinks about what is really important, not what is foolish.

I recently received a letter from a lady who thanked me because our radio program had helped her break a ten-year addiction to soap operas. She had learned to study and meditate on God's Word rather than indulge in her five-hour-a-day viewing habit. She expressed her praise to God for His grace in her life. I rejoice with her because she is learning to set her mind on what is worthy of thought.

Paul said, "Whatever things are true, whatever things are honest, whatever things are just, whatever things are pure, whatever things are lovely, whatever things are of good report; if there be any virtue, and if there be any praise, think on these things" (Phil. 4:8). That's the focus of an ordered and well-disciplined mind.

The sober-minded person overcomes the lusts of the flesh by training his mind to respond to God's truth. That is possible only through Christ's power reigning in His life (Phil. 4:13).

D. "Good Behavior"—Well-Organized (v. 2*e*)

1. Its definition

The Greek word translated "good behavior" is *kosmios*. It comes from the root word *kosmos*, which generally refers to the interplay between human, divine, and satanic values. A man of "good behavior" approaches all the aspects of his life in a systematic, orderly manner.

2. Its application

This kind of person diligently fulfills his many duties and responsibilities. His disciplined mind produces disciplined actions—"good behavior."

The opposite of *kosmos* is chaos. Elders can't have a chaotic lifestyle. That's because their work involves administration, oversight, scheduling, and establishing priorities.

The ministry is no place for a man whose life is a continual confusion of unaccomplished plans and unorganized activities. Over the years I have seen many men who have had difficulty ministering effectively because they couldn't get their lives in order. They couldn't concentrate on one task or systematically set and accomplish goals. Such disorder is a disqualification for the ministry.

E. "Given to Hospitality"—Hospitable (v. 2*f*)

1. Its definition

The Greek word translated "given to hospitality" is composed of the words *xenos* ("stranger") and *phileō* ("to love" or "show affection"). It means to love strangers.

Are You Hospitable in the Biblical Way?

Quite often I hear it said that So-and-so has the gift of hospitality because she is a great cook or because she likes to have friends over for a visit. As important as those virtues are, they are not examples of biblical hospitality.

Biblical hospitality is showing kindness to strangers, not to friends. In Luke 14:12-14 Jesus says, "When you give a luncheon or a dinner, do not invite your friends or your brothers or your relatives or rich neighbors, lest they also invite you in return, and repayment come to you. But when you give a reception, invite the poor, the crippled, the lame, the blind, and you will be blessed, since they do not have the means to repay you; for you will be repaid at the resurrection of the righteous" (NASB).

I realize that showing love toward strangers requires vulnerability, and can even be dangerous because some may take advantage of your kindness. While God doesn't ask us to discard wisdom and discernment in dealing with strangers (cf. Matt. 10:16), He does require us to love them. What about you? Do you practice biblical hospitality?

2. Its application

   a) To the early church

   The prevalence of persecution and poverty, and the high number of orphans and widows in the early church, made it necessary for Christians to open their homes to others. In addition, traveling Christians were dependent on the hospitality of other Christians, for most of the public inns were brothels in which lodgers were in danger of being robbed, beaten, or solicited to evil.

   Commentator William Barclay wrote, "In the ancient world, inns were notoriously bad. In one of Aristophanes' plays Heracles asks his companion where they will lodge for the night; and the answer is: 'Where the fleas are fewest.' Plato speaks of the innkeeper's being like a pirate who holds his guests to ransom. Inns tended to be dirty and expensive and, above all, immoral.

"The ancient world had a system of what were called *Guests Friendships*. Over generations families had arrangements to give each other accommodation and hospitality. Often the members of the families came in the end to be unknown to each other by sight and identified themselves by means of what were called *tallies*. The stranger seeking accommodation would produce one half of some object; the host would possess the other half of the tally; and when the two halves fitted each other the host knew that he had found his guest, and the guest knew that the host was indeed the ancestral friend of his household.

"In the Christian Church there were wandering teachers and preachers who needed hospitality. There were also many slaves with no homes of their own to whom it was a great privilege to have the right of entry to a Christian home. It was of the greatest blessing that Christians should have Christian homes ever open to them in which they could meet people like minded to themselves.

"We live in a world where there are still many who are far from home, many who are strangers in a strange place, many who live in conditions where it is hard to be a Christian. The door of the Christian home and the welcome of the Christian heart should be open to all such" (*The Letters to Timothy, Titus, and Philemon* [Philadelphia: Westminster, 1975], p. 82).

b) To the pastor and elder

The pastor must not be unapproachable or isolated from his people. Even his home is a tool for God's service. His availability makes it possible for his people to observe his true character as he interacts with the various aspects of life and ministry both inside and outside his home.

68

When I consider my responsibility to love strangers, I am reminded that God received into His family us who were "aliens from the commonwealth of Israel, and strangers from the covenants of promise, having no hope, and without God in the world" (Eph. 2:12). Since those of us who are Gentiles have been welcomed by God, how can we fail to welcome strangers into our homes? After all, everything we have belongs to God. We are simply His stewards.

Yet we need to exercise discretion in the stewardship of what we have. If a couple shows up at my door with eight little children and four new boxes of crayons, I will be a little leery! One time we had the walls of our home decorated by overzealous young artists, so we are sensitive to the problems that can arise from opening one's home to strangers. We don't want to be wasteful with the resources God has given us, but we must remember that those resources belong to Him. And He commands us to love strangers.

c) To all Christians

All Christians are commanded to show hospitality.

(1) Romans 12:13—Paul listed "given to hospitality" as a command for every true believer.

(2) Hebrews 13:2—"Do not neglect to show hospitality to strangers, for by this some have entertained angels without knowing it" (NASB). The writer has Abraham and Sarah in mind, who graciously served a meal to three strangers only to discover that they were none other than God Himself and two holy angels, who came in the form of men (Gen. 18:1-8).

(3) 1 Peter 4:9—"Use hospitality one to another without grudging." Our hospitality must flow from willing and gracious hearts.

Hospitality goes beyond opening your home to strangers—it includes opening your heart as well. Sometimes that's the best avenue for evangelism. We need to be sensitive to the spiritual and physical needs of others.

F. "Apt to Teach"—Skilled in Teaching (v. 2*g*)

1. Its definition

The Greek word translated "apt to teach" (*didaktikon*) is used only two times in the New Testament (once in the passage discussed in this lesson and once in 2 Tim. 2:24), and it means "skilled in teaching." It's the only qualification listed in 1 Timothy 3:2 that relates specifically to the function of an elder and sets the elder apart from the deacon (vv. 8-10), is highly qualified morally and spiritually, but is also skilled in teaching.

The stipulation that the leader be "apt to teach" is listed with the moral qualifications because teaching effectively is predicated on the character of the teacher. You cannot divorce what a teacher is from what he says when the content of his teaching is moral. He must exemplify what he teaches.

2. Its delineation

Paul repeatedly reminded Timothy of the priority of teaching.

a) 1 Timothy 5:17—"Let the elders that rule well be counted worthy of double honor, especially they who labor in the word and doctrine." The Greek word translated "labor" (*kopiaō*) means "to work to the point of exhaustion."

It saddens me to see ministers overly concerned about adequate leisure time when God's Word constrains us to labor to the point of exhaustion. Obviously there is need for proper rest, but the priority is clear.

b) Ephesians 4:11-12—Christ provides the church with evangelists and teaching pastors—the equivalent of elders—to mature the saints. Teaching God's Word is their means of accomplishing that end (2 Tim. 3:17).

c) 1 Timothy 4:6, 11, 16—"If thou put the brethren in remembrance of these things, thou shalt be a good minister of Jesus Christ. . . . These things command and teach. . . . Take heed unto thyself and unto the doctrine." A good minister reminds his people of divine truth by communicating God's Word.

d) 2 Timothy 1:13—"Hold fast the form of sound words, which thou hast heard of me."

e) 2 Timothy 2:15—"Study to show thyself approved unto God, a workman that needeth not to be ashamed, rightly dividing the word of truth." The elder must labor to interpret God's Word correctly.

f) 2 Timothy 2:2—"The things that thou hast heard from me among many witnesses, the same commit thou to faithful men, who shall be able to teach others also." As the church continued to grow and the apostles faded from the scene, there was a tremendous need for teachers. So Paul instructed Timothy to teach men who could teach others. That was the primary role of the elder.

Elders must be skilled in teaching. They must have the ability to communicate God's Word and the integrity to make their teaching believable.

3. Its limitation

The role of teaching the church is limited to those who have been called and gifted for that task. You do not need to be ashamed if you're not gifted to teach. God simply wants you to be faithful in using whatever gifts He has given you.

In 1 Corinthians 12 Paul discusses the gifts of the Spirit. Verse 28 says, "God hath set some in the church: first apostles, second prophets, third teachers; after that miracles, then gifts of healings, helps, governments, diversities of tongues." All church leadership is the work of God.

In verse 29 Paul asks, "Are all apostles? Are all prophets? Are all teachers? Are all workers of miracles?" The obvious answer is no. We are all teachers in an informal sense as we proclaim God's truth in our daily conversations, but not all are teachers in the formal sense.

I believe that those called to teach have innate human potential for leadership, and that they are refined and gifted by God's Spirit. They are then nurtured through education and other means to be fully qualified to lead the church.

Conclusion

An elder orders his priorities clearly, has a well-organized life, and has the gifts and integrity to be a skilled teacher of God's Word. That's the kind of person God has called to lead His church.

Establishing and maintaining godly leaders is the most important issue in the church because they set the pattern for the congregation to follow. Pray that God will maintain the purity of your church leaders and that He will raise up many more godly leaders for the church around the world.

Focusing on the Facts

1. What kind of leaders are needed in the church today (see p. 58)?
2. What characteristics did Field-Marshal Montgomery find necessary for an effective military leader (see p. 59)?
3. What questions did John R. Mott use to determine leadership potential (see p. 59)?
4. What questions and comments did J. Oswald Sanders offer for determining leadership potential (see pp. 59-61)?
5. What must occur before someone with natural leadership abilities is qualified to be an effective spiritual leader (see p. 61)?
6. Church leadership cannot be determined by _____ _____ but by _____ _____ (see p. 63).
7. What are the general characteristics of spiritual leaders (see p. 63)?

8. Define "sober-minded" (v. 2d; see p. 64).
9. How does being sober-minded relate to being temperate (v. 2c; see p. 64)?
10. In addition to elders, who else must be sober-minded (1 Tim. 3:11; Titus 2:2; see p. 64)?
11. How does being sober-minded relate to humor (see pp. 64-65)?
12. What should a person who wants a disciplined mind dwell on (Phil. 4:8; see p. 65)?
13. The sober-minded person overcomes the lusts of the flesh by training his mind to respond to _____ _____ (see p. 66).
14. Define "good behavior" (v. 2e; see p. 66).
15. What is the relationship of good behavior to sober-mindedness (see p. 66)?
16. Define "given to hospitality" (v. 2f; see p. 66).
17. How did Jesus define hospitality in Luke 14:12-14 (see p. 67)?
18. Why was hospitality especially important in the days of the early church (see pp. 67-68)?
19. Who are the special recipients of Abraham and Sarah's hospitality in Genesis 18:1-8 (Heb. 13:2; see p. 69)?
20. What is the relationship of hospitality to evangelism (see pp. 69-70)?
21. Define "apt to teach" (v. 2g; see p. 70).
22. Why is "apt to teach" listed among the moral qualification for elders (see p. 70)?
23. Define "labor" in 1 Timothy 5:17 (see p. 70).
24. What was the primary function of New Testament evangelists and teaching pastors (Eph. 4:12; see p. 70)?
25. To whom is the role of teaching the church limited (see p. 71)?
26. Is there a sense in which all Christians are teachers? Explain (see p. 72).

Pondering the Principles

1. We have seen that God grants innate leadership potential to those He calls to lead the church. That potential is often evident even before one is called, gifted, and trained for a specific leadership role. Perhaps you are such a person. Carefully read through the questions and comments by J. Oswald Sanders (see pp. 59-61). Are you encouraged by your responses? Do you desire to see those characteristics increase in your life? If so, take every opportunity to cultivate your leadership potential and

carefully consider the qualifications for spiritual leaders (1 Tim. 3:1-7). Aim at being that kind of person. Share your desire with a pastor or elder who can encourage you, guide your training, and hold you accountable.

2. A disciplined mind is the key to a disciplined life. Cultivating a disciplined mind requires that you constantly expose it to what is good. Read the following passages, making a list of what the psalmist meditated on: Psalm 1:1-2; 63:6; 77:12; 119:15, 27, 48, 97-105; 143:5. What things do you meditate on? Should some of those things be eliminated? If so, ask God to help you be more disciplined in your thinking as you learn to focus on what is true, honorable, right, pure, lovely, of good repute, excellent, and worthy of praise (Phil. 4:8).

3. Biblical hospitality is showing love for strangers—being sensitive to their needs and making sacrifices on their behalf when necessary. Can you think of some practical ways that you can express Christ's love to strangers? Pray for opportunities to do so, and take advantage of them as they arise. Remember, hospitality is an attitude as much as an action, and your sensitivity to a stranger's needs can bring about opportunities for evangelism.

5
The Call to Lead the Church—Elders
Part 5

Outline

Introduction
A. The Priorities of Ministry
    1. Evangelizing the lost
    2. Edifying believers
    3. Teaching God's Word
    4. Praying for God's people
    5. Strengthening families
    6. Attending to special needs
    7. Having Communion and baptism
    8. Promoting holy living
B. The Demands of Ministry
    1. Discipline
    2. Self-Denial
    3. Hard work
    4. Organizational skills
    5. Proper attitudes
    6. Patience

Review
I. An Elder Must Be Blameless in His Moral Character (vv. 2b-3)
    A. "The Husband of One Wife"—Sexually Pure (v. 2b)
    B. "Temperate"—Not Given to Excess (v. 2c)
    C. "Sober-Minded"—Self-Disciplined (v. 2d)
    D. "Good Behavior"—Well-Organized (v. 2e)

E. "Given to Hospitality"—Hospitable (v. 2f)
F. "Apt to Teach"—Skilled in Teaching (v. 2g)
   1. Its definition
   2. Its delineation
   3. Its limitation

Lesson
   4. Its identification
G. "Not Given to Wine"—Not a Drinker (v. 3a)
   1. Defined
   2. Defended
H. "Not Violent"—Not a Fighter (v. 3b)
   1. Defined
   2. Delineated
      a) Physical violence
      b) Verbal violence
I. "Patient"—Easily Pardons Human Failure (v. 3c)
   1. Defined
   2. Applied
J. "Not a Brawler"—Not Quarrelsome (v. 3d)
K. "Not Covetous"—Free from the Love of Money (v. 3e)
   1. The definition
   2. The danger
   3. The defense

Conclusion

Introduction

A. The Priorities of Ministry

In 1 Timothy 3:1-7 the apostle Paul lists the qualifications for elders. Once a man becomes an elder, his responsibilities include teaching, leading, praying, and ordaining other elders. In addition, Scripture gives several priorities for elders to uphold.

1. Evangelizing the lost

Elders are to seek the salvation of unbelievers. The various functions, programs, and ministries of their churches

76

should focus on that ultimate goal. In Acts 26:18 Paul says he was called "to open their eyes, and to turn them from darkness to light, and from the power of Satan unto God, that they may receive forgiveness of sins, and inheritance among them who are sanctified." All spiritual leaders share in that aspect of God's call.

You may be gifted in program development, administration, or some other area of ministry, but evangelism must not be forgotten. No matter what else is left undone, we must present Christ to the unsaved.

2. Edifying believers

Another priority for elders is to edify believers—to stimulate their spiritual growth, so that they become increasingly useful to the Lord. That includes warning the unruly, encouraging the fainthearted, supporting the weak, and being patient with everyone (1 Thess. 5:14).

Ephesians 4:12 says to equip "the saints for the work of the ministry for the edifying of the body of Christ." The context has primary reference to teaching sound doctrine.

Edification also involves confronting and restoring believers who fall into sin (Gal. 6:1), encouraging those who lose their zeal for ministry (2 Tim. 1:6-7), admonishing those who neglect their love for Christ (Rev. 2:4), and challenging faithful believers toward greater perseverance and strength (1 Thess. 4:1).

3. Teaching God's Word

Spiritual shepherds must faithfully feed their flock with the Word of God (Acts 20:28). A steady diet of divine truth is the core of church life.

4. Praying for God's people

Paul's concern for the spiritual maturity of the Galatians was so intense that he referred to it as birth pangs (Gal. 4:19). Agonizing over God's people is a mark of true spiritual leadership, and thus we should be motivated to intercede in prayer on their behalf.

5. Strengthening families

Our families must be taught what their biblical roles are, how to love and serve each other, and how to combat influences that tend to tear families apart. Family members need to be taught how to devote themselves to one another, to God, to His Word, to the church, and to personal ministry.

6. Attending to special needs

We must reach out in love and sympathy to those in distress, whether they be facing death, illness, divorce, or some other disappointment or disaster. Such caring is a great tradition in Christian ministry, and rightly so—Jesus Himself set the example when He responded with compassion to the special needs of those around Him.

Quite often a spiritual leader will be called away from the normal course of his ministry to attend to a special need that arises in someone's life. That's part of the ministry. Sad to say, some leaders see such things as intrusions into their schedules when in reality they are divinely appointed opportunities to demonstrate Christ's love. We need to see such situations in that light and respond accordingly.

7. Having Communion and baptism

I believe it is the responsibility of spiritual leaders to remind the congregation of Christ's death and resurrection through the ordinances of Communion and baptism. Communion reminds us of His death; baptism reminds us of His resurrection.

8. Promoting holy living

When God's people are holy in character and conduct, they are like salt and light in the world (Matt. 5:13-14). Only then can the church penetrate this evil generation with the light of God's truth. Spiritual leaders must exemplify holiness and encourage their people to pursue holiness in their own lives.

Those priorities indicate the serious nature of spiritual leadership; it is a high, holy, and sacred calling. In addition it's very demanding.

B. The Demands of Ministry

Several demands are placed upon spiritual leaders.

1. Discipline

Discipline has been defined as training that develops self-control and character, or orderliness and efficiency. That's an overarching requirement for effective ministry because it affects every area of one's life.

2. Self-Denial

A spiritual leader's life is not his own: he has been called to a task beyond himself. Contrary to the protagonist of Henley's *Invictus*, he is not the master of his own fate, the captain of his own soul, or the determiner of his own destiny. He moves at the bidding of God's Spirit. Therefore, he must practice self-denial.

3. Hard work

Rescuing the unsaved from the hand of Satan is not an easy task. Instructing the saints and working toward their maturity is equally demanding. Hard work is required in every aspect of the ministry.

4. Organizational skills

An elder must focus on what really matters, not on peripheral issues or distractions. He must have the ability to establish priorities and get things done.

5. Proper attitudes

His attitude must be gentle and humble while maintaining zeal, intensity, and seriousness. He must be confrontal, direct, and authoritative, while maintaining warmth, love, and compassion. That may seem like an impossible balance to maintain, but God gives us grace and a divine perspective that help to overcome our weaknesses.

6. Patience

The Puritan minister Richard Baxter understood the need for a pastor to have patience. He wrote, "We must bear with many abuses and injuries from those to whom we seek to do good. When we have studied for them, and prayed for them, and exhorted them, and beseeched them with all earnestness and condescension, and given them what we are able, and tended them as if they had been our children, we must look that many of them will requite us with scorn and hatred and contempt, and account us their enemies, because we 'tell them the truth.'

"Now, we must endure all this patiently, and we must unweariedly hold on in doing good, 'in meekness, instructing those that oppose themselves, if God, peradventure, will give them repentance to the acknowledging of the truth.' We have to deal with distracted men who will fly in the face of their physician, but we must not, therefore, neglect their cure. He is unworthy to be a physician, who will be driven away from a phrenetic patient by foul words" (*The Reformed Pastor* [Carlisle, Pa.: Banner of Truth, 1974], p. 119).

It takes a special man to understand the priorities and meet the demands of ministry. He must be empowered by the Holy Spirit, called by God, and qualified for leadership according to the standards in 1 Timothy 3:1-7.

Review

The overarching qualification for elders is blamelessness (1 Tim. 3:2; see pp. 34-40). There are four categories in which an elder must be blameless: moral character, family life, spiritual maturity, and public reputation.

I. AN ELDER MUST BE BLAMELESS IN HIS MORAL CHARAC-
TER (vv. 2b-3; see pp. 45-72)

A. "The Husband of One Wife"—Sexually Pure (v. 2b; see pp. 45-51)

B. "Temperate"—Not Given to Excess (v. 2c; see pp. 51-54)

C. "Sober-Minded"—Self-Disciplined (v. 2d; see pp. 64-66)

D. "Good Behavior"—Well-Organized (v. 2e; see p. 66)

E. "Given to Hospitality"—Hospitable (v. 2f; see pp. 66-70)

F. "Apt to Teach"—Skilled in Teaching (v. 2g)

  1. Its definition (see p. 70)

  2. Its delineation (see pp. 70-71)

  3. Its limitation (see pp. 71-72)

Lesson

  4. Its identification

Several qualities are common to all skilled Bible teachers. These qualities also serve as criteria with which to measure prospective teachers.

  a) He has credibility

The most powerful impetus to effective teaching is credibility. A skilled teacher will practice what he preaches. If you teach one thing and live another, you are contradicting and undermining your teaching.

Paul said to Timothy, "Let no man despise thy youth, but be thou an example [to] the believers" (1 Tim. 4:12). He wanted Timothy to be a model others could follow—a prototype of his own teaching. Paul went on to list the areas of life in which Timothy should be an example: "in word [what you say], in conduct [what you do], in love [what you feel], in spirit [what you think], in faith, [what you believe], in purity [what motivates you]" (v. 12*b*). That's exemplary behavior in every dimension of life, which is the first and foremost factor in skilled teaching.

In 1 Corinthians 11:1 Paul says, "Be ye followers of me, even as I also am of Christ." You are not a skilled teacher unless you can call on people to follow your example.

b) He has the gift of teaching

The Holy Spirit gives the gift of teaching to those called to teach the church (Rom. 12:7; 1 Cor. 12:28; Eph. 4:11). It is not a natural ability but a Spirit-given endowment that enables one to teach the Word of God effectively.

In 1 Timothy 4:14-16 Paul admonishes Timothy, saying, "Do not neglect the spiritual gift [of teaching] within you. . . . Pay close attention to yourself and to your teaching; persevere in these things" (NASB). In 2 Timothy 1:6 he says, "I put thee in remembrance that thou stir up the gift of God, which is in thee." Paul wanted Timothy to exercise his gift faithfully.

Do You Have the Gift of Teaching?

Though all believers are gifted by the Holy Spirit to minister to the Body of Christ (1 Cor. 12:7), not all have the gift of teaching (Rom. 12:7). How can you know if you have that gift? Ask yourself two questions: (1) Do I have a strong desire to teach? (2) Do my students affirm my giftedness? Those are important considerations. Some people who think they're gifted teachers may have students who disagree.

Remember, the gift of teaching is more than the natural ability to communicate information; it's a spiritual endowment given to those who are called by God to teach His Word. If you have the gift of teaching, be faithful to use it. If you don't, know that the gifts

82

you have are equally important. In either case, be a good steward of your gifts.

c) He has a reservoir of doctrinal understanding

First Timothy 4:6 describes a good minister as being "nourished up in the words of faith and of good doctrine." Even though Timothy was that kind of minister, Paul encouraged him to guard carefully the sound doctrine he had been taught. In 1 Timothy 6:20 Paul says, "O Timothy, keep that which is committed to thy trust." In 2 Timothy 1:13-14 he says, "Retain the standard of sound words which you have heard from me. . . . Guard, through the Holy Spirit . . . the treasure which has been entrusted to you" (NASB).

How Deep Is Your Doctrinal Reservoir?

Paul reminded Timothy that from childhood he (Timothy) had known the Holy Scriptures (2 Tim. 3:15). Even as a child, Timothy was being equipped for teaching. That reservoir of biblical knowledge was a crucial element in his ministry.

Generally speaking, the more doctrinal knowledge a teacher has, the more skilled his teaching will be. That doesn't mean a new Christian can't be a skilled teacher, but he will have to work hard to make up for his lack of knowledge.

Recently I met with other Christian leaders to consider six candidates for a significant ministry position. During our deliberations I noticed that the father of each candidate was a prominent pastor. Each candidate had grown up in a family that taught him biblical truth and exemplified it in their daily living.

That's a tremendous commentary on the richness and depth a Christian heritage adds to a spiritual leader. It also illustrates that a skilled teacher must first be a skilled pupil. Each candidate faithfully had learned and applied what his father taught him.

Are you a skilled learner? Even if you don't have a rich spiritual heritage, you can begin to develop your own doctrinal reservoir.

d) He is humble

A teacher's attitude is as important as his content. If you teach God's truth with arrogance, you undermine what you say. That's why humility is so essential to skilled teaching. Paul said, "The servant of the Lord must not strive, but be gentle unto all men, apt to teach, patient, in meekness instructing those that oppose him" (2 Tim. 2:24-25).

e) He lives a holy life

His life is marked by holiness—not sinless perfection but a commitment to true spirituality and the pursuit of righteousness. He focuses on things of eternal significance.

(1) 1 Timothy 4:7-8, 15-16—Paul said, "Discipline yourself for the purpose of godliness . . . godliness is profitable for all things, since it holds promise for the present life and also for the life to come. . . . Take pains with these things; be absorbed in them. . . . Pay close attention to yourself and to your teaching . . . for as you do this you will insure salvation both for yourself and for those who hear you" (NASB).

(2) 1 Timothy 6:11—Paul encouraged Timothy to "follow after righteousness, godliness, faith, love, patience, meekness."

(3) 2 Timothy 2:20-22—Paul said, "In a great house there are not only vessels of gold and of silver, but also of wood and of earth; and some to honor, and some to dishonor." Most homes are like that: you have good dishes and everyday dishes. When company comes you use the good dishes.

The servant of God seeks to be "a vessel unto honor, sanctified, and fit for the master's use, and prepared unto every good work" (v. 21). To do so you must "flee . . . youthful lusts, [and] follow righteousness, faith, love, peace, with them that call on the Lord out of a pure heart" (v. 22).

f) He is diligent in Bible study

No matter how deep his reservoir of doctrinal knowledge, or how gifted in teaching, a skilled teacher must also be committed to the discipline of study.

(1) 1 Timothy 5:17—Paul said that elders who rule well are worthy of double pay, "especially they who labor in the word and doctrine." The Greek word translated "labor" means working to the point of weariness.

(2) 2 Timothy 2:15—Paul said, "Study to show thyself approved unto God, a workman that needeth not to be ashamed, rightly dividing the word of truth." You must be a diligent student to avoid being ashamed of your work. You can preach and teach with confidence when you know your study has been thorough and accurate.

g) He avoids false doctrine

Many gifted young men who are called into the ministry attend secular or religious schools that overtly attempt to undermine the Christian faith. In doing so they often lose the courage of their convictions.

(1) 1 Timothy 1:4—Paul said, "[Don't] give heed to fables and endless genealogies, which minister questions rather than godly edifying."

(2) 1 Timothy 4:7—Paul said, "Refuse profane and old wives fables." The Greek work translated "refuse" means "to push away" or "don't listen."

(3) 1 Timothy 6:20-21—Paul said to avoid "profane and vain babblings, and oppositions of knowledge falsely so called, which some, professing, have erred concerning the faith." We must avoid false doctrine because it can confuse us and lead us away from biblical truth.

(4) 2 Timothy 2:16-17—Paul said, "Shun profane and vain babblings; for they will increase unto more ungodliness. And their word will eat as doth a gangrene."

If you expose yourself to such people, you are in danger of being victimized by their errors. That's what happened to those whose faith was overthrown by Hymenaeus and Philetus, who taught an unorthodox view of Christ's resurrection (vv. 17-18).

h) He teaches God's Word

The skilled teacher not only avoids error but also teaches the truth. That's why Paul said to Timothy, "I charge thee, therefore, before God, and the Lord Jesus Christ . . . preach the word; be diligent in season, out of season; reprove, rebuke, exhort with all long-suffering and doctrine" (2 Tim. 4:1 2).

i) He has courage and conviction

(1) 1 Timothy 1:18-20—Paul said, "This charge I commit unto thee . . . [hold] faith, and a good conscience, which some, having put away concerning faith, have made shipwreck; of whom are Hymenaeus and Alexander, whom I have delivered unto Satan, that they may learn not to blaspheme." The skilled teacher teaches with conviction and doesn't waver from sound doctrine.

(2) 1 Timothy 4:13, 15—Paul said, "Till I come, give attendance to reading, to exhortation [applying the text], to doctrine [explaining the text]. . . . Meditate upon these things."

(3) 2 Timothy 4:6-7—Paul said, "I am now ready to be offered, and the time of my departure is at hand. I have fought a good fight, I have finished my course, I have kept the faith." It wasn't easy for Paul, but he ended his spiritual journey still holding to the same courage and convictions with which he had started.

Contrast Paul's attitude with that of Demas, who forsook the faith because he loved this present world (v. 10).

G. "Not Given to Wine"—Not a Drinker (v. 3a)

1. Defined

The Greek word translated "given to wine" (*paroinos*) means "one who drinks." It doesn't refer to a drunkard—that had already been explained as an obvious disqualification. The issue here is the man's reputation: Is he known as a drinker?

We know that the Greek word translated "temperate" (v. 3c) refers in its literal sense to one who is not intoxicated. *Paroinos*, on the other hand, refers to one's associations: such a person doesn't frequent bars, taverns, or inns. He is not at home in the noisy scenes associated with drinking. His lifestyle is not that of a drinker.

2. Defended

The same qualification is required of deacons (v. 8). Proverbs 31:4 says, "It is not for kings to drink wine, nor for princes strong drink." Leviticus 10:9 forbids priests from drinking wine or strong drink while performing their sacred duties. Those in spiritual leadership must stay away from anything that distorts their judgment or distracts from their testimony. Their lifestyle must be exemplary.

H. "Not Violent"—Not a Fighter (v. 3b)

1. Defined

You can't be an elder if you settle disputes with your fists or in other violent ways. The Greek word translated "violent" (*plēktēs*) means "a giver of blows" or "a striker." An elder isn't quick-tempered and doesn't resort to unnecessary physical violence.

That qualification is closely related to "not given to wine" because such violence is usually connected with people who drink excessively.

2. Delineated

a) Physical violence

A spiritual leader must be able to handle tense situations with a cool mind and a gentle spirit. Paul said, "The servant of the Lord must not strive" (2 Tim. 2:24).

b) Verbal violence

The tongue can be an instrument of violence. I believe *plēktēs* in this context implies verbal as well as physical violence. In 1 Timothy 6:4-5 Paul says to beware of one who "has a morbid interest in controversial questions and disputes about words, out of which arise envy, strife, abusive language, evil suspicions, and constant friction" (NASB). James 3:6 warns, "The tongue is a fire, a world of iniquity."

A spiritual leader must not deal with difficulties through physical or verbal abuse.

I. "Patient"—Easily Pardons Human Failure (v. 3*c*)

We skipped "not greedy of filthy lucre," which appears in the King James Version but not in the better Greek manuscripts. That qualification is identical in meaning to "not covetous" (v. 3*e*), which we will soon cover in our study (see pp. 89-90).

1. Defined

The Greek word translated "patient" (*epieikēs*) means "to be considerate, genial, forbearing, gracious, or gentle." Aristotle said it speaks of a person who easily pardons human failure (William Barclay, *The Letters to Timothy, Titus and Philemon* [Philadelphia: Westminster, 1975], p. 83).

It's also used in 2 Timothy 2:24: "The servant of the Lord must not strive, but be gentle unto all men, apt to teach, patient."

2. Applied

In a practical sense, patience is the ability to remember good and forget evil. The patient man doesn't keep a record of wrongs people have committed against him (cf. 1 Cor. 13:5).

That's an important virtue for a spiritual leader. I know people who have left the ministry because they couldn't forgive someone who had criticized or upset them. They carry a list of grievances that eventually robs them of the joy of serving others.

Discipline yourself not to talk or even to think about wrongs done against you, because it serves no productive purpose. It simply rehearses the hurts and clouds your mind with anger.

A patient person is able to pardon human failure and focus on the good done by others. He doesn't dwell on getting even because he doesn't hold grudges. That's the kind of person we need in spiritual leadership.

J. "Not a Brawler"—Not Quarrelsome (v. 3*d*)

The Greek word translated "not a brawler" (*amachos*) is similar in meaning to *mēplēktēs* ("not violent," v. 3*b*). The difference is that the latter refers to not being physically violent, whereas the former refers to not being quarrelsome.

When you have a plurality of church leaders attempting to make decisions, you can't get very far if any of them are quarrelsome. That's why Paul said, "The servant of the Lord must not strive, but be gentle unto all men . . . patient" (2 Tim. 2:24). He must be a peacemaker.

K. "Not Covetous"—Free from the Love of Money (v. 3*e*)

1. The definition

The Greek word translated "not covetous" (*aphilarguros*) is a negation of the Greek words for "love" and "silver." It describes someone who doesn't love money.

2. The danger

Love of money can corrupt a man's ministry because it tempts him to view people as a means by which he can get more money. Paul said, "Godliness with contentment is great gain; for we brought nothing into this world, and it is certain we can carry nothing out. And having food and raiment let us be therewith content. But they that will be rich fall into temptation and a snare, and into many foolish and hurtful lusts, which drown men in destruction and perdition. For the love of money is the root of all evil, which, while some coveted after, they have erred from the faith, and pierced themselves through with many sorrows" (1 Tim. 6:6-10).

3. The defense

How do we avoid the love of money? Here's a simple principle I've used: don't place a price on your ministry. Sometimes people ask me how much I charge to teach or preach. I don't charge anything. If I'm paid, that's fine; if not, that's fine too. I leave that up to the Lord and those to whom I minister. I'll accept whatever He supplies, but I don't want my ministry to be influenced, distorted, or corrupted in any way by financial expectations.

If someone gives you a financial gift you didn't seek, you can accept it as from the Lord and be thankful for it. But if you pursue money, you'll never know if it came from Him or from your own efforts. That robs you of the joy of recognizing God's provision for your needs.

Conclusion

An elder must be morally qualified to lead the church. His desires must be focused on heavenly things. He can't allow earthly desires to cripple his faith, love, or spiritual power. He must not be greedy, indulgent, or ambitious for worldly gain or power.

I pray that God will raise up many such men for future spiritual leadership, and that He will make all of us who currently lead His church the kind of men He wants us to be. Be sure to pray for your leaders and for the church around the world. It's becoming increasingly difficult to find qualified spiritual leaders. But God still calls men to the ministry, and He will bless the church that doesn't compromise on His standards for leadership.

Focusing on the Facts

1. According to Acts 26:18, what did Jesus instruct Paul to do (see pp. 76-77)?
2. What does edifying others involve (see p. 77)?
3. A steady diet of _____ _____ is the core of church life (see p. 77).
4. What is an elder's responsibility toward the families in his congregation (see p. 78)?
5. How should an elder react to the special needs of his congregation (see p. 78)?
6. What is the purpose of baptism and Communion (see p. 78)?
7. Define "discipline" (see p. 79).
8. Why must an elder practice self-denial (see p. 79)?
9. What attitude must an elder have toward ministry (see pp. 79-80)?
10. The most powerful impetus to effective teaching is _____ (see p. 81).
11. What is the gift of teaching (see p. 82)?
12. How can you know if you have the gift of teaching (see p. 82)?
13. How did Paul describe a good minister (1 Tim. 4:6; see p. 83)?
14. A skilled teacher must first be a skilled _____ (see p. 83).
15. A teacher's _____ is as important as his content (see p. 84).
16. Define "labor" as used in 1 Timothy 5:17 (see p. 85).
17. Why is it important to avoid false doctrine (see pp. 85-86)?
18. Define *paroinos* (v. 3; see p. 87).
19. In what way does "not given to wine" differ from "temperate" (v. 3; see p. 87)?
20. A spiritual leader must not deal with difficulties through _____ or _____ _____ (see p. 88).
21. Give a practical definition of patience (v. 3; see p. 89).
22. How does *amachos* differ from *plēktēs* (v. 3; see p. 89)?
23. What danger does the love of money present to a spiritual leader (see p. 90)?

Pondering the Principles

1. Before Jesus ascended into heaven He commanded His disciples to "Go . . . make disciples of all the nations" (Matt. 28:19, NASB). In so doing He established evangelism as the number one priority for the church. But many Christians act as if the responsibility for evangelism belongs to the pastor or to the church evangelism committee. What about you? Are you concerned about the lost? When was the last time you spoke to an unbeliever about Christ? Are you currently praying for someone's salvation? Ask God to give you a concern for the lost. Cultivate friendships with unbelievers, and take every opportunity to speak to them about the Lord.

2. We have seen that credibility is the key to effective teaching; your life must model your lesson. That's true even if you aren't a preacher or teacher in the formal sense. We are all teaching something to those who watch us, and they often learn more from our actions than from our words. What are you teaching those who observe your life? Are they learning holiness or hypocrisy?

3. Timothy was a gifted teacher, but he needed encouragement to minister under difficult circumstances (2 Tim. 1:6-7). Perhaps you are experiencing discouragement in your ministry. That happens when we lose sight of our calling, focus on our circumstances, or seek encouragement from the wrong sources. Review these basics and ask God to give you a renewed sense of purpose and direction for the task He has called you to do:

   - To whom should I go for encouragement (Rom. 15:5, NASB)?
   - Where should I go for encouragement (Rom. 15:4, NASB)?
   - What should be the focus of my ministry (1 Cor. 4:1-2)?
   - Should I attempt to evaluate the effectiveness of my ministry (1 Cor. 4:3-4)?
   - What will be the result of my ministry (1 Cor. 4:5)?

6
The Call to Lead the Church—Elders
Part 6

Outline

Introduction
A. The Importance of Integrity in Leadership
   1. According to Dwight Eisenhower
   2. According to John Stott
   3. According to Henry Ward Beecher
B. The Power of Influence in Leadership
   1. Warnings to avoid evil influences
   2. Encouragements to follow godly influences
   3. Results of evil influences
   4. Results of godly influences
     a) The example of Jehoshaphat
     b) The example of Azariah
     c) The example of Jotham
C. The Peril of Hypocrisy in Leadership

Review
I. An Elder Must Be Blameless in His Moral Character (vv. 2*b*-3)

Lesson
II. An Elder Must Be Blameless in His Family Life (vv. 4-5)
A. His Leadership in the Family (v. 4)
   1. The nature of his rule
   2. The quality of his rule
   3. The sphere of his rule
     a) He's a good manager of his resources
     b) He's a good ruler of his family
       (1) His children are submissive
       (2) His children are believers
       (3) His children are respectful

B. His Leadership in the Church (v. 5)
    1. The sphere of his rule
    2. The nature of his rule

Conclusion

Introduction

Scripture places a high premium on qualified leaders. That's why in 1 Timothy 3:2-7 Paul specifies the qualifications of a true leader. The standards are high because spiritual leaders are models of Christian virtue for the congregation to follow. It's essential that they be men of great integrity.

A. The Importance of Integrity in Leadership

Integrity is a key ingredient for any successful leader, whether secular or spiritual.

1. According to Dwight Eisenhower

    Dwight David Eisenhower, former president and general of our armed services, believed the supreme quality for a leader to be integrity. Eisenhower knew that without integrity, no real success is possible for a leader, whether he be in a section gang, on a football field, in an army, or in an office. "The captain of such a team need only have their respect and affection: the team would follow him anywhere" (Peterlyon, *Eisenhower: Portrait of the Hero* [Boston: Little, Brown and Company, 1974], p. 207).

2. According to John Stott

    In his book *Between Two Worlds*, Christian author John Stott says, "Communication is by symbol as well as speech. For 'a man cannot only preach, he must also live. And the life that he lives, with all its little peculiarities, is one of two things: either it emasculates his preaching or it gives it flesh and blood' [J. H. Bavinck, *An Introduction to the Science of Missions* (Presbyterian and Reformed, 1960), p. 93]. We cannot hide what we are. Indeed, what we are speaks as plainly as what we say. When these two voices blend, the impact of the message is doubled. But when they contradict each other, even the positive witness of the one is [negated] by the other.

"This was the case with the man Spurgeon describes as a good preacher but a bad Christian: he 'preached so well and lived so badly, that when he was in the pulpit everybody said he ought never to come out again, and when he was out of it they all declared he never ought to enter it again' [*Lectures to My Students*, (Zondervan, 1980), 1:12-13]. It is at this point that a practical problem presents itself to us. Pastors are told to be models of Christian maturity" ([Grand Rapids: Eerdmans, 1982], p. 264).

The credibility of a spiritual leader depends upon his character. That's why Paul told Timothy and the Ephesian elders to guard their lives carefully (Acts 20:28; 1 Tim. 4:16).

3. According to Henry Ward Beecher

Henry Ward Beecher, a nineteenth-century American preacher, once said, "A preacher is, in some degree, a reproduction of the truth in personal form" (*Lectures on Preaching: Personal Elements in Preaching* [Nelson, 1872], p. 16; cited by Stott, p. 266). That's why a spiritual leader must live a blameless life that lends credibility to his message. In so doing he can have a profound influence for righteousness.

B. The Power of Influence in Leadership

I define leadership as influence, and one's influence is a direct result of his example. That's why the qualifications for spiritual leadership in 1 Timothy 3:2-7 deal with a man's character.

The influence that leaders have on their followers is illustrated throughout Scripture. Often those illustrations are accompanied by a warning to avoid an evil influence or an encouragement to follow a godly influence.

1. Warnings to avoid evil influences

   a) Leviticus 18:3

   God warned the Israelites to avoid pagan peoples: "After the doings of the land of Egypt, wherein ye dwelt, shall ye not do; and after the doings of the land of Canaan, to which I bring you, shall ye not do; neither shall ye walk in their ordinances." He knew the power of an evil influence and the tendency of people to mimic the behavior of those around them.

   b) Deuteronomy 18:9

   Moses said, "When thou art come into the land which the Lord thy God giveth thee, thou shalt not learn to do after the abominations of those nations."

   c) Proverbs 22:24-25

   Solomon said, "Make no friendship with an angry man; and with a furious man thou shalt not go, lest thou learn his ways, and get a snare to thy soul."

   d) Proverbs 29:12

   Solomon said, "If a ruler hearken to lies, all his servants are wicked." An evil ruler will produce evil followers.

   e) Ezekiel 20:18

   God said, "Walk not in the statutes of your fathers, neither observe their ordinances, nor defile yourselves with their idols." He wanted His people to be free from the influence of wicked fathers.

   f) Hosea 4:9

   Hosea said, "Like people, like priest." The people followed the evil example of their leaders, so God punished them all.

g) Matthew 23:2-3

Jesus said, "The scribes and the Pharisees sit in Moses' seat. All, therefore, whatever they bid you observe, that observe and do; but do not after their works; for they say, and do not." The leaders of Israel were hypocrites because they said one thing but did another.

2. Encouragements to follow godly influences

a) 1 Timothy 4:12

Paul said, " [Timothy] in speech, conduct, love, faith and purity, show yourself an example of those who believe" (NASB).

b) Titus 2:7

Paul similarly instructed Titus, "In all things show yourself to be an example of good deeds" (NASB).

c) Hebrews 13:7

The writer said, "Remember those who led you, who spoke the word of God to you; and considering the result of their conduct, imitate their faith" (NASB).

d) James 5:10

James said, "As an example, brethren, of suffering and patience, take the prophets who spoke in the name of the Lord" (NASB).

e) 1 Peter 5:3

Peter instructed all elders to be good examples to their congregations.

f) 1 Corinthians 11:1

Paul said, "Be ye followers of me, even as I also am of Christ."

g) Philippians 4:9

Paul said, "Those things which ye have both learned, and received, and heard, and seen in me, do, and the God of peace shall be with you."

We all influence others for good or evil. That's why Scripture deals so pointedly with the moral character of an elder. His godly example is the most important element in his leadership.

3. Results of evil influences

Some of the kings of Israel and Judah illustrate the tragic results of an evil influence.

a) The example of Nadab in Israel

First Kings 15:25-26 says, "Nadab, the son of Jeroboam began to reign over Israel in the second year of Asa, king of Judah, and reigned over Israel two years. And he did evil in the sight of the Lord, and walked in the way of his father, and in his sin with which he made Israel to sin." Nadab followed his father's evil example.

b) The example of Ahaziah in Israel

First Kings 22:51-53 says, "Ahaziah, the son of Ahab, began to reign over Israel in Samaria the seventeenth year of Jehoshaphat, king of Judah, and reigned two years over Israel. And he did evil in the sight of the Lord, and walked in the way of his father, and in the way of his mother, and in the way of Jeroboam, the son of Nebat, who made Israel to sin; for he served Baal, and worshiped him, and provoked to anger the Lord God of Israel, according to all that his father had done."

c) The example of Jehoram in Judah

In 2 Kings 8:16-18 we read, "In the fifth year of Joram, the son of Ahab, king of Israel, Jehoshaphat being then king of Judah, Jehoram, the son of Jehoshaphat, king of Judah, began to reign. Thirty and two years old was he when he began to reign, and he reigned eight years in Jerusalem. And he walked in the way of the kings of Israel, as did the house of Ahab; for the daughter of Ahab was his wife. And he did evil in the sight of the Lord."

d) The example of Ahaziah in Judah

Second Kings 8:25-27 says, "In the twelfth year of Joram, the son of Ahab, king of Israel, did Ahaziah, the son of Jehoram, king of Judah, begin to reign. Two and twenty years old was Ahaziah when he began to reign, and he reigned one year in Jerusalem. And his mother's name was Athaliah, the daughter of Omri, king of Israel. And he walked in the way of the house of Ahab, and did evil in the sight of the Lord, as did the house of Ahab; for he was the son-in-law of the house of Ahab." The wickedness of that family was perpetuated from generation to generation. That's the power of an evil influence.

e) The example of Jeroboam in Israel

In 2 Kings 17:21-22 we read, "[The Lord] forcibly removed Israel from the house of David; and they made Jeroboam, the son of Nebat, king; and Jeroboam drove Israel from following the Lord, and made them sin a great sin. For the children of Israel walked in all the sins of Jeroboam which he did; they departed not from them." The influence of Jeroboam changed the course of an entire nation.

f) The example of Manasseh in Judah

Second Chronicles 33:9 says, "Manasseh made Judah and the inhabitants of Jerusalem to err, and to do worse than the nations, whom the Lord had destroyed before the children of Israel." Manasseh made

God's people act worse than the heathen. What horrifying influence he had!

It's not enough for spiritual leaders to teach the truth; they must model it in their lives. That's what integrity is all about: living what you teach. And that's why the standards in 1 Timothy 3:2-3 relate to a church leader's moral character. His influence in the church will be tremendous, so he must be morally blameless.

Does God Curse Children?

Deuteronomy 5:9 says, "I the Lord thy God am a jealous God, visiting the iniquity of the fathers upon the children unto the third and fourth generation of them who hate me." Many people think that verse means that God automatically curses an evil man's children for three or four generations. Some even teach that you should never adopt a child, because he or she might be under a divine curse for the sins of his father, grandfather, or great grandfather.

I believe that's an incorrect interpretation of the verse. The issue is not a divine curse upon children but the power of an evil influence. Sin and unbelief can so thoroughly pollute a family that it can take three or four generations to root out and change the problem.

4. Results of godly influences

The godly kings of Judah illustrate the power of a good influence.

a) The example of Jehoshaphat

First Kings 22:42-43 says, "Jehoshaphat was thirty and five years old when he began to reign, and he reigned twenty and five years in Jerusalem. And his mother's name was Azubah, the daughter of Shilhi. And he walked in all the ways of Asa, his father; he turned not aside from it, doing that which was right in the eyes of the Lord." Even though Jehoshaphat failed at times, Scripture commends him for following his father's godly example.

b) The example of Azariah

In 2 Kings 15:1-3 we read, "In the twenty and seventh year of Jeroboam, king of Israel, began Azariah, son of Amaziah, king of Judah, to reign. Sixteen years old was he when he began to reign, and he reigned two and fifty years in Jerusalem. And his mother's name was Jecoliah, of Jerusalem. And he did that which was right in the sight of the Lord, according to all that his father, Amaziah, had done."

c) The example of Jotham

Second Kings 15:32-34 says, "In the second year of Pekah, the son of Remaliah, king of Israel, began Jotham, the son of Uzziah, king of Judah, to reign. Five and twenty years old was he when he began to reign, and he reigned sixteen years in Jerusalem. And his mother's name was Jerusha, the daughter of Zadok. And he did that which was right in the sight of the Lord; he did according to all that his father, Uzziah, had done."

Other godly leaders in Israel included Hezekiah, Josiah, Ezra, and Nehemiah.

What Kind of Influence Do You Have on Others?

Every leader has the power to influence others for good or evil through his example. That's why God requires elders to model a high standard of godliness. That's also why 1 Timothy 3 doesn't list qualifications typical of today's corporate leaders: diligence, foresight, conceptual vision, administrative skills, decisiveness, courage, humor, eloquence, friendliness, tact, diplomacy, and so on. Those human characteristics are helpful in secular situations, but the issue in spiritual leadership is modeling godly virtue.

An elder is to evangelize unbelievers, edify believers, feed the flock, strengthen families, and help the church act as salt and light in the world. Therefore the church must choose qualified elders. No one else is suitable for such a high calling.

C. The Peril of Hypocrisy in Leadership

John Stott wrote, "William Golding is a contemporary novelist who has vividly illustrated the negative power of hypocrisy. In his book *Free Fall* [Harcourt Brace, 1962] he tells the story of Sammy Mountjoy, an illegitimate child brought up in a slum, who became a famous artist. During his school days he was torn between two teachers and between the two worlds they represented. On the one hand there was Miss Rowena Pringle, a Christian who taught Scripture, and on the other Mr. Nick Shales, an atheist who taught science. Hers was the world of 'the burning bush,' of supernatural mystery, his of a rationally explicable universe.

"Instinctively, Sammy was drawn to the burning bush. Unfortunately, however, the advocate of this Christian interpretation of life was a frustrated spinster who had her knife into Sammy because he had been adopted by the clergyman she had hoped to marry. She took her revenge by being cruel to the boy. 'But how,' Sammy later asked himself, 'could she crucify a small boy . . . and then tell the story of that other crucifixion with every evidence in her voice of sorrow for human cruelty and wickedness? I can understand how she hated, but not how she kept on such apparent terms of intimacy with heaven' [p. 210]. It was this contradiction which kept Sammy from Christ."

Stott went on to quote Sammy as saying that Miss Pringle's life nullified her teaching: " 'She failed to convince, not by what she said but by what she was. Nick persuaded me to his natural scientific universe by what he was, not by what he said. I hung for an instant between two pictures of the universe; then the ripple passed over the burning bush and I ran towards my friend. In that moment a door closed behind me. I slammed it shut on Moses and Jehovah' " (*Between Two Worlds* [Grand Rapids: Eerdmans, 1982], pp. 268-69).

How many doors have been slammed shut on Moses and Jehovah because of hypocritical Christians? When such Christians are church leaders, the potential for harm is even greater due to the breadth of their influence. That's the power of an example, and that's why an elder's character is so important.

Review

We have seen that the overarching qualification for an elder is blamelessness (1 Tim. 3:2; see pp. 34-40): his life must be exemplary because others will follow his example. He must be blameless in his moral character, family life, maturity, and reputation.

I. AN ELDER MUST BE BLAMELESS IN HIS MORAL CHARACTER (vv. 2*b*-3; see pp. 45-54, 64-72, 81-91)

Paul paid careful attention to his moral character. He said, "I buffet my body and make it my slave, lest possibly, after I have preached to others, I myself should be disqualified" (1 Cor. 9:27, NASB). He admonished Timothy to "flee from youthful lusts, and pursue righteousness" (2 Tim. 2:22, NASB). Anyone desiring to lead in the church must give careful attention to his moral integrity.

Are There Weeds in Your Spiritual Garden?

I don't know much about gardening, but I recently read something that caught my attention. It said that it isn't enough for a gardener to love flowers; he must also hate weeds. That's analogous to our Christian commitment: it isn't enough for a church leader to love God's Word; he must also hate sin. If anything comes into his life that is at all doubtful, he must remove it, just as a gardener removes anything that might distract from the beauty of his garden or hinder the growth of his flowers.

That principle is illustrated in an incident involving Dr. Maltbie Babcock, former pastor of the Brick Presbyterian Church in New York City. Some years ago he was approached by a physician in his congregation who was concerned about Dr. Babcock's health. Handing him some theater tickets the physician said, "Take these. You need the recreation of going to see a play." Dr. Babcock looked at them. Seeing that they were tickets to a play of the kind he could not conscientiously attend, he said kindly, "Thank you, but I'm afraid I cannot take them." "Why not?" the physician asked. Dr. Babcock replied, "Doctor, it's this way. You're a physician—a surgeon, in fact. Before you operate, you scrub your hands meticulously. You wouldn't dare operate with dirty hands. I'm a servant of Christ. I deal with precious human souls. I wouldn't dare serve others with a dirty life."

That pastor understood the importance of a godly example. Do you? Do you guard your example closely, or have you allowed some weeds to take root in your spiritual garden?

Lesson

II. AN ELDER MUST BE BLAMELESS IN HIS FAMILY LIFE (vv. 4-5)

"One that ruleth well his own house, having his children in subjection with all gravity (for if a man know not how to rule his own house, how shall he take care of the church of God?)."

An elder's home life is an essential consideration. Before he can lead in the church he must demonstrate his spiritual leadership within the context of his family.

Does Scripture Teach Celibacy for Church Leaders?

The Roman Catholic Church teaches that church leaders must be celibate, but Scripture teaches that an elder must be a spiritual leader in his family.

The Catholic church was not the first religious group to advocate a celibate leadership. Apparently the same improper emphasis existed in Ephesus. In 1 Timothy 4 Paul warns about those who "shall depart from the faith, giving heed to seducing spirits, and doctrines of demons . . . forbidding to marry" (vv. 1, 3). They set a false standard of spirituality by advocating celibacy for those who wanted to rise above the spiritual level of others.

An elder's family is the proving ground for his leadership skills. That doesn't mean only men with families can be elders, but those who do have families must be godly leaders at home.

104

A. His Leadership in the Family (v. 4)

"One that ruleth well his own house, having his children in subjection with all gravity."

1. The nature of his rule

The Greek word translated "rule" means "to preside, have authority over, stand before, or manage." He is the manager of his home.

That affirms the consistent biblical teaching on male headship in the home. Obviously there are shared responsibilities between husband and wife, and there are many tasks that the wife manages within the home; but the husband must be the leader.

The same Greek word is used in 1 Timothy 5:17: "Let the elders that rule well be counted worthy of double honor." An elder's ability to rule the church is affirmed in his home. Therefore, he must be a strong spiritual leader in his home before he is qualified to lead in the church.

2. The quality of his rule

He must rule his home "well." There are many men who rule their home but they don't rule very well—they don't get the desired results.

The Greek word translated "well" (*kalōs*) is rich in meaning. It could be translated "excellently," but that wouldn't give us the full meaning. To understand its meaning, we need to compare it with *agathos*, a common word in the New Testament that means "inherently good, morally good, or practically good." *Kalōs* goes a step further to include the idea of being aesthetically good: it is beautiful, lovely, and appealing to the eye.

The idea is that an elder's leadership in the home is inherently good, and manifestly good to those who observe it.

3. The sphere of his rule

   a) He's a good manager of his resources

   By implication, a man's home includes his resources. A man may love the Lord and be spiritually and morally qualified to be an elder. He may even be skilled in teaching and have a believing wife and children who follow his leadership in the home, but let's say he has mismanaged his funds and is in the midst of bankruptcy. Somehow he can't seem to put his finances into proper order. Since in the area of finances he doesn't rule his household well, he is disqualified from spiritual leadership.

   Stewardship of possessions is a critical test of a man's leadership. His home is a proving ground where his administrative abilities can be clearly demonstrated.

   b) He's a good ruler of his family

   In addition to managing his resources, an elder must rule his family properly.

   (1) His children are submissive

   The Greek word translated "subjection" is a military term that speaks of lining up in rank under those in authority. His children are to be lined up under his authority—respectful, controlled, and disciplined.

   That qualification applies only if a man has children. He's not disqualified if he doesn't have children. But if God has given him children, they must be under control and respectful toward their parents.

   (2) His children are believers

   Titus 1:5-6 says an elder must have "children who believe, not accused of dissipation or rebellion" (NASB). The Greek word translated "believe" (*pistos*) refers in that context to believing the gospel.

An elder's children must believe the message he's preaching and teaching. If they are unbelievers, they rob his ministry of credibility.

The same standard is required of deacons: "Let the deacons be the husbands of one wife, ruling their children and their own houses well" (1 Tim. 3:12). That's an important issue to the Lord.

Before a man is qualified to lead in the church, he must first demonstrate his ability to rule his own household well. That includes the people and the resources God has entrusted to him. His children must be under control and respectful, and when they reach the age where they can make their own commitment to Christ, they must be believers.

(3) His children are respectful

The Greek word translated "gravity" refers to dignity and respect. It blends the concepts of dignity, courtesy, humility, and competence. It describes stateliness or refinement. His children bring honor to their parents.

Is It Unfair to Disqualify a Man Because of His Family's Sins?

It's possible that a man who is otherwise qualified for spiritual leadership can be disqualified on the family level. Perhaps his personal life is right before the Lord but he became a Christian after his wife or children had already established sinful patterns of behavior, so his family life is in chaos. In that case he is not qualified to lead in the church.

He may have children who are not favored with the sovereign electing grace of Christ. In that case he does not qualify to be an elder, but God has other plans for him. He is not relegated to an inferior ministry. Church leadership is of high priority, but *every* ministry is important (1 Cor. 12:12-25). The key is for him to faithfully pursue the ministry opportunities God brings his way, and refuse to regard his task as inferior in any sense.

In the Old Testament there were certain physical disqualifications for a priest. Leviticus 21:16-20 says, "The Lord spoke to Moses, saying, 'Speak to Aaron, saying, "No man of your offspring throughout their generations who has a defect shall approach to offer the bread of his God. For no one who has a defect shall approach: a blind man, or a lame man, or he who has a disfigured face, or any deformed limb, or a man who has a broken foot or broken hand, or a hunchback or a dwarf, or one who has a defect in his eye or eczema or scabs or crushed testicles" ' " (NASB).

An individual with a physical deformity was not permitted to perform priestly duties. That wasn't a commentary on the character or spiritual life of a deformed man, but simply a matter of God's selecting a certain kind of man to serve as priest. He wanted unblemished men as models of spiritual service. The same standard applies to church leadership. God wants elders to have unblemished and exemplary home lives.

Three Keys to Spiritual Leadership at Home

A. Authority

It's essential that a father exercise enough authority for his children to obey him. Where there's disobedience, there must be immediate and negative consequences. Because of the Fall, all human beings start out spiritually depraved. The only way you can train a depraved person to do what is right is to associate pain with disobedience (Prov. 13:24).

B. Wisdom

A father must have enough wisdom for it to be natural and reasonable for his children to obey him. Invariably a child will question his authority: "Why can't I do that?" or, "Why should I do this?" Whether you like it or not, the entire time you are rearing your children you are the neighborhood philosopher and theologian to them. That requires your being reasonable in what you expect of them.

C. Love

A father must have enough love to make it easy for his children to obey him. Your children should long to obey you because they don't ever want to do anything that would hinder their relationship with you.

As I reflect on my own children, I'm confident that they have obeyed because it was advisable to do so—we taught them that lesson. I hope they obeyed because it was reasonable and natural to do so. But most of all I hope they obeyed because it was a delight to do so and because they wanted to preserve the close bond we have with each other. I thank God for the wonderful relationship we all have.

The reason an elder must demonstrate authority, wisdom, and love at home is that he is called to do the same in the church. He must "speak, and exhort, and rebuke with all authority" (Titus 2:15). To do that he must have enough authority to make it advisable for the congregation to obey, enough wisdom to make it reasonable to obey, and enough love to make it easy to obey.

B. His Leadership in the Church (v. 5)

"If a man know not how to rule his own house, how shall he take care of the church of God?"

1. The sphere of his rule

That verse is a negative restatement of verse 4. In the Greek text, "the church of God" is literally "a church of God," and refers to a local assembly. A man isn't qualified to rule any local assembly if he can't rule his own house.

2. The nature of his rule

The Greek word translated "care" is beautifully illustrated in the parable of the Good Samaritan: "A certain man went down from Jerusalem to Jericho, and fell among thieves, who stripped him of his raiment, and wounded him, and departed, leaving him half dead. And by chance there came down a certain priest that way; and when he saw him, he passed by on the other side. And likewise a Levite, when he was at the place, came and looked on him, and passed by on the other side.

"But a certain Samaritan, as he journeyed, came where he was; and when he saw him, he had compassion on him, and went to him, and bound up his wounds, pouring in oil and wine, and set him on his own beast, and brought him to an inn, and took care of him" (Luke 10:30-34).

In that parable "care" is a verb that encompasses compassion, medical care, transportation, and the offering of time and money. It's sacrificial giving on behalf of others, and that's what church leadership is all about.

I believe there's no better place to see a man's commitment to meeting the needs of others than in his own home. Does he care about his family? Is he committed to each member? Does he work hard to meet their needs? If he doesn't, how will he ever care for the church?

Conclusion

Qualified elders are blameless in their moral character and family life. Their children love the Lord and submit to parental authority. Admittedly such men are uncommon, but God wants that caliber of man to lead his church. The standards are high because elders must be models of spiritual virtue so that their example and influence are godly.

Focusing on the Facts

1. What did President Eisenhower say about the importance of integrity in leadership (see p. 94)?
2. Leadership can be defined as _____ (see p. 95).
3. What warning does God give the Israelites in Leviticus 18:3 (see p. 96)?
4. According to Proverbs 29:12, what influence does an evil ruler have on his people (see p. 96)?

5. How does Jesus describe the scribes and Pharisees in Matthew 23:2-3 (see p. 97)?
6. Peter instructed all elders to be _____ _____ to their congregations (1 Pet. 5:3; see p. 97).
7. How does Nadab illustrate the influence of an evil example (1 Kings 15:26; see p. 98)?
8. It's not enough for spiritual leaders to _____ the truth; they must _____ it in their lives (see p. 100).
9. Does Deuteronomy 5:9 teach that God curses the children of a sinful man? Explain (see p. 100).
10. How does Azariah illustrate the influence of a godly example (2 Kings 15:1; see p. 101)?
11. In William Golding's novel *Free Fall*, how did Rowena Pringle demonstrate hypocrisy, and what impact did her example have on Sammy Mountjoy (see p. 102)?
12. What was Dr. Babcock's explanation for not accepting the theater tickets offered him (see pp. 103-4)?
13. How does 1 Timothy 3:4 refute the view that church leaders must be celibate (see p. 104)?
14. Define "rule" (v. 4; see p. 105).
15. Describe the difference between the Greek words *kalōs* and *agathos* (see p. 105)?
16. Is management of resources included in the idea of ruling one's home? Explain (see p. 106).
17. Define "subjection" (v. 5; see p. 106).
18. Can a man who does not have children be an elder? Explain (see p. 106).
19. What does it mean to have "children who believe" (Titus 1:6, NASB; see pp. 106-7)?
20. Define "gravity" (v. 4; see p. 107).
21. According to Leviticus 21:16-20, who couldn't perform priestly duties? Does that mean such people are inferior in God's eyes (see p. 108)?
22. What are the three keys to spiritual leadership in the home, and how do they relate to leadership in the church (see pp. 108-9)?
23. What does it mean to care for the church, and how did Jesus illustrate that principle (Luke 10:30-34; see pp. 109-10)?

Pondering the Principles

1. People are influenced by their companions, whether for good or evil. 1 Corinthians 15:33 says, "Do not be deceived: 'Bad company corrupts good morals' " (NASB). That principle is repeated throughout Scripture. Do you choose your companions carefully? Obviously you can't always avoid evil people, but you must guard yourself against their influence. Who are your closest companions? Do they share your love for the Lord, or do they regularly challenge your Christian principles? Remember, their influence may be subtle, but your companions will affect your attitudes and actions. Read these verses and ask God to give you wisdom as you evaluate the influence of your friends on your life, and be sure to thank Him for those who are godly examples to you: Proverbs 4:14-15; 12:11, 26; 13:20; 2 Corinthians 6:14-17.

2. William Golding's story of Sammy Mountjoy illustrates how our hypocrisy can destroy our credibility and drive people away from Christ (see p. 102). Conversely, a pure life brings glory to God. Jesus said, "Let your light so shine before men, that they may see your good works, and glorify your Father, who is in heaven" (Matt. 5:16). It has been rightly said that a believer's life is the only Bible some people ever read. What is your life telling others about Christ? Is the message clear, or is it distorted by hypocrisy? Do you attract people to Christ or turn them away?

3. We have seen that spiritual leadership in the home requires enough authority to make it advisable for our children to obey us, enough wisdom to make it reasonable for them to obey us, and enough love to make it easy for them to obey us (see pp. 108-9). Sadly, many parents today are authoritarian but lack the wisdom and love necessary to encourage a godly response in their children. Others are so "loving" that they disregard true authority and wisdom. Does your parenting reflect godly authority, wisdom, and love? That's a big task for any parent, but God has placed us in authority over our children (Eph. 6:1), promised us His wisdom (James 1:5), and given us His love (Rom. 5:5). Our responsibility is to seek His wisdom daily through prayer, and to learn His Word and exemplify it to our children.

7

The Call to Lead the Church—Elders
Part 7

Outline

Introduction
A. The Standards for Spiritual Leaders
B. The Struggles of Spiritual Leaders
 1. Discouragement
  a) Over our own failures
  b) Over the failures of others
 2. Indifference
 3. Busy laziness
  a) By avoiding priorities
  b) By pursuing recreation
 4. Compromise
 5. Pride

Review
 I. An Elder Must Be Blameless in His Moral Character (vv. 2*b*-3)
 II. An Elder Must Be Blameless in His Family Life (vv. 4-5)

Lesson
III. An Elder Must Be Blameless in His Spiritual Maturity (v. 6)
 A. The Definition (v. 6*a*)
  1. He must be humble
  2. He must not be a recent convert
  3. He must be spiritually mature
 B. The Rationale (v. 6*b*-*c*)
  1. To avoid pride (v. 6*b*)
   a) The situation at Ephesus
   b) The situation at Crete
   c) The situation at Grace Church

Introduction

A. The Standards for Spiritual Leaders

God requires elders to be men of integrity, wisdom, dignity, and virtue. But even though the standards are very high, God doesn't require perfection. If He did, no one would be qualified to lead the church, because we all fail.

James 3:1-2 says, "My brethren, be not many teachers, knowing that we shall receive the greater judgment. For in many things we all stumble. If any man offend not in word, the same is a perfect man, and able also to bridle the whole body." Only a perfect man doesn't stumble and offend. Therefore, we shouldn't rush into church leadership without first giving careful consideration to the severe judgment that comes upon leaders who fail.

Such warnings, however, should not discourage us from leadership if God has called us to that task. Even though we aren't perfect, by God's grace and the Spirit's power we can meet His standards. But it would be dishonest for any church leader to hold himself up as a perfect example of

114

godliness, as if he had no spiritual struggles, sins, or failures in life. Our fallen human flesh limits to some degree the success of our work, and we experience struggles just like every other believer.

B. The Struggles of Spiritual Leaders

In reflecting on my own life and ministry I can identify several struggles that are common to many church leaders.

1. Discouragement

   a) Over our own failures

   Succumbing to the temptation of discouragement is very easy for those in ministry because we have high hopes and expectations for ourselves. I have self-imposed standards for my own preaching, study, self-discipline, and my fulfillment of leadership responsibilities. And when I fail to meet my own standards, I tend to become discouraged.

   b) Over the failures of others

   Discouragement can also come when you have high hopes for your people's spiritual growth, yet you see them falling short of God's will.

   Discouragement is very common among church leaders. It has nothing to do with the size of your church, because it usually comes not from a desire to have more people but from a longing to see your people respond to God's Word as they should.

2. Indifference

   After you have lived with discouragement for a while, the tendency is to shield yourself by developing an attitude of indifference. You say to yourself, *What's the difference? They grasp only a few of the things I say anyway. Half of them are asleep, and the other half don't care.*

   Many older pastors whose ministries have been wonderfully blessed by God have become bitter and distant from their people because they've been hurt so many times. They've built a wall between themselves and people, so they can't feel the hurt anymore. That's always a temptation to one degree or another in the ministry.

3. Busy laziness

   a) By avoiding priorities

   "Busy laziness" is my term for the times when we are very busy but aren't accomplishing anything of real significance. It's easy to be busy in the ministry, but busyness can be a form of laziness when we are doing what we want to do rather than what needs to be done. It's a matter of priorities; a good test of our commitment and character is to be able to discern what's most important and to do it. It's always a temptation to follow the path of least resistance and remain busy doing things that are good but not important.

   b) By pursuing recreation

   There's also the temptation to say to yourself, *There are so many souls to bring to Christ, so many ministries to do, so much work, so many Christians to instruct, and so many things to teach!* You can get tired just thinking about it, so you may think, *I can't do it all. I need a break. I've got to get away.* Obviously we need a certain amount of relaxation, but we must avoid the temptation to use that as an excuse to neglect our responsibilities.

   I remember speaking at a conference where there were more than one thousand pastors in attendance. The conference organizers brought in several motivational speakers, and we were all told to say something that would stir those men to commitment. The organizers wanted to get them excited about the Lord and about their ministries so that they would return to their churches with renewed zeal.

116

We were having a great week of meetings, and the men were responding enthusiastically. Then came the final speaker of the conference. His topic was the pastor's need for recreation and leisure time. That single message drained the enthusiasm and energy out of everything that had been accomplished during the week! By the time he was finished, everyone was saying, "Yeah, that's what I've been waiting to hear. That's what I need: a break, a vacation."

Sometimes we *want* to hear that we're overworked, but that can be the flesh talking. Our busyness may be accomplishing very little of eternal consequence. It's tempting to get busy doing things that don't amount to much and then tell ourselves how much we need a break.

4. Compromise

When I say "compromise," I'm not referring to gross moral or doctrinal compromise but to the subtle temptation to refrain from speaking God's truth for the sake of pleasing others and gaining popularity.

Most of us desire approval—we like to have people applaud us. So the temptation is to limit our message in order to gain acceptance and be better liked in our community.

5. Pride

Pride is a constant temptation, especially where God has graciously blessed a man's ministry. Pride can lead a pastor to think, *Look what I've accomplished*. It is sinful self-congratulation.

Besides, there's always a multitude of general temptations that beset a spiritual leader. That's why we have to "put on the whole armor of God" (Eph. 6:11). Satan is unrelenting in his attempts to cause Christians to sin, and the prominence and influence of a spiritual leader make him a prime target for the enemy's attacks.

117

In light of all those temptations, what elder could remain sinless? We all fail. Sometime in the midst of the spiritual battle we feel like giving up, or we become indifferent or prideful. Perhaps we say unkind words to someone. There are so many areas in which a leader can fall, and we are all far from perfect.

The qualifications for spiritual leaders are very high, but they're not so high that everyone is disqualified. By His grace God can make us what He wants us to be. Our task is to faithfully pursue His standards.

Review

I. AN ELDER MUST BE BLAMELESS IN HIS MORAL CHARACTER (vv. 2b-3; see pp. 45-54, 64-72, 81-91)

II. AN ELDER MUST BE BLAMELESS IN HIS FAMILY LIFE (vv. 4-5; see pp. 104-10)

Lesson

III. AN ELDER MUST BE BLAMELESS IN HIS SPIRITUAL MATURITY (v. 6)

"Not a novice, lest being lifted up with pride he fall into the condemnation of the devil."

A. The Definition (v. 6a)

1. He must be humble

Humility is an extremely important spiritual characteristic, though it has not yet been mentioned in our consideration of leadership qualifications. Although Paul doesn't specifically mention humility in this passage, it is the obvious point of contrast in his caution against spiritual pride.

2. He must not be a recent convert

The Greek word translated "novice" (*neophutos*) means "newly planted." The idea is that an elder should not be a new convert or newly baptized. This is the only occurrence of *neophutos* in the New Testament. It is used in its literal sense outside the New Testament to speak of planting trees in the ground (Fritz Rienecker and Cleon Rogers, *Linguistic Key to the Greek New Testament* [Grand Rapids: Zondervan, 1982], p. 623).

3. He must be spiritually mature

The opposite of a new believer is a mature Christian. An elder must be mature in the faith. Of course maturity is relative, so the standard of maturity will vary from congregation to congregation. The point is that an elder must be more spiritually mature than the people he leads.

B. The Rationale (v. 6*b-c*)

1. To avoid pride (v. 6*b*)

The Greek word translated "lifted up" (*tuphoō*) means "to wrap in smoke" or "puff up." In its figurative sense it means "to be beclouded with pride" (Rienecker and Rogers, p. 623). We don't want new Christians to get puffed up with a false sense of spirituality. We don't want their thinking to become clouded with prideful thoughts.

The reason for restricting a new convert from spiritual leadership is not due to his inability to teach—he may be a fine Bible teacher. It's not because he can't be a good leader—he may have strong leadership characteristics. It's not because he has inadequate knowledge of God's Word—he may be a diligent Bible student. But if he is elevated to spiritual leadership alongside of mature godly men, he's going to have a battle with pride.

He may fulfill the qualifications of 1 Timothy 3 by having a blameless life and a marvelous family. But if he's a relatively new Christian, the tendency will be for him to feel proud about being elevated to the level of leadership occupied by older, more mature men who have been in the church for many years.

a) The situation at Ephesus

The Ephesian church had been in existence for several years and had trained its own elders. In fact, the first group of elders were personally discipled by Paul for three years (Acts 20:31).

By the time Paul wrote 1 Timothy, several years had passed, so there was a high level of maturity in that church. Consequently, the role of pastor or elder in Ephesus was reserved for very mature men.

Admittedly some leaders in Ephesus were not qualified, such as Hymenaeus and Alexander, who were delivered to Satan to learn not to blaspheme (1 Tim. 1:20). I believe they were two of the leading pastors in that church. There were others who also needed to be rebuked (1 Tim. 5:20), but that didn't change the fact that elders were to be spiritually mature. To have raised a new Christian to that level of leadership would have been to tempt him to think more highly of himself than he ought to have.

b) The situation at Crete

Titus ministered on the isle of Crete, and Paul instructed him to "ordain elders in every city" (Titus 1:5). The situation in Crete was different from that at Ephesus. The Ephesian church had been in existence for many years but the church at Crete was very young, so there weren't many mature believers there. Consequently, if a relatively new convert became an elder, the temptation toward pride was not so great because all the other elders were fairly new converts also.

To become an elder in Ephesus would give a new convert the idea that he had already reached a level of spiritual maturity that took the other men years to obtain, but the same was not true in Crete.

120

The primary issue in eldership is not the length of time a man has been a Christian, or his physical age (although maturity in years is implied in spiritual maturity), but his maturity level as it relates to the congregation he leads. Often the maturity level of a congregation is directly related to the age of the church.

c) The situation at Grace church

Grace Community Church is a mature church by comparison to many other churches. That's not a boastful statement—it's simply a matter of longevity and ministry priorities. Grace Community Church has existed for more than thirty years and has taught God's Word throughout that time. Consequently we have many third, fourth, fifth, and sixth generation Christians in our congregation—one "generation" of believers has brought new persons to Christ and those new believers have in turn led others to Christ, and so on, through the six generations. Our elders are mature men who know and teach the Word in great depth, and have spent many years preparing for that kind of leadership.

In that situation, if we made a relatively new Christian an elder, he would struggle with the temptation to see himself as having arrived at a high level of spiritual leadership rather rapidly and could easily fall into the sin of pride.

On the other hand, suppose you are a missionary who has led people to Christ in a primitive part of the world, established a church, ministered there for six months, and now have to return home. Before leaving you have to select someone to be its pastor. That person will have to be a new Christian, but you will look for someone who is mature in comparison to the rest of the congregation. It might take that same man ten years to become an elder at Grace Community Church, but in his own community he's rightfully pastoring a church because of the relative nature of what spiritual maturity means in any given congregation.

121

We have young seminary graduates ministering at Grace Church who are not elders because the church's perception of elder leadership is so high. Many of these men are excellent teachers and are qualified in their moral character and family life, but to place them into a position at that level of leadership so early in their ministry experience would tempt them to become proud.

Many of our young men have left our church to pastor other churches without ever having been an elder at Grace church. But they were seen by those churches as men of spiritual maturity who could lead and teach them in God's Word. Spiritual maturity in this sense is relative.

We must protect men from the temptation of pride. The issue isn't how long they've been believers but how they'll handle being placed into a high level of spiritual leadership too soon. Some men can handle it properly, but others will become prideful. Paul warned Timothy not to expose a man to that temptation.

2. To avoid condemnation (v. 6c)

You might expect Paul to say that prideful leaders will become ineffective or fall into sin, but instead he says they will fall into the "condemnation of the devil." That's a very serious situation.

a) The source of that condemnation

What is the "condemnation of the devil"? Some people think that Paul here means that a prideful leader will be condemned by the devil, but Scripture never portrays the devil as a judge who condemns people. Since Scripture presents God as Judge, it's best to understand the condemnation of the devil as a reference to the judgment that God pronounced on the devil. A prideful leader will incur that same type of condemnation. That conclusion is supported by the context, which deals with the issue of pride, and Scripture teaches that God opposes a proud man (James 4:6).

b) The nature of that condemnation

The condemnation of the devil was a demotion from high position because of his pride. God will do the same to any man whose thinking is clouded with pride and whose perception of his own spirituality is distorted because of a premature rise to spiritual leadership.

c) The history of that condemnation

A brief review of the devil's fall from spiritual privilege will help us understand the severity of Paul's warning.

(1) The existence of angels

The Bible talks about various kinds, ranks, and functions of angels: cherubim, seraphim, archangels, principalities, powers, and rulers.

(2) The names of angels

Some angels have higher ranks and capacities for service than others. Cherubim are the highest-ranked angels and are often portrayed as standing around the throne of God (cf. Ex. 25:18-22; Ezek. 1:5-26; 10:15, 20; Rev. 4:6-8). They possess surpassing beauty and power.

We know three cherubim by name.

(*a*) Gabriel

Gabriel revealed and interpreted God's purpose and program for His kingdom (Dan. 8:16; 9:21; Luke 1:19, 26).

(*b*) Michael

Michael is the commander-in-chief of the heavenly armies (Dan. 10:13; Jude 9).

Gabriel and Michael are common names for children because they represent two wonderful angels.

(c) Lucifer

The most beautiful, powerful, and glorious angel of all was Lucifer. His name means "son of the dawn," "son of the morning," or "morning star." Even though *Lucifer* is perhaps the most lovely name among the angels, it is despised because of what he became.

(3) The fall of Satan

Lucifer's sin was pride, for which God cast him out of heaven. We see his prideful character on display in Isaiah 14:12-14: "How art thou fallen from heaven, O Lucifer, son of the morning! How art thou cut down to the ground, who didst weaken the nations! For thou hast said in thine heart, I will ascend into heaven, I will exalt my throne above the stars of God; I will sit also upon the mount of the congregation, in the sides of the north, I will ascend above the heights of the clouds, I will be like the Most High."

Lucifer wanted to usurp God's authority. Five times he said, "I will," but God said in effect, "No, you won't." "Yet thou shalt be brought down to sheol, to the sides of the pit. They that see thee shall narrowly look upon thee, and consider thee, saying, Is this the man who made the earth to tremble?" (Isa. 14:15-16).

Satan was humiliated rather than exalted. To avoid exposing a man to that kind of condemnation, we must avoid placing him into spiritual leadership too quickly. A leader who becomes prideful will not lose his salvation, for that is impossible, but he will lose his esteemed position.

Are You a Diotrephes?

I believe God deals harshly with any Diotrephes in the church—anyone "who loveth to have the pre-eminence" (3 John 9). That's why we must exercise great caution in placing a man into spiritual leadership. We don't want to lift him up only to have God bring him down. God will do what is necessary to protect His church from the influence of prideful leaders. He loves His church and is deeply committed to the people He has purchased with His own precious blood (Acts 20:28).

Of course the safeguard against spiritual pride is humility. Jesus said, "Whosoever will be chief among you, let him be your servant" (Matt. 20:27). That's the sign of a mature leader, and that's what the Lord wants His church to have. In fact, His standard of maturity could rightly be called His standard of humility, because a mature leader is a humble servant.

As a man grows into more responsible leadership roles within the church, he must be protected from any position that will breed spiritual pride.

IV. AN ELDER MUST BE BLAMELESS IN HIS PUBLIC REPUTATION (v. 7)

"Moreover, he must have a good report of them who are outside, lest he fall into reproach and the snare of the devil."

A. The Quality of His Reputation

The Greek word translated "good" (*kalōs*), as was discussed previously, embraces the ideas of internal and external goodness. An elder must have a good internal character and a good external reputation or testimony.

The Greek word translated "report" (*martureō*) is the word from which we get *martyr*, but its basic meaning is "a certifying testimony." An elder's character must be certified by the testimony of other people.

125

B. The Evaluators of His Reputation

"Outside" has reference to those who are not in the church. An elder must have a reputation for integrity, love, kindness, generosity, and goodness among those in the community who know him.

That doesn't mean all people agree with his theology. In fact, there might even be some antagonism toward his Christian convictions, but he is seen as a man of character.

That's an important qualification because an elder can't have a godly influence on his community if he is not respected. That would bring reproach on Christ.

C. The Consequences of His Reputation

1. The potential for disgrace

The Greek word translated "reproach" means "disgrace." It is sad to consider how many men have disgraced the Lord and His church because of their sins. That's why an elder must be blameless in his reputation.

Incidentally, that qualification isn't limited to sins committed as an elder. It also includes any sins in the past that have given him a bad reputation. A man's ongoing reputation in the community must be considered before he is placed into spiritual leadership.

The importance of a good reputation in the community is illustrated throughout the New Testament.

a) Romans 2:24

Paul said to Israel, "The name of God is blasphemed among the Gentiles through you." Israel's sin brought reproach upon their God, and we are no different.

I'm constantly aware that many people know who I am and what I do. Consequently, I must carefully guard my testimony in the community. For example,

126

I was in a store recently with my family, and we were discussing the purchase of a few furniture items. The salesman waited patiently as everyone contributed comments and opinions about the various options available. When we had finally reached a consensus I told the salesman we were ready. He smiled and said to me, "I know who you are." I immediately thought, *Oh no, what impression have we left on him?* He then said, "I appreciate your ministry very much." I was relieved that our somewhat lengthy family discussion had not hindered our testimony.

Every Christian has to deal with some level of visibility. And people need to see a blameless life. They do not have to agree with your beliefs, but they must see your godly character.

b) Philippians 2:15

Paul wanted the Philippians to be "blameless and harmless, children of God, without rebuke, in the midst of a crooked and perverse nation . . . [shining] as lights in the world, holding forth the word of life." The quality of their lives would bear witness to the reality of their God. That's a high calling and a sacred responsibility.

c) Colossians 4:5-6

Paul said, "Walk in wisdom toward them that are outside [unbelievers]. . . . Let your speech be always with grace, seasoned with salt, that ye may know how ye ought to answer every man." A good reputation includes wise words as well as godly deeds.

2. The potential for entrapment

Elders need to have a good reputation with those outside the church so that they don't fall into "the snare of the devil." Satan tries hard to entrap spiritual leaders in order to destroy their credibility and integrity. He's like a roaring lion seeking to devour (1 Pet. 5:8), and spiritual leaders are a primary target.

"The snare of the devil" obviously refers to the traps set by the enemy, for God does not entrap believers (James 1:13). We all must be very cautious.

Like all Christians, elders have areas of weakness and vulnerability, and they sometimes fall into one of Satan's traps. Only a perfect man doesn't stumble (James 3:2). Elders must be particularly discerning and cautious to avoid the snares of the enemy so that they are not victimized by him. Then they can be effective in leading others away from his traps.

Conclusion

God has identified the moral character, family life, maturity, and reputation He requires of elders. For the church to be all that God designed it to be, it must be led by qualified men. God requires qualified leadership for His church because He wants to mediate His rule through holy vessels and because they are the models of what every believer should be. The qualifications apply to every believer, but the congregation will learn only what they see modeled in their leadership. It must begin with the leaders.

The Ephesian church needed to examine its leaders, and the same holds true for us. The future of the church depends upon the quality of today's leaders.

Some years ago I gave my sons this poem (Dale Martin Stone, "The Shaping of a Disciple," in *Sourcebook of Poetry* [Grand Rapids: Zondervan, 1968], p. 409) to illustrate how God molds His leaders:

> When God wants to drill a man
> And thrill a man, and skill a man,
> When God wants to mold a man
> To play for Him the noblest part,
> When He yearns with all His heart
> To build so great and bold a man
> That all the world shall be amazed,
> Then watch God's methods, watch His ways!
> How He ruthlessly perfects
> Whom He royally elects!

How He hammers him and hurts him,
  And with mighty blows converts him,
Making shapes and forms which only
  God Himself can understand,
Even while His man is crying,
  Lifting a beseeching hand . . .
Yet God bends but never breaks
  When man's good He undertakes;
When He uses whom He chooses
  And with every purposes fuses
Man to act, and act to man,
  As it was when He began;
When God tries His splendor out,
  Man will know what He's about!

I believe God is building such men, and we must identify them, place them into leadership, pray for them, and follow their example. In so doing we will bring glory to God.

Focusing on the Facts

1. What warning does James 3:1 give to prospective teachers and why (see p. 114)?
2. What are two sources of discouragement for an elder (see p. 115)?
3. Why are elders tempted to be indifferent toward people (see pp. 115-16)?
4. Define "busy laziness" (see p. 116).
5. Compromise can be defined as the temptation to refrain from speaking God's truth for the sake of _____ _____ and gaining _____ (see p. 117).
6. How can an elder shield himself from Satan's attacks (Eph. 6:11; see p. 117)?
7. What does Paul mean by "novice" in verse 6 (see p. 119)?
8. The opposite of a new believer is a _____ _____ (see p. 119).
9. What does "lifted up" picture (see p. 119)?
10. What was the Ephesian church's perception of an elder (see p. 120)?
11. How did the leadership situation at Ephesus differ from that of Crete (see p. 120)?
12. What is "the condemnation of the devil" (see p. 122)?

13. How does God respond to a proud man (James 4:6, see p. 122)?
14. What are the highest-ranked angels (see p. 123)?
15. Who are Gabriel and Michael (see p. 123)?
16. What does "Lucifer" mean (see p. 124)?
17. What was Lucifer's sin (Isa. 14:12-16; see p. 124)?
18. Who was Diotrephes (3 John 9; see p. 125)?
19. What is the safeguard against spiritual pride (Matt. 20:27; see p. 125)?
20. What does the command that an elder be of "good report" mean (v. 7; see p. 125)?
21. Who are the outsiders referred to in verse 7 (see p. 126)?
22. What does it mean for a leader to fall into reproach (see p. 126)?
23. What kind of impact did Israel's reputation have on the Gentile nations (Rom. 2:24; see p. 126)?
24. What admonition does Paul give in Philippians 2:15 (see p. 127)?
25. What does it mean to fall into "the snare of the devil" (v. 7; see pp. 127-28)?
26. How do the qualifications required of elders apply to the congregation (see p. 128)?

Pondering the Principles

1. We have seen that discouragement is a common problem among church leaders because they have such high expectations for themselves and for their congregations. Apparently Timothy struggled with discouragement and needed encouragement from Paul (2 Tim. 1:6-7). Perhaps the greatest source of encouragement for a church leader is an obedient and responsive congregation. Read 1 Thessalonians 5:12-13 and Hebrews 13:7, 17. How does God want you to respond to your leaders, and what will be the results if you obey Him? Pray that God will make you a continual source of encouragement to your spiritual leaders.

2. "Busy laziness" is a term describing activities that accomplish little of real significance. Take time to rethink your priorities. Are you neglecting important tasks for the sake of the trivial? It might be helpful to make a list of personal, family, and ministry goals and then evaluate your daily activities in light of those goals. Commit your time and energy to the Lord each day in prayer, asking Him for wisdom and discernment in doing the most important things first.

8
Qualified Servants
for the Church—Deacons
Part 1

Outline

Introduction

Lesson
I. A Study of Deacons
   A. An Overview of *Diakonos*
      1. Its original meaning
      2. Its specific meaning
      3. Its general meaning
   B. An Example of *Diakonos*
   C. The Meaning of *Diakonos*
      1. Level one—general service
      2. Level two—gifted service
      3. Level three—official service
         a) The similarity to elders
         b) The difference from elders
   D. The Alleged References to *Diakonos*
      1. Regarding certain men
         a) Paul
         b) Timothy
         c) Tychicus
         d) Epaphras
      2. Regarding Acts 6
         a) The account
            (1) The problem
            (2) The solution
               (*a*) The dilemma of the twelve
               (*b*) The decision of the twelve
               (*c*) The delegation of the twelve

Introduction

When I think of the word *deacon* I remember a certain austere man who grabbed me by the ear and marched me out of my Sunday school class. I hate to admit it, but that happened on several occasions! In my younger days deacons represented authority in the church. In most of the churches I grew up in deacons were the spiritual leaders of the church. In many churches today they are the ruling body; even the pastor may be employed by and accountable to the deacons.

Many people in churches seek to attain the title of deacon, for with the title comes honor and respect in the community. Other churches have no deacons. In still other churches, particularly liturgical churches, deacons are identified as a sub-order to the priests. They serve as a clerical order maintaining the facilities or administrating the business of the church.

Lesson

I. A STUDY OF DEACONS

If we're to understand the biblical meaning of deacon, we need to eliminate any preconceived definitions. Paul refers to the office of deacon four times in 1 Timothy 3 (vv. 8, 10, 12, 13). In that passage we will study the responsibility of the deacons in the church. Understand that in no sense does Scripture present deacons as inferior to elders, overseers, or pastors. In fact, you will find that the qualifications for being a deacon are not unlike those for being an elder. The qualifications for both offices require examination of a man's character, personal life, home life, leadership ability, and commitment to serving the Lord's church.

In 1 Timothy 3:8-13 Paul says, "In like manner must the deacons be grave, not double-tongued, not given to much wine, not greedy of filthy lucre, holding the mystery of the faith in a pure conscience. And let these also first be proved; then let them use the office of a deacon, being found blameless. Even so must their wives be grave, not slanderers, sober-minded, faithful in all things. Let the deacons be the husbands of one wife, ruling their children and their own houses well. For they that have used the office of a deacon well purchase to themselves a good standing, and great boldness in the faith which is in Christ Jesus." As you can see, there is no less a premium on spiritual maturity and moral purity for a deacon than for an elder.

A. An Overview of *Diakonos*

The Greek words *diakonos* ("servant"), *diakonia* ("service"), and *diakoneō* ("to serve") are used at least one hundred times in the New Testament. The original sense of those words referred to serving. In 1 Timothy 3 *diakonos* is transliterated (spelled in the characters of another alphabet) rather than translated. In only that New Testament passage (3:8-13) and Philippians 1:1 did the translators of the King James version choose to transliterate the Greek terms rather than translate them.

1. Its original meaning

Diakonia originally referred to serving tables. *Diakonos* was probably the word for waiter. Eventually *diakonia* was broadened to mean any kind of service.

2. Its specific meaning

The meaning of *diakonos* is primarily general except for its uses in 1 Timothy 3 and Philippians 1:1. Only in those two cases did the editors transliterate it, as if to set it apart in a specific sense to refer to a group of select people called to serve the church.

3. Its general meaning

Every other use of *diakonos*, *diakonia*, and *diakoneō* is general, not necessarily referring to any specific office in the church. The New Testament writers used those words the same way we use the words *servant*, *serve*, and *service*. We go to a service station for gas. When we play tennis we serve the ball. We serve our employer. We serve our nation.

For the most part *diakonia* is translated "service" or "ministry." In some cases it is translated "administration" because of the context. In Acts 11:29 it is translated "relief" because the service referred to was giving resources to people suffering from a famine.

B. An Example of *Diakonos*

The original and most limited meaning of *diakonia* has to do with serving food.

1. John 2:5, 9—When Jesus was at a wedding in Cana, "His mother saith unto the servants [Gk., *diakonos*—the waiters], Whatever he saith unto you, do it" (v. 5). Then verse 9 says, "When the ruler [head waiter] of the feast had tasted the water that was made wine, and knew not from where it was (but the servants who drew the water knew), the governor of the feast called the bridegroom." In that passage *diakonos* was used for a group of waiters at a wedding.

2. Luke 4:39—Peter's mother-in-law became very ill. After Jesus healed her, the text says, "Immediately she arose and ministered [Gk., *diakoneō*] unto them." The context implies she ministered by serving a meal.

Three other texts in the gospels use *diakonos* in reference to serving a meal (Luke 10:40; 17:8; John 12:2).

134

C. The Meaning of *Diakonos*

1. Level one—general service

Diakonos was broadened from its limited meaning to apply to all kinds of general service.

a) Romans 13:4—Here *diakonos* is used to describe a government official or servant. Such officials punish evildoers and reward those who do well.

b) John 12:26—Jesus said, "If any man serve me, let him follow me." Following Jesus constitutes *diakonia*— service or ministry.

As the gospel and epistle writers adapted the term, they used it in a broad sense for all kinds of spiritual service. Based on what Jesus said, they identified following Christ with serving Him. Spiritual service is the major emphasis of the Christian life. Anything we do in obedience to God's Word is service. In that sense we're all in the ministry. In no sense do deacons serve while everyone else watches. There isn't a leadership level made up of elders and pastors, a service level made up of deacons, and a spectator level made up of all other believers. There is no audience in the church—we are all in the ministry. We've all been called to submit ourselves to the Lord Jesus Christ. He said, "Where I am, there shall also my servant be: if any man serve me, him will my Father honor" (John 12:26). We all are His servants.

c) 1 Corinthians 12:4-5—Within this broad range of service, "there are diversities of gifts, but the same Spirit. And there are differences of administrations [Gk., *diakonia*]." All Christians are in some form of spiritual service. All are deacons in a general sense because we all are instructed to serve in a variety of ways.

d) 2 Corinthians 9:1—"As touching the ministering to the saints . . . " Here Paul begins a discussion about our common role of serving the saints. We're all to be engaged in service. We serve God every time we obey His Word and His Spirit. Every time I do that which is

135

right, I offer service to Him. And we serve one another when we meet each other's needs.

e) Ephesians 4:11-12—"He gave some, apostles; and some, prophets; and some, evangelists; and some, pastors and teachers; for the perfecting [maturing] of the saints for the work of the ministry [Gk., *diakonia*]." My job as an elder and pastor is to mature the saints so that they can serve others.

All of us are called as servants of Christ. We're under orders. Christ is our Lord and master. He has called us into spiritual service. We serve Him by obeying the Word of God, following the promptings of the Spirit of God, coming under the authority of the church, and meeting the needs of those around us. It's one thing to say, "I'm proud to be able to serve my country," or, "I'm proud to have served this great cause." But that doesn't come close to being able to say, "I have been called into service by the King of kings and Lord of lords—Jesus Christ Himself." That is our high and holy calling—the vocation to which we are called (Eph. 4:1).

2. Level two—gifted service

In Romans 12:4-7 Paul says, "As we have many members in one body, and all members have not the same office, so we, being many, are one body in Christ, and every one members one of another. Having then gifts differing according to the grace that is given to us, whether prophecy, let us prophesy according to the proportion of faith; or ministry [Gk., *diakonia*], let us wait on our ministering [Gk., *diakoneō*]." Here Paul identifies special gifts of service. It is parallel to his use of the gifts of helps in 1 Corinthians 12:28. God has uniquely designed some people to serve. While everyone is in the service of Christ, some have been specially gifted by the Spirit of God to serve.

In 1 Corinthians 16:15 Paul says, "I beseech you, brethren (ye know the house of Stephanas, that it is the first fruits of Achaia [the first converts in the province of Achaia], and that they have devoted themselves to the ministry [Gk., *diakonia*] of the saints)." The entire family was characterized by serving others. We all are to be

136

serving others, but some of us are especially gifted in that area.

3. Level three—official service

In my judgment the only specific scriptural discussion of the office of deacon is in 1 Timothy 3. It constitutes a third level of spiritual service in addition to every believer's general service and the gifted service of specific believers. Deacons serve in an official capacity as servants of the church. We could just as easily call them servants.

a) The similarity to elders

Although they are servants, deacons aren't supposed to do all the work—they are to be models of spiritual virtue for everyone else. In that sense they stand alongside the elders. Elders and deacons are not on different spiritual planes. Elders have been given authority because they exercise the power of God's Word in their teaching. But deacons are to be equal to elders in every other respect. In fact, there's no difference in their spiritual qualifications.

b) The difference from elders

While deacons are to be as godly as elders, they differ from elders in terms of their ability to teach. The authority of pastors and elders is based on their proclamation and exposition of God's Word. Yet alongside the elders are those who implement what's been taught and whose lives are no less godly. Deacons are to seek to raise the congregation to the highest level of spiritual virtue, not to set themselves apart as especially pious people whom the congregation can never expect to imitate.

In Philippians 1:1 Paul addresses his letter to "bishops and deacons [Gk., *diakonos*]" at Philippi. That could be a reference to official deacons, or it could be simply a reference to the leaders and followers in a general sense. However, the references in 1 Timothy 3 are definitely specific to the office of deacon.

D. The Alleged References to *Diakonos*

Some have argued that there are other specific references to deacons elsewhere in Scripture. Let us examine those alleged references.

1. Regarding certain men

a) Paul

Some believe Paul was a deacon. That's a major defense used by those who advocate deacon rulership in the church. But Paul was an apostle, not a deacon. He himself said, "I am the apostle of the Gentiles, I magnify mine office" (Rom. 11:13). The Greek word translated "office" is *diakonia*. Paul was saying that he gloried in serving Christ. He was a deacon in a general sense. All of us, whatever our ministry involvement may be, are to render service to God. But Paul's office was that of an apostle. He talked about his service many times, but he was always careful to specify that he was an apostle (e.g., 2 Cor. 10-12).

b) Timothy

In 1 Timothy 4:6 Paul says to Timothy, "If thou put the brethren in remembrance of these things, thou shalt be a good minister [Gk., *diakonos*] of Jesus Christ, nourished up in the words of faith and of good doctrine, unto which thou hast attained." Based on that verse some have said Timothy was a deacon, and a good deacon at that. But we know that Timothy was not a deacon in the traditional sense. In 2 Timothy 4:5 Paul says to him, "Do the work of an evangelist, make full proof of thy ministry [Gk., *diakonia*]." Timothy's *diakonia* was his office as an evangelist—a proclaimer and preacher—a role quite distinct from the office of deacon.

c) Tychicus

In Ephesians 6:21 Paul calls Tychicus a "faithful minister [Gk., *diakonos*]." Three times in Ephesians Paul used *diakonos*, but never in a technical way. He always

138

used it in reference to general service. Therefore we can't assume Tychicus was a deacon.

d) Epaphras

In Colossians 1:7 Paul called Epaphras "a faithful minister [Gk., *diakonos*]." Paul also referred to himself as a *diakonos* in Colossians 1:23, 25. Since we are certain Paul wasn't calling himself a deacon, it is also unlikely he was calling Epaphras one.

2. Regarding Acts 6

Many people believe that the first deacons in the church are the seven men referred to in Acts 6. However those men are never called deacons.

a) The account

Acts 6:1 says, "In those days [the time of Passover] . . . the number of the disciples was multiplied." There were as many as twenty thousand believers in Jerusalem, a good percentage of them pilgrims who had come to the city for the feasts. When they believed in Christ, many remained and became part of the church.

There were two kinds of Jews in the world—Palestinian Jews (those who lived in Palestine) and Hellenistic Jews (those who had been born and raised outside of Palestine in the Greek world). The Hellenistic Jews traveled to Jerusalem for the Passover.

(1) The problem

With such a large number of Hellenistic Jews joining Palestinian Jews as Christians within a rapidly growing church body, a problem surfaced. Acts 6:1 says, "There arose a murmuring of the Grecians [the Hellenistic Jews] against the Hebrews [the Palestinian Jews], because their widows were neglected in the daily ministration." There may have been several hundred widows in the church who needed care—many of them Hellenistic Jews.

Caring for the Poor and Needy

Christian widows came under the care of the church—a function the church inherited from a common Jewish practice. The Jewish people had—and still have—a strong commitment to care for the poor and the needy. That commitment was based on God's instruction in the Old Testament. Over the years the Jews developed sophisticated means for meeting needs. William Barclay tells us that every Friday morning in the synagogue two collectors went to the marketplace and to homes to collect money and goods to give to the poor and needy. Those resources were then distributed to those in need in the community. Those who had a temporary need received just enough to see them through their difficulty; those who required regular support received enough for fourteen meals—two meals a day for seven days. They called that distribution the *Kuppah,* or the Basket. In addition a daily collection of food was made from house to house for those who were in an emergency situation and needed food for that day. That distribution was called the *Tamhui,* or the Tray (*The Acts of the Apostles,* rev. ed. [Philadelphia: Westminster, 1976], p. 51).

The Jewish people didn't emphasize one person's giving to another in need; they emphasized that the resources should be given to the synagogue so that wise men in positions of leadership could distribute it properly.

The church adopted the practice of the synagogue. But an argument ensued in the church when the Hellenistic Jews complained that their widows weren't receiving their fair share of the food that was being distributed.

(2) The solution

How were the leaders of the church going to solve that problem?

(a) The dilemma of the twelve

Acts 6:2 says, "The twelve called the multitude of the disciples unto them, and said, It is not fitting that we should leave the word of God, and serve tables." That is a stated line of de-

140

marcation: some people in the church need to teach the Word of God, and others need to take care of the business of the church. That line of demarcation stands intact in the pastoral epistles. The priority for the apostles was not to leave the Word of God to distribute food. They were trying to disciple thousands of brand-new converts. That was a tremendous task—one they couldn't leave to spend time determining how to bring equity to the matter of food distribution.

(b) The decision of the twelve

Acts 6:3 says, "Wherefore, brethren, look among you for seven men of honest report, full of the Holy Spirit and wisdom, whom we may appoint over this business." Notice that they were appointed for a specific task. There's no reference to an office in that verse. Then verse 4 says, "We will give ourselves continually to prayer, and to the ministry [Gk., *diakonia*] of the word."

The only uses of *diakonia* were in reference to the apostles (v. 4) and to the daily *diakonia* of serving the widows (v. 1). There is no place where the seven men are called deacons. The apostles performed their service (proclaiming the Word), and the people performed theirs (passing out food to the widows). But neither of the verses refers to deacons specifically.

Based on Acts 6:2, the post-apostolic church of Rome allowed for only seven deacons to pass out goods to the poor. But I don't believe the Holy Spirit intended for Acts 6:2 to establish an ongoing order.

(c) The delegation of the twelve

> Acts 6:5-6 says, "The saying pleased the whole multitude; and they chose Stephen, a man full of faith and of the Holy Spirit, and Philip, and Prochorus, and Nicanor, and Timon, and Parmenas, and Nicolas, a proselyte of Antioch, whom they set before the apostles; and when they had prayed, they laid their hands on them."

b) The answer

There are three reasons I don't believe those seven men were actual deacons.

(1) The general use of *diakonia*

Luke (the author of Acts) used *diakonia* in a general sense to mean service. The only time it is used in reference to certain individuals is in verse 4, where it is connected with the apostles.

The New Testament never refers to the seven men as deacons. In fact, the book of Acts never refers to deacons, although we would expect such a reference if those seven men were the first of a new order. One would expect them to be in office in Acts 11 when a famine occurred in Judea. Acts 11:29-30 indicates that the the church at Antioch as a whole—not a special order of deacons—sent relief to the elders in Judea.

(2) The specific nature of the task

Those seven men were chosen for a specific task. They were honest, so they could be trusted with money, and they were full of the Spirit and wisdom, so they could discern the needs of people. They were chosen for a one-time crisis, not installed into a full-time office. If they had been chosen as deacons, we can be confident they would have appeared later in the book of Acts.

Interestingly, all seven men had Greek names. If they were to be an ongoing group of deacons in the church at Jerusalem, it seems strange that they would have all been Greek Jews. But if they were appointed for the specific task of relieving Hellenistic widows, it makes sense that the people would choose Greeks to do that.

However, Acts 6 does provide us with a preliminary look at the function of deacons. The apostles were devoted to the Word and to prayer while the seven cared for a specific task. That kind of organization is basic to the church. According to 1 Timothy 3, the elders are to focus on teaching the Word and overseeing the church, whereas the deacons are to focus on implementing and applying the Word.

(3) The implied elder role of the men

Acts 6 does give us a historic precedent of the function of deacons, but the seven men were not actual deacons. In many ways they were more like elders. Acts 6:7 says, "The word of God increased." Why did it increase? Because the apostles were free to devote their time to the Word and to prayer. Verses 7-8 continue, "The number of the disciples multiplied in Jerusalem greatly; and a great company of the priests were obedient to the faith. And Stephen [one of the seven], full of faith and power, did great wonders and miracles among the people." Could it be that the other six did the same? Those seven men may well have been specially gifted evangelists who went out into the city performing signs, and wonders, and mighty deeds as they preached. We know that Philip, another of the seven, was a powerful, wonder-working preacher (Acts 8:5-8). If the other five were like Stephen and Philip, they were more like apostles than deacons.

II. THE SETTING OF 1 TIMOTHY 3

Paul wrote 1 Timothy sometime around A.D. 64. The church had been in existence for approximately thirty years. (Christ was crucified just after A.D. 30.) Timothy was serving as the pastor of the church at Ephesus—a church that had grown and developed initially under Paul for three years (Acts 20:31), and later under leaders trained by Paul.

It had become apparent to Paul that the church at Ephesus needed not only teachers of the Word who served as overseers and elders but also administrators and workers to implement what the elders taught. A growing number of people had risen into places of official service. So Paul instructed Timothy regarding the type of man he should choose to do that work.

There is a level of service we're all to be engaged in, a level of service for those specifically gifted to serve, and a level of service for properly qualified people who represent and implement the authority of the elders and pastors of the church. We don't know exactly when elders and deacons became established roles in the church, but we do know that by the time Paul wrote 1 Timothy those offices were recognized and filled by models of spiritual virtue.

Elders and Deacons Compared and Contrasted

If I had to define my task as a pastor and elder, I would sum it up simply by saying this: win, teach, train, send. We pastors and elders don't have to work hard to determine what we're supposed to do. We are to teach the Word of God. Why? To win people to Christ. Why? So they can grow in the faith. Why? So they can be trained to win people to Christ. Then we send them out to do that very thing.

Deacons help the elders implement their task. The distinction between the two ministry roles lies in the fact that Scripture says elders must be able to teach. That doesn't mean deacons can't teach or shouldn't teach. They certainly should be strong in sound doctrine. Also, they should be full of faith, full of the Spirit, full of wisdom, and possessing a good reputation—like the men in Acts 6. They ought to be people of integrity. To state that deacons are not the primary teachers in the church is not to say that they are ignorant theologically. First Timothy 3:9 says they hold "the mystery of the faith in a pure conscience." That means they not only know the truth but also live the truth.

Conclusion

Everyone in the church is to serve in some way. Some serve with unique gifts, and some serve in an official capacity as deacons. They are models of service to Christ and His church. The qualifications for both elders and deacons are the same, but deacons function under the leadership of the elders. Nevertheless deacons are leaders in the church in this sense: they are to lead by example. Every church needs both pastoral leadership and servant leadership. We couldn't accomplish anything if it weren't for the men and women who carry out the administration, implementation, and application of God's Word.

Focusing on the Facts

1. In what ways are the qualifications for elders and deacons parallel (see pp. 132-33)?
2. Define *diakonia* and the related words *diakonos* and *diakoneō*. For the most part, how did the New Testament writers use those words (see p. 133)?
3. What was the original and most limited meaning of *diakonia* (see p. 134)?
4. In what sense are all Christians involved in ministry (see p. 135)?
5. What does Romans 12:7 indicate about the service rendered by some people (see p. 136)?
6. In what function do elders differ from deacons (see p. 137)?
7. Why couldn't Paul have been a deacon (see p. 138)?
8. Why couldn't Timothy have been a deacon (see p. 138)?
9. What do many people assume happened in Acts 6 (see p. 139)?
10. According to Acts 6:1, what problem surfaced in the church at Jerusalem (see p. 139)?
11. What practice did the church adapt from the synagogue? Explain (see p. 140).
12. How did the leaders of the Jerusalem church solve the problem (see pp. 140-42)?

13. Why were the seven men mentioned in Acts 6:5 probably not deacons? Explain each reason (see pp. 142-43).
14. Why did Paul write to Timothy about the qualifications for elders and deacons (see p. 144)?
15. Compare and contrast elders to deacons (see pp. 144-45).

Pondering the Principles

1. Read John 12:26. What kind of people does God honor? Does that mean He honors elders and deacons only, or all believers? What does it mean to follow Christ? Based on your answers, does your life prove that you are a follower of Christ? A true believer cannot merely come to church, listen to the sermon, enjoy fellowship with the people, and then leave. He or she must be actively involved in serving Christ. What can you do today to begin to fulfill your role as a follower of Christ? To help you in your task, memorize John 12:26: "If anyone serves Me, let him follow Me; and where I am, there shall My servant also be; if anyone serves Me, the Father will honor him" (NASB).

2. According to Acts 6:3, the people were to look for men who were "of honest report, full of the Holy Spirit and wisdom." Acts 6:5 mentions that Stephen was also "full of faith." Those characteristics identify seven men of integrity. Can you be characterized as a person of integrity? On a scale of 1 to 10, how would you rate yourself in each of those four characteristics? In which one are you weakest? Make it your goal this week to improve your Christian walk in that area. For example, if you are weakest in your faith, look up "faith" in a concordance and do a word study on that topic. Or, you might make a list of all the times God has been faithful in blessing your life; in turn, that will increase your faith in Him.

9
Qualified Servants
for the Church—Deacons
Part 2

Outline

Introduction
A. Models of Spiritual Leadership
   1. Abraham
   2. David
   3. Solomon
   4. Josiah
   5. Ezra
   6. The prophets
   7. John the Baptist
   8. Paul
B. The Issue of Spiritual Leadership

Review

Lesson
I. Deacons Who Are Men (vv. 8-10, 12)
   A. Their Personal Character (v. 8)
      1. "Grave"—Dignified
      2. "Not double-tongued"—Not a malicious gossip
      3. "Not given to much wine"—Not a drunkard
      4. "Not greedy of filthy lucre"—Not a greedy person
   B. Their Spiritual Life (v. 9)
      1. Defining the mystery
      2. Describing the commitment
         a) To doctrine
         b) To a pure conscience

Introduction

A. Models of Spiritual Leadership

In seeking spiritual leaders, what kind of person does God look for?

1. Abraham

God blessed Abram when He called him to be the leader of the nation Israel—those who would come from his loins and from whom the Messiah would come. Nehemiah 9:8 tells us why: God "foundest his heart faithful before [Him]." The qualification for leadership that God saw in Abraham was a faithful heart.

2. David

When the Lord sent Samuel to look among the sons of a man named Jesse and identify one to be the king of Israel, He gave Samuel this standard: "Look not on his countenance, or on the height of his stature" (1 Sam. 16:7). God warned Samuel not to use those external features as a standard, because that was how the people had chosen Saul, their current king. First Samuel 9:2 says that there was not a man in Israel who was more handsome or taller than Saul. Yet he turned out to be an evil, unsuccessful king. So God said to Samuel, "The Lord seeth not as man seeth; for man looketh on the outward appearance, but the Lord looketh on the heart" (1 Sam. 16:7). Samuel chose David, a man with a heart that was right before God.

3. Solomon

Toward the end of David's life, God gave him a son by the name of Solomon. It was David's task to pass the throne on to Solomon. These are the words of wisdom that David said to him: "Thou, Solomon, my son, know thou the God of thy father, and serve him with a perfect heart and with a willing mind" (1 Chron. 28:9).

4. Josiah

One of the most familiar and beloved kings of Judah was Josiah. He began his rule as a boy, yet God used him to bring about great revival and reform, and a new spirit of worship and obedience among the people. He repaired the Temple and restored the law of God. Second Kings 22:19 explains why God used Josiah so mightily: "Thine heart was tender, and thou hast humbled thyself before the Lord." He wept before the Lord when God planned to destroy the people. Josiah was sensitive, humble, and tenderhearted.

5. Ezra

God used Ezra to lead Israel to repentance, revival, and restoration. This is why: "Ezra had prepared his heart to seek the law of the Lord, and to do it" (Ezra 7:10).

6. The prophets

The father of John the Baptist was a priest named Zacharias. He accurately described the Old Testament prophets as God's "holy prophets" (Luke 1:70). Holiness was the key to their ministry.

7. John the Baptist

John the Baptist had the supreme task of announcing the coming of Messiah. He was an effective leader, bringing about great repentance in Israel. All the people of Jerusalem and Judea went out to see him. They were baptized, and they began to prepare their hearts for the coming of Messiah. What made John effective was his spiritual virtue. Even Herod, who had John beheaded, "feared John, knowing that he was a righteous man, and holy" (Mark 6:20). The mark of John's leadership was his spiritual devotion.

8. Paul

Many Bible scholars have enjoyed studying Paul's leadership skills. What particularly stand out are his courage and the strength of his convictions. But in writing to the Thessalonians, Paul identified the key to his effectiveness by saying that his behavior was holy, just, and blameless (1 Thess. 2:10).

B. The Issue of Spiritual Leadership

Those passages, and many others as well, show us that when the Lord looks for men or women to serve Him, He looks to the spiritual dimension of their lives. He looks at the heart, and He chooses people with integrity, purity, and virtue.

As Paul wrote to Timothy about establishing leaders in the church at Ephesus, the essential issues are all spiritual. In fact, throughout 1 Timothy Paul emphasizes the necessity of holy, pure, godly, blameless, and righteous living. Of extreme importance to Paul was that godliness and virtue be maintained among those who lead the church (1 Tim. 3:3-13).

Who Is a Man After God's Own Heart?

First Samuel 13:14 says, "The Lord hath sought him a man after his own heart." What kind of a man is that? One who desires to think as He thinks, feel as He feels, and respond as He responds. He is a man with a heart that beats like Christ's, a heart that loves righteousness and hates sin, a heart that loves the sinner but rejects his deeds, a heart that reaches out in mercy to those who are hurting, a heart that cares, a heart that knows righteousness and obedience, and a heart that is consumed with extending the Father's glory. That's exactly the kind of heart Christ has. In Ezekiel 22:30 God says, "I sought for a man among them, that should . . . stand in the gap before me." He wants someone to stand in His place and represent Him. From Abraham on, God has always sought that kind of person for leadership.

Review

We have already studied the spiritual character of elders in 1 Timothy 3:1-7. Now we'll look at the character of deacons. The English word "deacon" is transliterated from the Greek word *diakonos*, which is usually translated "servant." By the time Paul wrote 1 Timothy, the Ephesian church had grown to the point that certain people were serving in the church in official capacities. Paul referred to them as *diakonos*, and we call them deacons.

It's essential that official servants be qualified. Although a deacon is not a pastor or an elder, he is still a leader in the church because he serves the Lord by implementing what the elders decide. He is a model servant of Christ.

The New Testament says little about the organization and structure concerning who is accountable to whom. However, it does say that elders are to lead the church, that deacons are to serve the church, and that those in both roles are to meet certain qualifications.

Lesson

I. DEACONS WHO ARE MEN (vv. 8-10, 12)

Verse 8 says, "In like manner." That simply means that Paul is introducing a new category. First came the overseers; now, in like manner, come the deacons.

151

A. Their Personal Character (v. 8)

1. "Grave"—Dignified

The Greek word translated "grave" (*semnos*) means "serious." It could be translated "dignified" or "stately." It carries the idea of being serious in mind as well as serious in character. *Semnos* comes from the root verb *sebomai*, which means "to venerate" or "to worship." So *semnos* refers to a person who has a stateliness about him that demands respect. Such a person has a majestic quality about him that causes people to stand in awe. A synonym of *semnos* is *hieroprepēs*, which means "to act like a sacred person." That kind of individual, by virtue of his spiritual character, has a certain mystique about him.

One who serves as a deacon understands the seriousness of spiritual issues. He is not flippant or frivolous—he doesn't make light of serious matters. I confess that the older I get, the more serious life becomes to me.

2. "Not double-tongued"—Not a malicious gossip

This is the only place in Scripture where *dilogos* appears. It simply means "two-tongued." What is a two-tongued person? A gossip—someone who is quick to discuss private matters. Also, such a person is apt to say one thing to one person and another to someone else to achieve his or her own personal goals.

Because deacons are privy to certain private matters and grave spiritual issues, they need to know how to speak with integrity at the appropriate times. There needs to be a high premium on verbal honesty and integrity among spiritual leaders. They are not to speak hypocritically but consistently, righteously, and honestly. Spinning lies among God's people is a serious matter.

3. "Not given to much wine"—Not a drunkard

The Greek phrase could be translated "not holding near much wine." Wine was practically the only drink available in Paul's day. It was mixed in a ten-to-one ratio with water to prevent intoxication, but it was still necessary to exercise caution when drinking it.

The Greek word translated "given to much wine" (*prosechō*) means "to hold near." Using it in a metaphorical sense, it means "to turn one's mind to" or "to occupy oneself with." It was a necessity to drink wine, but not to indulge in it. The present active nature of the participle indicates it is to be the person's habitual practice. He is to be known as someone who doesn't allow drink to influence his life.

Why Isn't Teetotaling a Qualification?

Couldn't the Lord have solved the problem by simply saying that we can't drink wine at all? As difficult as it may be for a twentieth-century American to understand and appreciate, wine was the common drink in the society of Paul's day. As a result Christians were not told to be total abstainers, but to be temperate. The evils that accompany drinking were not attached to the moderate use of mixed wine in that day. However, because of modern refrigeration capabilities, drinking wine is no longer necessary, and it is potentially dangerous since it is unmixed.

4. "Not greedy of filthy lucre"—Not a greedy person

In New Testament times those who served in the church were involved in passing out money to widows, orphans, and needy people. They also collected money and dispensed it for various purposes to carry on the business of the church. There were no banks or audit firms, so every transaction was made in cash. The people who handled the money actually carried it in a little purse on their belt. The temptation was always present to use the money for one's own purposes. So an official servant in the church had to be free of the love of money.

B. Their Spiritual Life (v. 9)

"Holding the mystery of the faith in a pure conscience."

1. Defining the mystery

The Greek word translated "mystery" (*musterion*) refers to something that was once hidden and is now revealed. The "mystery of the faith" is New Testament revelation—that which was hidden from past generations before the coming of Christ. It is God's redemptive truth. There is much New Testament teaching on that mystery, beginning in Matthew 13, continuing throughout the New Testament, and culminating in the book of Revelation.

2. Describing the commitment

a) To doctrine

The deacon must hold to all New Testament revelation. He must know and understand the truth revealed in the New Covenant. The spiritual character of a deacon begins with an affirmation of New Testament doctrine. He holds to the mystery of *the* faith. "The faith" simply refers to the whole of Christian truth.

b) To a pure conscience

The deacon is to hold "the mystery of the faith with a pure conscience." He has a clear conscience because he obeys the truth. When a person who is strong doctrinally violates that doctrine, he has a strong conscience reprimanding him. Show me a person who is weak in his conviction of God's truth, and I'll show you a person with a weak conscience. A person's conscience reacts to the body of truth to which he is committed.

A godly deacon holds strongly to the revealed New Testament faith and therefore maintains a pure conscience. A pure conscience exists only when a person lives out his biblical convictions. By God's grace and power, and by confessing sin, we all can have a pure conscience and be an example to others.

C. Their Spiritual Service (v. 10*a*)

"Let these also first be proved [tested]; then let them use the office of a deacon."

This is an imperative: let them be tested. The Greek word translated "be proved" (*dokimazō*) means "to approve after testing." The verb is in the present passive tense, which implies an ongoing test—not a single test or probationary period.

Then Paul issues another imperative: "Let them use the office of [serve as] a deacon." Deacons are to be continually tested. That test is an ongoing general assessment by the church of each deacon's service to Christ. "Also" in verse 10 means that that truth applies to elders and pastors as well.

D. Their Moral Purity (v. 10*b*, 12*a*)

1. Being blameless (v. 10*b*)

"Being found blameless."

The requirement is not any lower for a servant. His function is different—he implements what the elders design, but his qualification is the same—he is to be blameless. He is to be without reproach, without spot, and without blemish. There should be nothing in his life for which he could be accused and thus disqualified.

As we have already discovered, the only difference between a deacon and an elder or pastor is that the elder must be a skilled teacher (v. 2). A unique function of an elder is the public teaching of God's Word. A deacon may teach, and may do so very effectively. Perhaps he may one day become a pastor or elder, but as a deacon his primary function is to implement the teaching of the pastors and elders through his service. We could say that elders focus on teaching and deacons focus on administration. They all work on meeting the personal needs of the flock. Skilled teachers need to be free to pray and study, so God equips servers to come alongside them and enable them to do just that.

2. Being one-woman men (v. 12*a*)

"Let the deacons be the husbands of one wife."

This is the same moral qualification for an elder (v. 2). A deacon is not to be unfaithful either in action or in attitude to the woman who is his wife. Are his heart and life totally devoted to her? His sexual morality, or lack thereof, must be taken into consideration.

E. Their Home Life (v. 12*b*)

"Ruling their children and their own houses well."

Just as an elder has to demonstrate leadership in his home, so does a deacon. The deacon and his wife must manage their children and possessions well. The deacon proves he has leadership ability by how capably he and his wife handle situations and solve problems in their home. They are to be models for everyone to follow.

II. DEACONS WHO ARE WOMEN (v. 11)

A. Their Office (v. 11*a*)

"Even so must their wives [the women]."

The Greek word translated "even so" is the same word translated "in like manner" in verse 8, and it indicates that we are now introduced to a third category of people. The King James Version says, "Even so must their wives." I believe that's an inadequate translation. There's no word in Greek that we can always translate as "wives." Verse 11 uses *gunaikeios*, which means "women." Paul didn't say, "their women," as if referring to the deacons' wives. The Greek text literally says, "Likewise women." But to which women is Paul referring?

In addition to the poor translation of the Greek text, it's unlikely that there would be qualifications for the wives of deacons and not for the wives of elders. Also the use of

156

"likewise" in verse 11 indicates that Paul is introducing a new category, just as he did in verse 8: first overseers, likewise deacons, likewise women. The church is to recognize that there are women in the church who may serve in an official capacity.

To avoid confusion, why didn't Paul refer to those women as deaconesses? Because there's no Greek word for that. Phoebe is called a deacon in Romans 16:1 because there is no feminine form of *diakonos*. The only other word Paul could have used would have been *diakonos*, but we would not have known that he was referring to women. Clearly Paul introduced another category of deacons: what we have come to know as deaconesses. I prefer to call them women deacons because that maintains the New Testament terminology.

B. Their Qualifications (v. 11*b*)

These qualifications parallel those of deacons in verse 8.

1. "Grave"—Dignified

Women deacons are to have a sense of dignity and stateliness. They should command respect because of their spiritual devotion.

2. "Not slanderers"—Discreet

The Greek word translated "slanderers" (*diabolos*) is often translated "devil." The devil is the supreme slanderer. Women deacons are not to act like his children. They must watch what they say. Just as men deacons are not to be "double-tongued" (v. 8), the women are not to pervert the knowledge they are privileged to possess by slandering and gossiping.

3. "Sober-minded"—Sensible

The same Greek word was used of elders in verse 2, and it parallels the third qualification of deacons in verse 8— "not given to much wine." Women deacons are to be sober and sensible in their judgments. That's impossible if they're not sober physically.

157

4. "Faithful in all things"—Trustworthy

This qualification parallels that of deacons in verse 8—
"not greedy of filthy lucre." If a deacon were greedy, he
couldn't be trusted.

So the four qualifications for the women parallel the qualifications given for the men. God has ordained that elders be
men, but among deacons there are to be both men and
women.

Conclusion

Paul closes his treatment of men and women deacons in verse 13
with a promise: "They that have used the office of a deacon well
purchase to themselves a good standing, and great boldness in the
faith which is in Christ Jesus."

A. A Good Standing

Those who serve well "purchase to themselves a good
standing." The Greek word translated "purchase" means
"to achieve" or "to acquire" By their effective and faithful
service, they achieve a good standing. The Greek word
translated "standing" (bathmos) means "step." It came to refer to stepping above everyone else. It could also refer to a
pedestal or an elevated platform. Paul is saying that when
you serve well as a deacon, you are put on a pedestal. While
at first glance that might seem sinful, it's not—if you didn't
seek to be elevated. If you serve humbly and faithfully, you
will be lifted up. James 4:10 says, "Humble yourselves in
the sight of the Lord, and he shall lift you up."

Who exalts the deacon? Both God and men. If you serve
well as a deacon, the people who have known about your
faithful service will respect and honor you. That doesn't
mean they'll give you earthly reward, but you will gain spiritual respect from them, which is the key to being a spiritual
example. When a person is respected, he is emulated. People don't pattern themselves after individuals they don't respect. Furthermore, God also will show you honor and

respect. Some day you'll hear, "Well done, good and faithful servant."

B. Great Boldness

The second reward is "great boldness in the faith which is in Christ Jesus" (v. 13). The phrase "the faith which is in Christ Jesus" refers to the Christian realm: Christian truth, salvation, and the church. If you serve God well, you will see His power and grace at work in your life, and that will energize you for greater service. Seeing God active in your life makes you more bold. Successful service builds confidence and assurance. The Greek word translated "boldness" (*parrhesia*) is often used in reference to boldness of speech.

Two things accrue to the faithful deacon: respect and confidence. One leads to his or her becoming a model that others emulate, and the other leads to greater usefulness and effectiveness. Looking back and remembering what God has done in the past allows me to accept another challenge in ministry, prepares me to face a seemingly impossible task, and gives me confidence, assurance, and boldness. Because I know His hand is on my life, I can accept the future, even though I feel inadequate. That is the confidence that comes from serving Christ. God needs faithful servants in His church. May God supply those people so that they can be models for all the rest.

Focusing on the Facts

1. Why did God choose the men referred to in the section on models of spiritual leadership (see pp. 148-50)?
2. Describe a man after God's own heart (see pp. 150-51).
3. How would you characterize a "grave" person (see p. 152)?
4. How should a deacon speak (see p. 152)?
5. How should a deacon view drinking (see pp. 152-53)?
6. Why is it important that a deacon be free from the love of money (see p. 153)?
7. Define the "mystery of the faith" (see p. 154).
8. Why is it important for a believer to have a pure conscience regarding New Testament doctrine (see pp. 154-55)?

9. How often should the church examine a deacon's qualifications for service (see p. 155)?

10. In what ways is the moral purity of deacons to be like that of elders (see pp. 155-56)?

11. What should characterize the home life of a deacon (1 Tim. 3:12; see p. 156)?

12. Why is it likely that Paul was referring to a category of women deacons in 1 Timothy 3:11 and not to the wives of deacons (see pp. 156-57)?

13. What are the qualifications of women deacons (1 Tim. 3:11; see pp. 157-58)?

14. According to 1 Timothy 3:13, what do deacons achieve for themselves when they serve well? Explain (see pp. 158-59).

Pondering the Principles

1. Perhaps you don't feel that God has gifted you with the ability to teach, but don't let that dissuade you from seeking to serve the church. Examine the personal character qualifications of a deacon (vv. 8-10, 12). How would you rate yourself in each of those areas? What kind of changes would you need to make in order to be known as righteous in those areas? Are you above reproach? That quality of life was an overarching qualification for an elder, and it is to be equally true of deacons. Are you faithful both in attitude and action toward your wife? And are you a strong leader in your home? Do some serious self-examination in all those areas. As you do, realize that the outcome of your examination holds greater significance than merely the possibility of a future role as a deacon. It means you will have a greater capacity for glorifying God.

2. If you're a woman, perhaps you've wondered what kind of role God has for you in the church. As we have studied 1 Timothy 3:11, you have seen that there is a specific role you can fulfill. Yet as with the men, you must meet certain qualifications. How would you rate yourself in the qualifications for women deacons? What changes do you need to make in those areas? Begin today to make your life one that not only pleases God but also prepares you to serve Him in the church.

Scripture Index

164

Topical Index

Manasseh, evil influence of, 99-100

Marriage
    divorce. *See* Divorce
    remarriage. *See* Remarriage
    sexual purity in, 45-51, 54, 56

Mather, Cotton, on the worthiness of the ministry, 31-32

Michael, the angel, 123

Ministers. *See* Deacons, Elders

Ministry
    call to the. *See* Calling to the ministry
    demands of, 79-80
    leadership in. *See* Leadership
    ordination to the. *See* Ordination

Moderation, 51-54

Money, love of. *See* Greed

Montgomery, Bernard L., on leadership, 59

Mott, John R., on leadership, 59

Mountjoy, Sammy, character in *Free Fall*, 102, 112

Mystery, of faith, 154-55

Nadab, evil influence of, 98

Ordination
    bestowers of, 34
    definition of, 32
    qualifications for, 34
    safeguards regarding, 33-34
    symbol of, 33

Organization, 66, 79

Pastors. *See* Elders

Patience, 80, 88-89

Paul
    diakonos and, 138
    leadership example of, 149

Philo, on self-discipline, 64

Polygamy, 46

Prayer
    for leaders. *See* Leadership
    importance of, 40

Pride, of church leaders, 117-25

Pringle, Miss Rowena, character in *Free Fall*, 102, 112

Recreation, overemphasis on, 116-17

Reinecker, Fritz, on *neophutos*, 119

Remarriage, circumstances permitting, 46-51

Reputation, of elders, 125-28

Rest. *See* Recreation

Restoration, of fallen leaders, 44, 55

Rogers, Cleon, on *neophutos*, 119

Sanders, J. Oswald
    on being willing to suffer, 19
    on leadership, 59-61

Sangster, Will, on the worthiness of the ministry, 32

Satan. *See* Devil, the

Scripture
    studying, 39-40, 85
    understanding, 83

Self-Denial, 79

Self-Discipline, 64-66, 74, 79

Seriousness, 64-65, 152, 157

"Sermon of the Plow," 17-18

Service
    diakonos and, 135-37, 146
    gift of, 136-37
    necessity of, 135-37, 146
    what God looks for, 150-51
    See also Elders, Deacons

Sexual purity, 45-51, 54, 56

Slander. *See* Gossip

Soap operas, addiction to, 65

Sober-mindedness. *See* Self-Discipline

ROOKWOOD II

Featuring important Museum Quality pieces from the
Florence I. Balasny-Barnes Collection,
the Edwin W. Henderson and Robert G. Bougrain Collection,
the Estate of Carl Schmidt's daughter
and other fine consignors.

Auction

May 30th and May 31st from 9:30 AM - 5:30 PM
each day in the Music Hall Ballroom
14th and Elm Streets, Cincinnati, Ohio

Preview

May 29th from 9:00 AM - 7:00 PM

Auctioneer

J. Louis Karp

Sale Coordinator

Riley Humler

Auction Consultants

Louis Aronoff
Jack Kircher

Cincinnati Art Galleries

Michele and Randy Sandler
635 Main Street
Cincinnati, OH 45202
(513) 381-2128
Fax (513) 381-7527

ISBN: 0-943633-04-4
Library of Congress Catalog Card Number:
92-071315

Terms of Sale

The buyer is the person making the final and highest bid. In the event of a disputed bid, the auctioneer shall determine who is the successful bidder, or the auctioneer may resell the lot in dispute, but in all instances the judgment of the auctioneer shall be final.

Sales Tax

A 5.5% Ohio Sales Tax applies to all retail purchases. Ohio Sales Tax exemption forms must be executed and filed with the auction clerk at the time of auction registration.

Withdrawal

The auctioneer reserves the right to withdraw any lot before or at the time of the sale.

Credit, Methods of Payment

Cash, Visa, Mastercard, certified check and bank letters of credit are acceptable methods of payment. If you are known to us, your credit, and your credit only, can be established. Please check with the sale clerk. No company or personal references are accepted. We would appreciate credit arrangements being made in advance of the auction dates. Persons not making prior credit arrangements can pay by personal check, but no merchandise can be removed until all checks have cleared. Any packing and shipping expenses will be borne by the purchaser.

Bidding

Lots will be sold in the order in which they appear in the catalog. The bidding shall be in increments as follows:

Up to $500	Bids will increase in $25 increments
$500-$1000	Bids will increase in $50 increments
$1000-$5000	Bids will increase in $100 increments
$5000-$10000	Bids will increase in $250 increments
$10000 up	Bids will increase in $500 increments

The final bid is the price at which the lot is knocked down to the buyer.

This final bid, in all cases, is subject to a 10% buyer premium, the purchase price being the total of the two sums.

If the purchase price is not paid in full, the auctioneer may either cancel the sale, and any partial payment already made shall be there upon forfeited as liquidated damages or the auctioneer may resell the lot, without notice to the buyer.

Absentee, Written and Telephone bids

Absentee bids are welcomed. Absentee bids will be executed as if the bidder were present at the auction with the earliest bid received having preference in case of a tie between absentee bidders. Floor bids will be taken over absentee bids in case of a tie. Absentee, written or telephone bids are subject to the same 10% buyer's premium, and all credit requirements as listed above. The auctioneer, Cincinnati Art Galleries, and their employees are not responsible for absentee, written or telephone bids that are not properly executed. Due to the limited number of telephone lines available during the auction, we may be unable to accept bids on lots having low estimates of $1,000 or less. All packing and shipping costs will be borne by the purchaser.

Buyer's Premium

The final bid ("hammer" price) is subject to a 10% premium. The purchase price is the total of these two sums.

Reserves and Estimates

The estimated value of each lot is printed in the catalog, and merely reflects the price range into which a lot might fall. All lots have a reserve price below which they will not be sold. The reserve price is not published in the catalog, but in no case is it higher than the lower amount of the estimated price.

Removal

All lots are to be removed by their buyers not later than 7:00 PM, Sunday, May 31, 1992. Lots are released to buyers upon presentation of proof of payment. All packing and shipping is the responsibility of the buyer.

Packing and Shipping

We have made arrangements with P.K.G.'s to be on hand to assist in packing and shipping your purchases should you desire. P.K.G.'s will pack any item and arrange shipping through U.P.S., Federal Express or other shippers, as long as the items are insured. International shipping is available through P.K.G.'s. Should you wish information about their capabilities, call Jeff Sizer, the Cincinnati Area Manager for P.K.G.'s at (800) 543-7547 or (513) 489-7547 and fax (513) 489-3874. Contractual arrangements for packing and shipping are the responsibility of the buyer and shipper. For those of you who wish to pack and carry, we will have limited packing materials available, such as boxes and wraps.

Guarantee

All lots in this catalogue are guaranteed as described and are guaranteed to be free of other problems or repairs. Crazing is only mentioned if objectionable. Sizes are approximate. (See Peck Book II for shape number references). We guarantee the authenticity of all lots in this auction.

Advice to Bidders

The Cincinnati Art Galleries staff is available to discuss all lots with intending buyers at all presale exhibitions, or by telephone (513-381-2128) Monday thru Friday 9AM-5PM, Saturday 9AM-4PM.

Prices Realized

The list of prices realized at the auction will be mailed shortly after the sale. Lots that have been withdrawn from the sale or that have failed to reach the reserve price will be excluded from the prices realized.

CONSIGNMENTS WANTED FOR ROOKWOOD III

Cincinnati Art Galleries is now accepting consignments for Rookwood III. There is no better venue for selling Rookwood than Cincinnati Art Galleries. We have established a new level of excellence in the Art Pottery world, first with our stunning Glover Collection Sale and now with the equally impressive offering of Rookwood II.

Cincinnati Art Galleries offers the consignor something very special. We have expertise in dealing with Rookwood that is unmatched and we operate our sales with the greatest attention to detail, honesty and scholarship. No one can offer consignors and sellers alike, a more friendly and efficient opportunity to either buy or sell Rookwood.

Cincinnati Art Galleries also offers extensive advertising for its sales. We target a number of National and Regional magazines and newspapers, ensuring that everyone is aware of our Auctions. Below are listed most of the ads produced for Rookwood II.

MAGAZINES & JOURNALS

February	Arts & Crafts Conference Grove Park Inn	Half Page, B&W
March/April	Arts & Crafts Quarterly	Full Page, Color
March/April	Antiques & Fine Art	Half Page, Color
March/April	Journal of American Art Pottery	Full Page, B&W
April	The Magazine Antiques	Half Page, Color
April	Art & Auction	Half Page, Color
April	Antique Monthly	Half Page, Color
May/June	Journal of American Art Pottery	Full Page, B&W
May/June	Antiques & Fine Art	Full Page, Color
May	The Magazine Antiques	Full Page, Color
May	Art & Auction	Full Page, Color
May	Antique Monthly	Full Page, Color

NEWSPAPERS

March	Antique Review (Monthly)	Full Page, B&W
March 2	Antique Week	Full Page, B&W
March 11	Antique Trader Weekly	Full Page, B&W
March 13	Newtown Bee (Antique & the Arts Weekly)	Full Page, B&W
March 16	Antique Week	Full Page, B&W
March 25	Antique Trader Weekly	Full Page, B&W
March 27	Newtown Bee	Full Page, B&W
March 30	Antique Week	Full Page, B&W
April	Antique Review (Monthly)	Full Page, B&W
April	Maine Antique Digest (Monthly)	Full Page, B&W
April 8	Antique Trader Weekly	Full Page, B&W
April 10	Newtown Bee	Full Page, B&W
April 13	Antique Week	Full Page, B&W
April 22	Antique Trader Weekly	Full Page, B&W
April 24	Newtown Bee	Full Page, B&W
April 27	Antique Week	Full Page, B&W
May	Antique Review (Monthy)	Full Page, B&W
May	Maine Antique Digest (Monthly)	Full Page, B&W
May 6	Antique Trader Weekly	Full Page, B&W
May 8	Newtown Bee	Full Page, B&W
May 11	Antique Week	Full Page, B&W
May 20	Antique Trader Weekly	Full Page, B&W
May 22	Newtown Bee	Full Page, B&W
May 25	Antique Week	Full Page, B&W

Should you have any questions about consignments of Rookwood for Rookwood III, call Randy Sandler, Riley Humler or Jack Kircher. We are actively planning for the next great sale of Rookwood and would be pleased to include pieces from your collection.

CONSIGNMENTS WANTED FOR OUR WINTER 1992 ART POTTERY SALE

Cincinnati Art Galleries also plans a sale of American and European Art Potteries in the Winter of 1992. We are interested in handling fine examples of Potteries other than Rookwood and will offer the same professionalism you have come to expect from us.

We are looking for examples of all major American and European Potteries and good studio pottery. Please call if you wish to discuss consignments.

SELECTED BIBLIOGRAPHY

ROOKWOOD: ITS GOLDEN ERA OF ART POTTERY 1880-1929, Edwin J. Kircher and Barbara and Joseph Agranoff, Cincinnati, Ohio, Privately Published, 1969.

THE BOOK OF ROOKWOOD POTTERY, Herbert Peck, Cincinnati, Ohio, Cincinnati Art Galleries, Publisher, reprinted 1991.

THE SECOND BOOK OF ROOKWOOD POTTERY, Herbert Peck, Cincinnati, Ohio, Cincinnati Art Galleries, Publisher, 1985.

ROOKWOOD POTTERY POTPOURRI, Virginia Cummins, Cincinnati, Ohio, Cincinnati Art Galleries, Publisher, Reprinted in 1991.

FROM OUR NATIVE CLAY, Martin Eidelberg, editor for the American Ceramic Arts Society, New York, Published by Turn of the Century Editions, 1987.

MR. S.G. BURT'S RECORD BOOK OF WARE AT ART MUSEUM, 2292 PIECES OF EARLY ROOKWOOD POTTERY IN THE CINCINNATI ART MUSEUM IN 1916. Reprinted for the Cincinnati Historical Society by Herbert Peck, 1978.

THE KOVELS' COLLECTOR'S GUIDE TO AMERICAN ART POTTERY, Ralph and Terry Kovel, New York, Crown Publishers, Inc., 1974.

ART POTTERY OF THE UNITED STATES, Second Edition, Paul Evans, New York, New York, Feingold & Lewis Publishing Corp., 1987.

ROOKWOOD POTTERY, AN EXPLANATION OF ITS MARKS AND SYMBOLS, Edwin J. Kircher, Cincinnati, Ohio, Published by the Author, 1984.

THE GLOVER COLLECTION ROOKWOOD POTTERY, Cincinnati Art Galleries, Cincinnati, Ohio, Cincinnati Art Galleries, Publisher, 1991.

FRAGILE BLOSSOMS, ENDURING EARTH, The Japanese Influence on American Ceramics, Everson Museum of Art, Syracuse, NY, 1989.

THE NEWARK MUSEUM COLLECTION OF AMERICAN ART POTTERY, Ulysses G. Dietz, The Newark Museum, Newark, NJ, 1984.

ROOKWOOD POTTERY
An Explanation of Its Marks and Symbols
by Edwin J. Kircher

HISTORY

The Rookwood Pottery was founded in 1880 at Cincinnati, Ohio by Mrs. Maria Longworth Storer. The establishment was named for the Longworth Estate in the nearby countryside. The family home had large numbers of crows roosting in the trees on its grounds, and acquired its name from their presence.

The first plant was an abandoned schoolhouse at 207 Eastern Avenue. This address has been changed due to street renumbering, and the building has been razed, but the location was near the present intersection of Kemper Lane and Eastern Avenue. The factory remained in this location until construction of its Mount Adams site in 1893.

Mrs. Storer was the granddaughter of Nicholas Longworth, a wealthy pillar of the early Cincinnati community, and daughter of Joseph Longworth who endowed the Cincinnati Art School. Her husband, Bellamy Storer, was the son of a prominent judge, and himself a barrister. He served two terms as Congressional Representative before being appointed in 1887 by President McKinley to the post of Ambassador to Belgium. He later became Minister to Spain.

Mrs. Storer had been an active participant in the development of artistic interest in Cincinnati in the decade preceding the founding of Rookwood. She had worked at the Frederick Dallas Pottery as did members of the Cincinnati Women's "Pottery Club" of which Mrs. Storer was not a member, but from which she later drew heavily for artists with which to stock her company.

Admiration of the Japanese ceramics exhibit at the 1876 Centennial Exposition in Philadelphia crystallized Mrs. Storer's intention to manufacture "Art Pottery" in Cincinnati. Her experience made her realize that the existing local equipment and potteries were not adequately designed to fulfill this objective. She then set about assembling her plant and equipment, and Rookwood Pottery was born.

Mrs. Storer gathered around her the finest chemists, potters and decorators available in the local area. She also brought in the Japanese artist, Kataro Shirayamadani, to inject the influence of an advanced pottery technique which she had admired so much.

At the Paris Exposition of 1889 Rookwood Pottery received a gold medal and "the world awakened" to Rookwood. The Pottery began to pay its own way by 1890 and monetary support by the Longworth family was no longer necessary. In 1891 Mrs. Storer turned over management of the Pottery to the capable direction of W. W. Taylor. It was under the leadership of Mr. Taylor that the Pottery attained its greatest significance in pursuit of a unique American contribution to western culture.

During the years 1890-1925 Rookwood probably realized its greatest profit both in money and talent. At this time the Vellum finish was developed; the Iris glaze and Rookwood Porcelain came into being. It was also at this time that the Rookwood Faience architectural tiles and ornaments were fully developed. Such talents as Carl Schmidt, E. T. Hurley, Fred Rothenbusch, Ed. Diers, and Sturgis Lawrence were at their zenith. Kataro Shirayamadani, Matt Daly, and A. R. Valentien enjoyed international reputations. An extraordinary array of experience and talent underpinned by the many years of technical development had built the finest Art Pottery the world has ever known.

FACTORY MARKS

The factory mark identifies the manufacturer of the ware. Rookwood has used a number of factory marks. It has employed both its name, in various forms, as well as the picture-symbol type of representation associated with most European furnaces. The symbol that comes quickly to mind is the world famous monogram mark of the reversed R and P, with its wreath of flames.

This unique factory mark was used longer than any other, and was in use at the time the pottery enjoyed its greatest prestige. As a result it is this mark that is most often found on the finest of Rookwood productions. Prior to its institution the factory marks were widely varied in design and survived but a short time. They are herein explained and illustrated in the order of their occurrence, beginning with the earliest.

The most common marks prior to 1882 were the name of the pottery and the date of manufacture, either painted or incised on the base of the piece by perhaps the decorators or potters. A variation of this consisted of the initials of the Pottery, and of the founder: R.P.C.O.M.L.N. (Rookwood Pottery, Cincinnati, Ohio, Maria Longworth Nichols. Mrs. Nichols remarried in 1886 and became Mrs. Storer.) Illustrations of two of these marks are below:

From 1880 to 1882 another design used was that prepared by the famous Cincinnati artist, H. F. Farny. This factory mark was printed in black beneath the glaze, and represents a kiln with two Rooks.

The following oval mark bearing the name and address of the factory was also used for a short time.

In 1882 the following two types of marks were used. Both were impressed in a raised ribbon, and the upper one appeared on a commercial project - a large beer tankard made for the Cincinnati Cooperage Company.

Prior to 1883 an anchor was sometimes impressed or placed in relief. It occasionally occurred in connection with an impressed date, and often in conjunction with a decorator's mark. (The illustration to the left is impressed; the one to the right appears in relief.)

The regular mark adopted in 1882 was the word ROOKWOOD and the date in arabic numerals, impressed. This mark was in continuous use until 1886, the date being changed each year.

**ROOKWOOD
1882**

In the year 1883 a small kiln mark was impressed in the ware, and may or may not appear with the word ROOKWOOD and the date, also impressed.

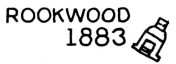

The monogram mark of the reversed R, and P was adopted in 1886, although it has been found upon ware dated as early as 1882. The monogram mark and the "ROOKWOOD 1886" both exist denoting the year 1886, the ROOKWOOD mark having been used in the earlier part of the year. In 1887 a flame point was placed above the RP monogram, and one point was added each year until 1900, at which time the monogram mark was encircled by 14 flame points.

In 1901 the same mark used to indicate 1900 was continued, and the Roman numeral I was added below, to indicate the first year of the new century. The Roman numeral was subsequently changed to denote the correct year.

SHAPE NUMBERS AND SIZE SYMBOLS

Shape numbers are impressed in the clay just below the factory mark, and are usually followed by the size symbol if applicable. These numbers were assigned consecutively, and bear no direct relationship to year of manufacture or quantity produced. On early pieces the size symbol sometimes precedes the pattern number. It is also known to have appeared immediately below the pattern number, particularly on items upon which the area available for marking is limited. An example of each arrangement is shown on the following page:

568B   A7   9 0 1
C

There are three categories of shapes. 1.) The regular series which comprise the majority of the pieces produced. 2.) The "Trial" series, in which the pattern number is preceded by a "T". ("E" for experimental could not be used — "E" is a size symbol.) 3.) Those items bearing no pattern numbers at all. (These were often the result of gifts for friends, etc., and in these cases were singular items.) Each of the categories excepting #3 were numbered consecutively.

2191   T1250

Clarence Cook, in "The Studio," said "Rookwood Pottery shows good taste in adhering to the principles which are the foundation of the system of forms called classical." In later years some patterns were duplicated, (same shape different pattern number) but despite exceptions, the patterns over the years have been generally quite artistic and tastefully executed.

Size symbols are impressed in the clay next to the pattern number and are represented by six letters. The sizes of the patterns were always lettered with A representing the largest, diminishing through F. If no size letter is shown, only the one size of the pattern exists. If an A exists, at least a B must have been constructed. However, there is no basis for assuming a C existed. Likewise, if an E is encountered, an A, B, C, and D were created, but not necessarily an F. Occasionally another was created at a later date, necessitating an insertion of a new size, such as "BB". An example of each single letter is shown:

A   B   C   D   E   F

Different pattern numbers having the same size letters bear no relation to each other. That is, a 907C and a 6308C have no relation in size, the former being a 14" high vase, and the latter a 7" high vase. Size ratio exists only within the category of a particular pattern or shape and is of no defined scale.

CLAY SYMBOLS

Rookwood Pottery employed a series of letter-symbols to indicate the clay used in the manufacture of the body. The clays were classified only in regard to color. The symbols were six in number and were impressed. The following letters were employed:

G   O   R   S   W   Y

These indicate Ginger, Olive, Red, Sage Green, White, and Yellow. The Ginger colored clay is one that would be termed a "Buff" clay. The letter "G" and the title Ginger" were employed to avoid confusion with the size symbol "B". The letter "S" is also used in another category, that of a special symbol.

The symbols refer only to the color of the various bodies, and as such do not take into consideration the possible chemical variations within a color. The White body was the most popular and undoubtedly the one most frequently used by the potters. This color was developed and compounded in at least seven chemically different varieties to fit glazes in use at the Pottery. Often no distinction was made in them when marking the ware. In later years the clay symbol "W" was sometimes omitted.

Rookwood experimented with artificially tinted bodies as have most of the world's leading potteries, but their existence in relation to the total production is quite small. Tinted grey, blue and black bodies were utilized for the most part after 1920.

Rookwood also experimented with foreign clays to some extent; but domestic clays, and particularly those from the Ohio Valley, were most popular. The Ohio region is rich in fine clays. These are naturally colored, having been stained by the mineral deposits of the area. The Red clay was from Buena Vista, Ohio and the Yellow from Hanging Rock, Ohio.

A Yellow clay was obtained from Georgia, and a Cream colored one from Chattanooga, Tennessee; still another clay came from Florida. The existence of a Cream colored clay, as well as examples of Cream colored ware, creates speculation that there may have been a symbol for "Cream" clay in use at one time, for relatively early pieces have been found marked with a double "C".

PROCESS MARKS

At Rookwood all experiments or changes in clay, decorative materials, and glaze were carefully recorded and studied. To do so, it was necessary to identify the items after their return from the fire. Therefore the chemists, and sometimes the potters, placed identifying symbols on the pieces. They did this by incising or impressing impromptu, but recognizable designs, much as Westerners brand cattle. The precise meaning of these symbols could only be known through access to the notebooks kept by these men. For the benefit of those who may come across such symbols a few are illustrated:

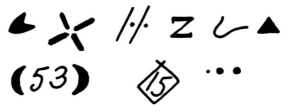

SPECIAL MARKS AND SYMBOLS

In the following paragraphs are collected and defined those marks and symbols which do not fit precisely into a prior category. These marks are not to be considered of any lesser importance than those comprising the other categories, because they also contribute invaluably to the understanding of the history and significance of the piece of Rookwood Pottery in question. Some are old. Others are of more recent composition. None are without precise meaning and purpose, though that be temporarily unknown.

The first mark to be considered, is the one that will be encountered most frequently. This is the "X" mark used to indicate a piece of secondary quality. Rookwood ware from its inception was graded into three classifications. These are: (1.) Those items of the best quality, that is, most nearly flawless. (No critisism of art work was involved, according to my friend Virginia Cummins, who was employed in the salesroom.) (2.) Those items displaying obvious technical faults, such as glaze bubbles, minor discolorations, kiln cracks, warp, and other manufacturing defects. It was this category of ware which was so designated by the "X" mark. (3.) Those items defective to the point of ruination of either their utility, decoration, or both. These were destroyed.

The "X" mark indicating secondary quality was usually cut into the underside of the piece, by means of a grinding wheel, much the same as that used to remove excess glaze from the resting surface of an item. The mark was also known to have been cut into the decorated surface of some pieces, and in these cases, undoubtedly contributes additionally to the undesirableness of the piece. The mark was not generally accurately cut, and as a result may appear as a "V" like score in the body, however, there is no reason to confuse this with the Vellum "V" mark, which is explained later in this same category. The "X" mark is generally large, and appears as a deeply ground score in the body, as follows:

The category of second quality was usually determined in the showroom, by those in charge. The sales personnel had access to a grinding wheel, and cut the second mark themselves. It is presumed that the decorators could also request that an item of their work be adjudged as secondary quality. The extent to which this was done, if any, is not known. The third example from the left is a wheel ground "X" with an additional cut through the center which was used for items to be given away. "Give away" recipients ranged from visitors of note to unsold pieces "raffled" at company sponsored parties for employees. In later examples (circa 1940) a single wheel ground line has been found, which may have been the equivalent of an "X".

As any collector can attest, the judgment of secondary items over a period of years as represented by pieces of varying age, appears rather whimsical. Many items so marked contain only flaws of a very minor nature. In contrast, items are known with kiln cracks of several inches or more, and are not marked seconds. Regardless of the apparent overlapping of categories, and inconsistent application of standards, a second is less valuable. The second quality items were placed on a separate table at the Pottery, and marked down, in relation to items of first quality.

The examples above show the two varieties of the "V" mark which was used to designate the Vellum line. This particular glaze was first introduced in 1904 and is credited to the efforts of the plant chemist Stanley G. Burt.

The Vellum mark always appears on the bottom of the item, apart from the factory mark, so that it can never be confused with the date 1905 (V). It is either impressed, in which case it is in the form of a printed "V", or incised. It is believed the impressed "V" refers to a "vellum" body, and the hand incised "V" refers to the decorators desire to have the piece "vellum" glazed. This explanation is based upon empirical evidence, and the double "V" occurs mostly within the mid-range years of vellum production. The possibility of mismarked items is rather remote, and although this has undoubtedly occurred, the Pottery was rather well organized at the time Vellum was manufactured, and an error of this type would be unusual. After seeing several Vellum pieces and examining them closely, it becomes increasingly easier to identify, and reference to the "V" mark serves only as a verification of one's knowledge.

The Vellums are one of the most beautiful and unusual of all the Rookwood creations. To describe Vellum in its simplest terms Rookwood's master potter, Earl Menzel, said, "It is merely a transparent mat, developed in the fire." The implication of this, is that Rookwood was the first pottery to develop this glaze without the aid of chemical or mechanical means. The Vellum glaze won a Gold Medal at the St. Louis World's Fair in 1904.

S

The above letter "S" was impressed in the clay of Rookwood as an indication that the particular item had been created as a "special" shape (perhaps at the request of a decorator) and was not assigned a normal sequential shape number. However, one must be careful to distinguish between the "S" indicating the Sage Green clay (see: clay marks) and the "S" indicating the potter's handiwork. This is a relatively easy distinction to make, for the Sage Green clay is a pale olive color, and is easily recognized on the unglazed portions of the under surface. In addition, Sage Green bodies usually lent themselves to decoration in tones of green, brown, and yellow.

In the case of a Sage Green clay piece which was thrown by hand, the piece would bear two "S's". Examples of this nature do in fact exist, as do all the other combinations of clay marks and the potter's "S".

P

The above letter, impressed in the paste, represents the term, "Porcelain." It was introduced at Easter, 1915, after Rookwood had developed a "porcelainized" body, and accompanying high gloss glaze. The body is not a true porcelain, but should be more correctly termed a "soft-porcelain" or "semi-porcelain."

These pieces were generally decorated in light colors. This was probably due to the high glaze maturity and body vitrification temperatures, conditions which tend to "burn out" deeper colors. This body has a slightly irridescent appearance, and in the thinner pieces a translucence will be evident when exposed to a strong light. The colors and manner of decoration surpassed those of the Copenhagen furnaces, and magnificent blues had been developed. The ware was quite costly to produce, and was subsequently abandoned for a ware referred to as "Jewel Porcelain."

Jewel Porcelain was also a "porcelainized" or vitreous body, but employed a distinctively different glaze, which was characterized by a running of the colors. This ware was manufactured for quite some time. It bore no body or glaze mark of its own, nor did it bear the "P" mark.

The "L" mark, as illustrated above, is found incised into older pieces of Rookwood in conjunction with the "Standard" glaze. The items are decorated, and the "L" is often under the decorator's mark, as shown in the second example, having been incised by the decorator himself. There is no apparent relationship between this mark and that of a specific decorator. It is found with the marks of all decorators of the period.

The letter refers to the decorator's choice of glaze to be employed. "L" refers to a lightly colored standard glaze and an M (not illustrated) refers to a Mahogany tinted standard glaze, The "D" for a dark standard glaze, was also used, and the script "G" (example 3) refers to the sea green glaze. The sea green glaze "G" is also found impressed as a capital G.

The above examples of the printed name "CINCINNATI" were used in an effort to identify the name of Rookwood with the city in which it was founded and had prospered. The impressions were always used in addition to the other standard symbols, factory marks, etc. This practice was originated circa 1920, and the symbol used from time to time on various productions. The mark on the extreme left appeared as a wreath over the factory symbol, RP with flames. The marks to the right appeared as later examples. The correlation between years and the use of these marks does not have any significance beyond the fact that the Pottery was attempting to hold its position of prestige in relation to its competitors; hence the inclusion of the name of the Pottery. Other varieties of the city name are known to exist.

The above marks were created for the pieces of Rookwood ware produced during the year of an anniversary. The first such anniversary mark is the one signifying Rookwood's Fiftieth Year, 1930. This mark was usually applied in the form of an underglaze color, (blue or black) and represents a kiln with the number 50 within it. The mark used for the Seventieth Year is also a kiln with the number 70 contained in it, but differs in that it is also found impressed in the clay, and often accompanied by the name ROOKWOOD impressed alongside. The third anniversary mark at the right took the form of a diamond and signified Rookwood Pottery's 75th birthday.

This mark appears on the underside of a Rookwood ashtray depicting one of the masks of drama, but is not a Rookwood mark. The pattern is an exact reproduction of an item brought from Italy by Mr. J.D. Wareham, director of the Pottery. The original pattern bore the mark in question, and therefore, it was preserved in the reproduction. The relief form represents Romulus, Remus and their Wolf Mother of Roman Mythology.

The above marks were instituted by Rookwood's master potter, Earl Menzel. The whorl was impressed on the underside of many thrown pieces and was merely an idiosyncrasy of the potter. The mark was made on the lathe, and is usually unaccompanied by Mr. Menzel's signature. It can be assumed to be a synonym for his mark, for these pieces were produced by his hand. The circle was applied, as an impression, to pieces whose shape might make them suitable for use as lamps, and was intended as a guide for drilling.

Initials, names, and inscriptions are also found incised into the decorative surface of some Rookwood. These are not marks, but the results of creation of pieces for friends, and commemoration of special events, and as such do not require further explanation.

ARTISTS' AND DECORATORS' MARKS

It became the custom at the Rookwood Pottery for the artists to incise or paint their initials or monograms on the pieces decorated or sculptured by them but this was not always so. In the fledgling days of the Pottery the signing of work was discouraged. Soon, however, a preference for the signed pieces made itself felt in the market, and the Pottery changes its policy. One must remember that these Artists' initials are presented here in their most ideal state — many hurriedly written examples exist, making the commonest of monograms sometimes impossible to decipher.

The artists not only cut their initials into the bottom of the ware, but painted them on, using some of the underglaze "paint" or engobe that was in use at the moment. This method was also employed when the artists signed pieces on the decorated surface. Many used their full names if their pieces were a special effort.

Marks were also impressed. This was done through the construction of a die, much the same as that employed to impress the factory mark. The decorators or potters formed these from clay, and once fired, they were permanent in nature and could be used repeatedly. It was necessary, of course, to construct them in reverse, the same as a rubber stamp. One artist intentionally failed to observe this rule, and as a result Carl Schmidt's mark is "mirrored," or reversed.

The use of dies was practiced primarily by the decorators of later years. Readily recognizable examples of these dies are the marks of Margaret Helen McDonald and Mary Graze Denzler.

There are decorators in the accompanying list. Some of these have as many as four different marks attributed to them. They are presented in the order of what is believed to be their earliest mark, first. An effort has been made to limit this presentation to only those marks and symbols which have been positively identified, and no full signatures have been included for these are self-explanatory.

Approximately one dozen other "decorators" marks will be found accompanying ware, circa 1946. These people are not identified in the following listing for they were designated as "junior artists" and did not participate in projects of original composition as did the staff artists. Their marks are found applied in underglaze color, and their duties consisted of applying specific colors to prepared designs.

Name	Monogram
Abel, Edward	*E·A·*
Abel, Louise	*(A)*
Altman, Howard	*HA·*
Asbury, Lenore	*L·A·*
Auckland, Fannie	*FA*
Auckland, William	*WA WA*
Baker, Constance A.	*C·A·B·*
Barrett, Elizabeth	*EB*
Bishop, Irene	*I·B·*
Bonsall, Caroline F.	*C·F·B·*
Bookprinter, Anna M.	*AMB AB*
Brain, Elizabeth W.	*EWB*
Brennan, Alfred	*AB*
Breuer, W. H.	*WHB WB*
Caven, Alice	*(AC)*
Conant, Arthur P.	*[C]*
Conant, Patti M.	*(PC)*
Cook, Daniel	*DC·*
Covalenco, Catherine	*CC*
Coyne, Sallie E.	*S·E·C· SEC*
Crabtree, Catherine	*(C)*
Cranch, E. Bertha I.	*E·B·I·C·*
Cranch, Edward P.	*EPC EPC E*
Crofton, Cora	
Daly, Matt A.	*MAD MDaly*
Demarest, Virginia B.	*VBD VGD*
Denzler, Mary Grace	
Dibowski, Charles John	*CJ·D·*
Diers, Edward	*ED·*
Duell, Cecil A.	*(AD*
Epply, Lorinda	*E*
Fechheimer, Rose	*R·F· R*
Felten, Edith R.	*E·R·F·*
Foertmeyer, Emma D.	*E·D·F·*
Foglesong, Mattie	*MF*
Fry, Laura A.	*LA LAF*
Furukawa, Lois	*LF*
Glass, William T.	*WJG*
Goetting, Arthur	*AG*
Hall, Grace M.	*G·H·*
Hanscom, Lena E.	*L·E·H·*
Harris, Janet	*JH*

Name	Mark
Hentschel, W. E.	(monogram)
Hickman, Katharine	KH
Hicks, Orville	Hicks
Hirschfeld, N. J.	NJH N.J.H.
Holtkamp, Loretta	4
Horsfall, Bruce	B—
Horton, Hattie	H.H.
Humphreys, Albert	A.H.
Hurley, Edward T.	E.T.H.
Jensen, Jens	(J)
Jones, Katherine	KJ
King, Flora	FK.
King, Ora	OT
Klemm, William	W.K.
Klinger, Charles	(K)
Koehler, F. D.	K FDK
Laurence, Sturgis	S.L.
Lawrence, ELiza C.	ECL
Ley, Kay	LEY
Lincoln, Elizabeth N.	LNL
Lindeman, Clara C.	CCL
Lindeman, Laura E.	L.E.L. LEL
Lunt, Tom	TOM
Lyons, Helen M.	HL.
Markland, Sadie	S.M.
Matchette, Kate C.	K.C.M.
McDermott, Elizabeth F.	EFM
McDonald, Margaret Heler	MM (MEH)
McDonald, William P.	WCD WPMCD
McLaughlin, Charles J.	TM
Menzel, Reuben Earl	REM
Mitchell, Marianne D.	MM
Moos, Herman	HM
Munson, Albert	AM
Newton, Clara Chipman	C.N. (monogram)
Nichols, Maria Longworth	M L N
Noonan, Edith	EN.
Nourse, Mary	M.N.
Perkins, Mary Luella	M.L.P. MP MP
Peters-Baurer, Pauline	PB
Pons, Albert	AP
Pullman, J. Wesley	WP

Name	Mark
Rauchfuss, Marie	
Reed, O. Geneva	
Rehm, Wilhelmine	
Rettig, Martin	
Rothenbusch, Fred	
Sacksteder, Jane	
Sax, Sara	
Scalf, Virginia	
Schmidt, Carl	
Sehon, Adeliza D.	
Seyler, David W.	
Shirayamadani, Kataro	
Smalley, Marian H.	
Sprague, Amelia B.	
Stegner, Carolyn	
Steinle, Carrie F.	
Storer, Maria Longworth (Nichols)	
Strafer, Harriette R.	
Stuntz, H. Pabodie	
Swing, Jeanette	
Taylor, Mary A.	
Tischler, Vera	
Todd, Charles S.	
Toohey, Sallie	
Valentien, Albert R.	
Valentien, Anna M.	
Van Briggle, Artus	
Van Briggle, Leona	
Van Horne, Katherine	
Vreeland, Francis W.	
Wareham, John D.	
Wenderoth, Harriet	
Wilcox, Harriet E.	
Wildman, Edith L.	
Willitts, Alice	
Workum, Delia	
Young, Grace	
Zanetta, Clotilda	
Zettel, Josephine E.	

THE STAFF OF CINCINNATI ART GALLERIES

Ballard Borich	Terry Boyle
Tim Boyle	Edie Buschle
Riley Humler	Jack Kircher
Pam Kirchner	Michele Sandler
Randy Sandler	

ALPHABETICAL LIST OF ARTISTS AND THEIR WORKS BY CATALOG NUMBER

ALPHABETICAL LIST OF ARTISTS AND THEIR WORKS BY CATALOG NUMBER

SATURDAY
MAY 30th
1992
LOTS 1-424

10% Buyers Premium
will be added to all lots purchased

1   Standard glaze vase by Harriet Wilcox, decorated in 1889 with dogwood. Marks on the base include the $300-$400
    Rookwood logo, the date, shape number 513, W for white clay, LY for light yellow (Standard) glaze and the
    artist's initials. Height 5⅜ inches.

2   Cameo glaze creamer decorated with sprays of white flowers by Sallie Toohey in 1887. Marks on the base $200-$300
    include the Rookwood logo, the date, shape number 47, W 7 for a type of white clay, W for white glaze and the
    artist's monogram. Height 1⅞ inches.

3   Vellum glaze vase decorated with Japanese maple leaves by Elizabeth Lincoln in 1910. Marks on the base $400-$600
    include the Rookwood logo, the date, shape number 900 D, V for Vellum glaze body, V for Vellum glaze and the
    artist's initials. Height 6¼ inches. Glaze peppering, bruise on lip and very tight line descending about 1 inch from
    the lip.

4   Standard glaze ewer decorated with rose hips by Carl Schmidt in 1896. Marks on the base include the Rookwood $250-$350
    logo, the date, shape number 746 D and the artist's monogram. Height 5⅛ inches. Tight crack in handle.

5   Mat glaze vase with fruit blossom decoration, done by Elizabeth Lincoln in 1925. Marks on the base include the $300-$400
    Rookwood logo, the date, shape number 2191 and the artist's initials. Height 5 inches.

6   Standard glaze three handled candy box, decorated with fruit blossoms by Amelia Sprague in 1893. Marks on the $250-$450
    base include the Rookwood logo, the date, shape number 232 A, R for red clay and the artist's monogram. Height
    2⅝ inches. Roughness to rim of base and a small flake off the edge of the top.

7   Mat glaze vase with floral decoration, painted in 1939 by Margaret McDonald. Marks on the base include the Rookwood logo, the date, shape number 6748 and the artist's initials. Height 5⅞ inches. $300-$500

8   High glaze vase with water lily decoration, done in 1930 by Sallie Coyne. Marks on the base include the Rookwood logo, the date, shape number 6144 and the artist's monogram. Height 2⅞ inches. Several small glaze skips. $200-$400

9   Standard glaze vase decorated with poppies by Leona Van Briggle in 1901. Marks on the base include the Rookwood logo, the date, shape number 917 E and the artist's monogram. Height 5⅝ inches. Bruise and crack at rim. $150-$250

10 Unusual Iris glaze horn pitcher, decorated with clover by Carl Schmidt in 1901. Marks on the base include the Rookwood logo, the date, shape number 647, W for white glaze and the artist's monogram. Height 4¼ inches. $400-$600

11 Standard glaze pitcher decorated with clover by Harriet Wilcox in 1889. Marks on the base include the Rookwood logo, the date, shape number 461, S for sage green clay, LY for light yellow (Standard) glaze and the artist's initials. Height 3¾ inches. $300-$400

12 Mat glaze vase with water lily decoration, done in 1925 by Sallie Coyne. Marks on the base include the Rookwood logo, the date, shape number 1909 and the artist's initials. Height 7⅛ inches. $300-$500

13   Iris glaze vase decorated with clover by Carrie Steinle in 1906. Marks on the base include the Rookwood logo, $600-$900
      the date, shape number 30 F, W for white glaze and the artist's monogram. Height 6¼ inches.

14   Mat glaze vase with stylized floral decoration, done in 1925 by Elizabeth Barrett. Marks on the base include the $300-$400
      Rookwood logo, the date, shape number 356 F and the artist's monogram. Height 5½ inches.

15   Mat glaze vase decorated with cherry blossoms by Elizabeth Lincoln in 1927. Marks on the base include the $300-$500
      Rookwood logo, the date, shape number 2963 and the artist's initials. Height 7¼. Very minor grinding roughness
      on base.

16   Standard glaze vase decorated with trailing apple blossoms, painted in 1885 by Martin Rettig. Marks on the base $200-$300
      include Rookwood in block letters, the date, shape number 76, O for orange clay and the artist's initials. Height
      2¾ inches.

17   Vellum glaze vase decorated with lilies of the valley by Sallie Coyne in 1919. Marks on the base include the $500-$700
      Rookwood logo, the date, shape number 1871, V for Vellum glaze body and the artist's monogram. Height 6⅛
      inches.

18   Standard glaze ewer decorated with mistletoe by Leona Van Briggle in 1900. Marks on the base include the $250-$350
      Rookwood logo, the date, shape number 844 and the artist's monogram. Height 5⅜ inches.

19   Standard glaze ewer with clover decoration, done in 1888 by Luella Perkins. Marks on the base include the $300-$400
Rookwood logo, the date, shape number 40, S for sage green clay, L for light Standard glaze and the artist's
monogram. Height 6⅜ inches.

20   Vellum glaze vase decorated with a band of stylized irises near the rim by Carrie Steinle in 1918. Marks on the $400-$600
base include the Rookwood logo, the date, shape number 1781 and the artist's monogram. Height 6¼ inches.

21   Standard glaze lidded candy dish with three strap handles, decorated by both Emma Foertmeyer and Mary $800-$1200
Nourse in 1892. The base, signed by Nourse, has the Rookwood logo, the date, W for white clay, L for light
Standard glaze and the artist's initials. The lid, possibly married to the base, is decorated with the image of a
young girl and her doll and initialled by Foertmeyer on the underside. Height 2½ inches. A short, tight line appears
at the rim near one of the handles.

22   High glaze vase decorated with magnolia leaves by Jens Jensen in 1944. Marks on the base include the $700-$900
Rookwood logo, the date, shape number 6357 and the artist's monogram. Height 6½ inches. A single burst glaze
bubble is present on the underside of the rim.

23   Vellum glaze vase decorated with faint swirlled patterns by Carl Schmidt in 1905. Marks on the base include the $150-$250
Rookwood logo, the date, shape number 1063, V for Vellum glaze body, V for Vellum glaze and the artist's
monogram. Height 3½ inches.

24   Unusual Butterfat glaze vase, decorated by Elizabeth Barrett in 1946 with boldly painted flowers. Marks on the $500-$700
base include the Rookwood logo, the date, shape number 6325, the number 3351 and the artist's monogram.
Height 7⅛ inches.

25   Standard glaze two handled vase painted with oak leaves by Irene Bishop in 1901. Marks on the base include the $250-$350
Rookwood logo, the date, shape number 906 E and the artist's initials. Height 4 inches.

26   Vellum glaze scenic plaque decorated by Carl Schmidt in 1920. The artist's name appears in the lower right hand $3000-$4000
corner. Marks on the back include the Rookwood logo and the date. Affixed to the frame is an original Rookwood
label with the title, "Sunset Glow C. Schmidt". Size is 8 x 5 inches.

27   Vellum glaze vase decorated with an Arts & Crafts style woodland scene by Sallie Coyne in 1921. Marks on the $600-$800
base include the Rookwood logo, the date, shape number 551, V for Vellum glaze body, a wheel ground x and
the artist's monogram. Height 6¾ inches. Bruise on lip, very tight dark craze line inside and some glaze separation
on the body.

28   Unusual incised and painted mat glaze vase with stylized floral decoration, painted in 1929 by Kataro $900-$1100
Shirayamadani. Marks on the base include the Rookwood logo, the date, shape number 2831 and the artist's
cypher. Height 5⅜ inches.

29   Unusual carved Mat glaze vase, made by Sallie Toohey in 1907 with seahorses swimming through sea grasses. $600-$800
     Marks on the base include the Rookwood logo, the date, shape number 950 F and the artist's monogram. Height
     5⅝ inches. Minor surface scratches and unobtrusive glaze dimples.

30   Iris glaze vase with daisy decoration, painted by Rose Fechheimer in 1905. Marks on the base include the $700-$900
     Rookwood logo, the date, shape number 951 E, W for white glaze and the artist's initials. Height 6¾ inches.

31   Standard glaze with two handles and three ball feet, painted with fruit blossoms by Laura Fry in 1885. Marks on $300-$500
     the base include Rookwood in block letters, the date, W for white clay, the number 526 and the artist's
     monogram. Height 4⅞ inches. Exhibitions: "Art Pottery of the Midwest" University Art Museum University of
     Minnesota, Minneapolis, 1988 - 1989, Item 9, Figure 2 in the catalog, photo on page 3.

32   Standard glaze two handled vase decorated circa 1889 by Albert Valentien with crisply painted leaves, vines and $500-$700
     berries. Marks on the base include the Rookwood logo, the partially obscured date, shape number 459, W for
     white clay, L for light Standard glaze and the artist's initials. Height 6⅝ inches. Minor glaze bubbles.

33   Drip glaze multicolor vase made at Rookwood in 1932. Marks on the base include the Rookwood logo, the date $300-$500
     and shape number 6308 C. Height 6¾ inches.

34   Dull finish vase decorated with lotus blossoms in 1886 by M.A. Daly. Marks on the base include the Rookwood $1000-$1500
logo, the date, shape number 30 B, W for white clay and the artist's initials. Height 11⅜ inches.

35   Large Standard glaze ewer with poppy decoration, done by Kataro Shirayamadani in 1891. Marks on the base $2500-$3500
include the Rookwood logo, the date, shape number 578 C, W for white clay and the artist's cypher. Height 12⅞
inches. Grinding chips on base, glaze discoloration and small pimples in glaze.

36   Sea Green vase decorated with four nicely detailed fish by M.A. Daly in 1897. The initials, HCRSL appear $2250-$2750
conjoined, incised on the vase's side. Marks on the base include the Rookwood logo, the date, G for Sea Green
glaze and the artist's full name. Height 5½ inches.

37   Vellum glaze scenic vase, decorated by Fred Rothenbusch in 1913. Marks on the base include the Rookwood $1500-$2000
logo, the date, shape number 2089 C, V for Vellum glaze body, V for Vellum glaze and the artist's monogram.
Height 11⅜ inches.

38   Vellum glaze vase with stylized poppy decoration, painted in 1907 by Laura Lindeman. Marks on the base $600-$800
include the Rookwood logo, the date, shape number 941 D, V for Vellum glaze body and the artist's initials.
Height 8⅜ inches.

39   Standard glaze three piece tea service decorated by Carl Schmidt in 1902 with mushrooms. Marks on the bases $800-$1200
      include the Rookwood logo, the date, shape number 615 and the artist's monogram. Height of the tallest piece is
      6 inches. Teapot has a chip on its finial, the creamer has glaze flaws and the wrong lid and the sugar bowl has
      chips on its handles and finial.

40   Large Limoges style glaze basket painted on one side with bats and the other with spiders by Maria Longworth $1000-$1500
      Nichols in 1882. The basket's feet are in the form of lion heads. Marks on the base include Rookwood in block
      letters and the date. The artist's initials appear inside the basket, high on the spiders' side. Height 8 inches. An old
      staple repair binds a crack on one end and one handle has been broken and repaired.

41   Unusual Vellum glaze bowl decorated with flowers and three circular panels, each with a view of a different tree $1100-$1300
      lined stream, painted in 1916 by Mary Grace Denzler. Marks on the base include the Rookwood logo, the date,
      shape number 214 B, V for Vellum glaze body and the artist's monogram. Height 3⅝ inches. Some glaze
      peppering.

42   Mat glaze vase painted with small blue flowers by John Wesley Pullman in 1929. Marks on the base include the $300-$500
      Rookwood logo, the date, shape number 900 D and the artist's monogram. Height 6⅞ inches.

43   Arts and Crafts Mat glaze low vase, decorated by C.S. Todd in 1913 with three incised and painted fish encircling the shoulder of the piece. Marks on the base include the Rookwood logo, the date, shape number 158 and the artist's initials. Height 6 inches. $900-$1100

44   Rookwood Architectural Faience tile in mat glaze, made circa 1915. Marks on the back include the Rookwood Faience logo and the number 1226 Y. Size 12 x 12 inches. $800-$1200

45   Standard glaze mug decorated with the portrait of a Native American by Sturgis Laurence in 1899. Marks on the base include the Rookwood logo, the date, shape number 587 C, what is probably L for light Standard glaze, the title, "Sertenta" Kiowa and the artist's initials. Height 4⅝ inches. Moderate glaze scratches. $800-$1200

46   Standard glaze vase with Gorham silver overlay, decorated with daisies by Artus Van Briggle in 1890. Marks on the base include the Rookwood logo, the date, shape number 565, S for sage green clay, L for light Standard glaze, the number 8 in a circle and the artist's initials. The silver is marked, "Gorham Mfg. Co. R 682". Some small burst glaze bubbles are evident. $3500-$4500

47   Handsome Iris glaze vase decorated with day lilies by Sara Sax in 1903. Marks on the base include the Rookwood logo, the date, shape number 932 C, W for white glaze and the artist's monogram. Height 11½ inches. $3000-$5000

48   Vellum glaze Venetian harbor scene vase, decorated by Carl Schmidt in 1923. Marks on the base include the Rookwood logo, the date, shape number 2064, V for Vellum glaze, P for porcelain body and the artist's monogram. Height 7½ inches. Slight glaze run near rim. Uncrazed. $2500-$3500

49   Vellum glaze vase with wild rose decoration, done in 1922 by Ed Diers. Marks on the base include the $800-$1000
       Rookwood logo, the date, shape number 2544, V for Vellum glaze body and the artist's initials. Height 8⅛ inches.

50   Standard glaze vase decorated with blue irises by Irene Bishop in 1902. Marks on the base include the Rookwood $300-$500
       logo, the date, shape number 926 D and the artist's initials. Height 6¾ inches.

51   Mat glaze vase with abstract floral decoration, carved and painted in 1916 by C.S. Todd. Marks on the base $500-$700
       include the Rookwood logo, the date, shape number 1920 and the artist's initials. Height 9 inches. Minor glaze
       dimples.

52   Standard glaze vase with hydrangea decoration, painted by Carl Schmidt in 1898. Marks on the base include the $400-$600
       Rookwood logo, the date, shape number 695 and the artist's monogram. Height 6⅛ inches.

53   High glaze vase decorated with magnolia by Jens Jensen in 1945. Marks on the base include the Rookwood logo, $400-$600
       the date, shape number 6938, the number 8489 and the artist's monogram. Height 7 inches. Chip on base with
       older repair.

54 Limoges style glaze horn pitcher decorated in 1883 by N.J. Hirschfeld with grasses and dragonflies. Marks on the base include Rookwood in block letters, the date, shape number 116, G for ginger clay, an impressed anchor mark and the artist's monogram. Height 6⅛ inches. This piece is from Rookwood Pottery's Museum, descending in the family of one of Rookwood's last owners and has never been offered for sale until now. $800-$1200

55 Commercial mat glaze lidded inkwell with repeating geometric line decoration, made at Rookwood in 1905. Marks on the base include the Rookwood logo, the date and shape number 418 B. Height 3⅛ inches. Missing inner cup. $200-$300

56 Iris glaze vase decorated with white poppies by Elizabeth W. Brain in 1904. Marks on the base include the Rookwood logo, the date, shape number 926 C, W for white glaze and the artist's initials. Height 8⅛ inches. $1200-$1500

57 Commercial mat glaze vase designed with classical figures by Louise Abel and made at Rookwood in 1920. Marks on the base include the Rookwood logo, the date, shape number 2522 and the artist's monogram. Height 4⅝ inches. Some pitting in the interior glaze. $300-$400

58 Standard glaze humidor with sterling lid, decorated by Constance Baker in 1897 with trumpet creepers. The lid, which must have been made for the base, is circled with repousse' trumpet creepers and fits perfectly. Marks on the base include the Rookwood logo, the date, shape number 805, a small triangular shaped esoteric mark and the artist's initials. Marks on the lid include three hall marks, the word "sterling" and the number 5. Height 4½ inches. $800-$1200

59   Mat glaze vase painted by Wilhelmine Rehm in 1946, depicting flowers and several leaping deer. Marks on the base include the Rookwood logo, the date, S for special shape, the number 7215 and the artist's initials. Height 5⅞ inches. $700-$900

60   Standard glaze vase decorated with violets for Columbian Exposition in 1893 by Sadie Markland. Marks on the base include the Rookwood logo, the date, shape number 686, W for white clay, L for light Standard glaze, a paper label which reads, "Rookwood Pottery Cincinnati, U.S.A. World's Columbian Exposition 1893" and the artist's initials. Height 3⅛ inches. $400-$600

61   Vellum glaze scenic plaque decorated by Ed Diers in 1913. The artist's name appears in the lower left hand corner. Marks on the back include the Rookwood logo, the date and V for Vellum glaze body. Affixed to the back is an original Rookwood label with the title, "The Riverlet E. Diers". Size is approximately 10½ x 8½ inches. $2500-$3500

62   Vellum glaze vase with floral decoration, painted in 1925 by Harriet Wilcox. Marks on the base include the Rookwood logo, the date, shape number 295 E, V for Vellum glaze and the artist's initials. Height 7½ inches. Uncrazed. $500-$700

63   Arts and Crafts mat glaze vase with carved and painted panels, done in 1913 by William Hentschel. Marks on the base include the Rookwood logo, the date, shape number 1864 and the artist's monogram. Height 4⅞ inches. $400-$600

64   Standard glaze vase decorated by Albert Valentien in 1885 with several Japanesque fish swimming through $2000-$3000
undulating sea currents and grasses. Marks on the base include Rookwood in block letters, the date, shape
number 28 C and the artist's initials. Height 6⅝ inches.

65   Unusual Iris glaze vase painted with a single peacock feather by Carl Schmidt in 1911. Marks on the base include $1500-$2000
the Rookwood logo, the date, shape number 918 E, W for white glaze, a wheel ground x and the artist's
monogram. Height 6 inches. Small areas of underglaze background color loss account for the x.

66   Exotic yellow tinted high glaze vase decorated with fruit blossoms on a black ground by Kataro Shirayamadani in $1500-$2000
1925. Marks on the base include the Rookwood logo, the date, shape number 2720 and the artist's cypher.
Height 6½ inches.

67   High glaze vase decorated with three angel fish by Jens Jensen in 1934. Marks on the base include the Rookwood $1000-$1500
logo, the date, S for special shape and the artist's monogram. Height 5½ inches. Uncrazed.

68   Dull finish vase decorated with fruit blossoms and oriental designs by Kataro Shirayamadani in 1887. Marks on $3000-$5000
the base include the Rookwood logo, the date, shape number 346, W 7 for a type of white clay and S for smear
(dull) glaze. Height 6⅛ inches. A tight crack descends from the rim. Exhibitions: "Fragile Blossoms, Enduring
Earth" The Everson Museum of Art, 1989, Item 25 in the catalog, Color plate on page 23.

69 Unusual copperdust glaze vase, made at Rookwood in 1930. Marks on the base include the Rookwood logo, the date, shape number 6194 and a small fan shaped esoteric mark. Height 6⅛ inches. — $500-$700

70 Mat glaze vase with floral decoration, painted in 1939 by Kataro Shirayamadani. Marks on the base include the Rookwood logo, the date, shape number 6197 F and the artist's cypher. Height 4¾ inches. — $600-$800

71 Black Opal type glaze compote with floral decor, done by Sara Sax in 1918. Marks on the base include the Rookwood logo, the date, shape number 1666 D, P for porcelain body and the artist's monogram. Height 6⅜ inches. — $500-$700

72 Bowl decorated with small flowers in what may be French Red slip by Sara Sax in 1919. Marks on the base include the Rookwood logo, the date, shape number 214 D and the artist's monogram. Height 2¾ inches. — $400-$600

73 Arts and Crafts mug decorated with a repeating border of incised and painted leaves in a mat glaze by Albert Pons in 1907. Marks on the base include the Rookwood logo, the date, shape number 1071 and the artist's monogram. Height 5⅛ inches. — $350-$550

74 Cameo glaze lidded pitcher, decorated with mums and oriental motifs by Kataro Shirayamadani in 1887. Marks on the base include the Rookwood logo, the date, shape number 335 B, W 3 for a type of white clay and the artist's cypher. Height 8¼ inches. Minor glaze roughness. $1500-$2500

75 Standard glaze pitcher with dogwood decoration, painted in 1893 by Carrie Steinle. Marks on the base include the Rookwood logo, the date, shape number 259 E, W for white clay and the artist's monogram. Height 4 inches. One burst glaze bubble under handle. $300-$400

76 Vellum glaze vase decorated with a twilight view of a small cottage beside a tree lined lake, painted in 1911 by Fred Rothenbusch. Marks on the base include the Rookwood logo, the date, shape number 1655 F, V for Vellum glaze body, V for Vellum glaze and the artist's monogram. Height 6½ inches. $1500-$1800

77 Standard glaze whiskey jug decorated with corn by Carrie Steinle in 1900. Marks on the base include the Rookwood logo, the date, shape number 512 C and the artist's initials. Height 5½ inches. $300-$500

78 Dull finish lidded tea caddy decorated with repeating die stamped patterns by Fannie Auckland in 1882. Marks on the base include Rookwood in block letters, the date and the artist's initials. Height 6⅜ inches. $800-$1200

79   Early high glaze Commercial ware lidded chocolate pot decorated with a single kingfisher and a panel with $600-$800
     oriental characters, made at Rookwood in 1887. Marks on the base include the Rookwood logo, the date, shape
     number 100 and S for sage green clay. Height 8 inches.

80   Iris glaze vase decorated by Olga Reed in 1895 with dandelions on a deep blue ground. Marks on the base $1000-$1500
     include the Rookwood logo, the date, shape number 568 C and the artist's initials. Height 6¾ inches. Some firing
     cracks in the glaze.

81   Standard glaze vase decorated in 1900 by Kataro Shirayamadani with large orange flowers. Marks on the base $2000-$3000
     include the Rookwood logo, the date, shape number 886 D and the artist's cypher. Height 8½ inches.

82   Coromandel glaze vase, made at Rookwood circa 1932. Marks on the base which are slightly obscured by the $600-$800
     glaze include the Rookwood logo, the date and shape number 6308 C. Height 6¾ inches.

83   Rare early commercial vase made at Rookwood in 1882 with what may be a platinum glaze. The vase, listed as $4000-$6000
     shape 20 in the Shape Record Book has two small handles and dragons in relief on each side. Marks on the base
     include Rookwood in block letters, the date, Cincinnati Art Museum accession numbers 500: '00 and remnants of
     three paper labels. Height 8⅛ inches. This vase was undoubtly in the Rookwood collection at the Cincinnati Art
     Museum and in Rookwood's own museum and is thought to have been sold in Cincinnati in the early 1980's
     with other items from the Williams family, one time owners of Rookwood. Listed: S.G. Burt's book, "2,292 pieces
     of early Rookwood Pottery in the Cincinnati Art Museum in 1916" as item 19 for the year 1882.

84   Commercial mat glaze bust made at Rookwood in 1942. Marks on the base include the Rookwood logo, the date $200-$300
and shape number 2026. Height 7½ inches.

85   Standard glaze pocket vase with daisy decoration, painted in 1892 by Sallie Coyne. Marks on the base include $250-$350
the Rookwood logo, the date, shape number 90 C, W for white clay and the artist's initials. Height 4 inches.
Minor roughness on feet.

86   Standard glaze tri-cornered pitcher decorated by M.A. Daly in 1892 with the portrait of a monk tasting a sample $2000-$3000
of wine. Marks on the base include the Rookwood logo, the date, shape number 259 B and the artist's initials.
Height 8¼ inches. There is a firing flaw in the handle and some glaze scratches.

87   Standard glaze tray decorated by Jeanette Swing in 1902 with cigarettes, pansies and matches. Marks on the base $300-$400
include the Rookwood logo, the date, shape number 930 D and the artist's monogram. Length 5¾ inches.

88   Colorful Painted Mat glaze vase, decorated with a single poppy by Harriet Wilcox in 1901. Marks on the base $1200-$1500
include the Rookwood logo, the date, shape number 4 DZ and the artist's initials. Height 7⅜ inches. One tiny
glaze skip.

89   Vellum glaze scenic vase, painted in 1910 by Kataro Shirayamadani with several small birds flying through a $3000-$4000
lakeside forest. Marks on the base include the Rookwood logo, the date, shape number 1661, V for Vellum glaze
body and the artist's cypher. Height 8¼ inches.

90   High glaze bowl lined in yellow and decorated with stylized dandelions by Sara Sax in 1916. Marks on the base $1200-$1500
include the Rookwood logo, the date, shape number 2260 C, P for porcelain body and the artist's monogram.
Height 6⅛ inches. Glaze pooling around the base.

91   Unusual vase decorated with abstract designs by John Dee Wareham in 1937 in what may be "Sung Plum" glaze. $4000-$6000
Marks on the base include the Rookwood logo, the date, S for Special shape and the name D. Wareham. Height
5¼ inches. Exhibitions: "Toward the Modern Style Rookwood Pottery the Later Years: 1915-1950" The Jordan-
Volpe Gallery, 1983, Item 85 in the catalog, Color plate 4. Refer to page 29 of the Jordan-Volpe book for a
contemporary description of Sung Plum glaze. Whatever the name, this glaze is a direct descendant of Black
Opal.

92   Tall Vellum glaze vase decorated with a band of exotic foliage by Elizabeth McDermott in 1919. Marks on the $1200-$1500
      base include the Rookwood logo, the date, shape number 1919, V for Vellum glaze body and the artist's
      monogram. Height 14⅛ inches.

93   Large Art Deco vase with two small loop handles, decorated with repeating bands of stylized flowers by William $800-$1000
      Hentschel in 1927. Marks on the base include the Rookwood logo, the date, shape number 2640 C and the
      artist's monogram. Height 13⅜ inches. Several grinding chips on the base, two that are thumb nail size.

94   Tall Vellum glaze vase with woodland scene, painted in 1938 by E.T. Hurley. Marks on the base include the $2500-$3500
      Rookwood logo, the date, shape number 2032 C and the artist's initials. Height 11½ inches. Uncrazed.

95   Important Black Iris glaze scenic vase, decorated in an Arts and Crafts manner with several cranes flying through $12000-$15000
a pine forest by Kataro Shirayamadani in 1910. Marks on the base include the Rookwood logo, the date, shape
number 951 B and the artist's cypher. Height 12⅛ inches.

96   Painted Mat glaze vase decorated by Olga Reed in 1904 with poppies. Marks on the base include the Rookwood $2000-$3000
      logo, the date, shape number 188 CZ and the artist's initials. Height 10⅜ inches. Minor grinding chips on base.

97   Standard glaze whiskey jug with wheat decoration, painted in 1895 by Harriette Strafer. Marks on the base $400-$600
      include the Rookwood logo, the date, shape number 676, L for light Standard glaze and the artist's initials. Height
      5¼ inches.

98   Large Iris glaze vase decorated in 1901 with lavender lilies by Albert Valentien. Marks on the base include the $5000-$7000
      Rookwood logo, the date, shape number 904 B, a wheel ground x and the artist's full name. Height 13⅜ inches.

99   Dull finish vase with dandelion decoration, painted in heavy slip by Albert Valentien in 1891. Marks on the base $3000-$4000
      include the Rookwood logo, the date, shape number 617 C, W for white clay, L for light Standard glaze and the
      artist's initials. Height 10⅜ inches. Exhibitions: "Ode to Nature: Flowers and Landscapes of the Rookwood Pottery
      1880 - 1940" The Jordan - Volpe Gallery, 1980, Catalog Number 11, Color Plate 4. Although Valentien clearly
      marked this piece to receive a light Standard glaze, it ended up with a dull or smear glaze which allows us a rare
      glimpse at what decorated Rookwood must have looked like before application of the thicker gloss glazes.

100   Good Iris glaze vase by Carl Schmidt, painted in 1907 with roses. Marks on the base include the Rookwood logo, $4000-$6000
the date, shape number 904 C, W for white glaze and the artist's monogram. Height 12⅛ inches. This piece is
from Rookwood Pottery's Museum, descending in the family of one of Rookwood's last owners and has never
been offered for sale until now.

101   Standard glaze ewer with fruit decoration by Harriette Strafer, painted in 1890. Marks on the base include the $200-$400
Rookwood logo, the date, shape number 304, W for white clay, L for light Standard glaze and the artist's initials.
Height 8 inches. Some glaze bubbles near the base and a small chip under the lip.

102   Vellum glaze plaque decorated by Lenore Asbury in 1916. The artist's initials appear in the lower right hand $4000-$6000
corner. Marks on the back include the Rookwood logo, the date and V for Vellum glaze body. Attached to the
frame is an original paper label entitled, "The First Thaw L. Asbury". Size 12⅛ x 9¼ inches.

103   Limoges style glaze vase in the manner of E.P. Cranch, decorated in 1882 with a rabbit jumping a haltered fox $2000-$3000
across a log. Marks on the base include Rookwood in block letters and the date. Height 10¼ inches.

104 Standard glaze two handled vase decorated in 1896 with wild roses by M.A. Daly. Marks on the base include the Rookwood logo, the date, shape number 583 D and the artist's initials. Height 8½ inches. $700-$900

105 Unusual Art Deco mat glaze vase decorated in 1931 by William Hentschel with the faces of a man and a woman. Marks on the base include the Rookwood logo, the date, shape number 2831, a wheel ground x, a fan shaped esoteric mark and the artist's monogram. Height 5⅜ inches. A long crack nearly encircles the vase. $300-$500

106 Large Standard glaze vase with two loop handles, decorated in 1898 with lotus blossoms and pads by Amelia Sprague. Marks on the base include the Rookwood logo, the date, shape number 664 B, a small star shaped esoteric mark and the artist's monogram. Height 10¼ inches. Minor bubbles and one ¼ inch clay inclusion on the shoulder. $2000-$3000

107 Mat glaze vase by Kataro Shirayamadani, painted in 1942 with orchids. Marks on the base include the Rookwood logo, the date, shape number 6311 and the artist's initials. Height 7⅜ inches. $800-$1000

108 Iris glaze vase with thistle decoration, done in 1897 by John Dee Wareham. Marks on the base include the Rookwood logo, the date, shape number S 1357, a wheel ground X, Cincinnati Art Museum accession number 293: 02, a small diamond shaped esoteric mark and the artist's initials. Height 11¾ inches. Listed: S.G. Burt's, "2,292 pieces of early Rookwood Pottery in the Cincinnati Art Museum in 1916", as item five for 1897. "S-1357-Iris Has Mr Burt's mark of a (diamond) no crz (crazing) but bad slip crk (crack). The piece now shows nominal crazing as well as several slip and glaze cracks. $2000-$3000

109 Large stoppered whiskey jug decorated with corn in 1897 by Olga Reed. Marks on the base include the Rookwood logo, the date, shape number 512 A, a small diamond shaped esoteric mark and the artist's initials. Height 10⅛ inches. $800-$1000

110 Unusual mat glaze vase decorated with three panels, each showing a different view of women's volleyball. Done with heavy slip and squeezebag technique in mat and semigloss glazes, the piece was made by Wilhelmine Rehm in 1934. Marks on the base include the Rookwood logo, the date, S for special shape and the artist's initials. Height 6¼ inches. $1500-$2500

111 Iris glaze vase with floral decoration, painted in 1897 by John Dee Wareham. Marks on the base include the Rookwood logo, the date, shape number 216, a small diamond shaped esoteric mark, a wheel ground x and the artist's initials. Height 12⅜ inches. Tight firing cracks in base, slight slip crazing and minor glaze discoloration. $2000-$3000

112 Vellum glaze vase with blueberry decoration, painted in 1916 by Elizabeth McDermott. Marks on the base include the Rookwood logo, the date, shape number 995 E, V for Vellum glaze body and the artist's monogram. Height 5½ inches. $500-$700

113 Rare Standard glaze vase depicting "The Enchantress" after a painting by G.P.J. Hood entitled, ""Hexentanz" (The Witches' Dance)", done by Bruce Horsfall in 1894. Marks on the base include the Rookwood logo, the date, shape number 644 C, the title, "Hexentanz" and the artist's monogram. Height 14⅜ inches. Broken and repaired. Pictured: "Rookwood Pottery Potpourri" Virginia Raymond Cummins, copyright 1991, Cincinnati Art Galleries. Color plate on page 126. Originally in the important collection of Edward Atlee Barber and sold at auction in Philadelphia after his death in 1917. A copy of the 1917 auction catalog accompanies the vase. $6000-$8000

114   Large Vellum glaze banded vase, decorated with a woodland scene by Ed Diers in 1918. Marks on the base $2500-$3500
      include the Rookwood logo, the date, shape number 857, a wheel ground X and the artist's initials. Height 15⅝
      inches. There are three small areas of glaze burnout which account for the X, but all blend nicely into the
      foreground.

115   Monumental Standard glaze vase decorated in 1890 by Albert Valentien with finely detailed lotus plants. Marks $3000-$4000
      on the base include the Rookwood logo, the date, shape number 463, L for light Standard glaze and the artist's
      initials. Height 20⅝ inches.

116   Tall Vellum glaze vase decorated with red hollyhocks by Lorinda Epply in 1923. Marks on the base include the $3000-$5000
      Rookwood logo, the date, shape number 2523, V for Vellum glaze body, P for Porcelain body and the artist's
      monogram. Height 17⅛ inches. A few glaze bubbles are present but the piece is uncrazed and very clean.

117 Rare and beautiful dull finish covered jar decorated in 1888 by Artus Van Briggle with butterflies, spider webs and pink oriental ribbons. Marks on the base include the Rookwood logo, the date, shape number 400, W for white clay, S for smear (dull finish) glaze and the artist's initials. Height 6⅛ inches. Very minor roughness on one handle. $1000-$1500

118 Vellum glaze plaque decorated with a Venetian harbor scene by Carl Schmidt in 1922. The artist's name appears in the lower right hand corner. Marks on the back include the Rookwood logo, the date and P for porcelain body. Size 9 x 7 inches. Uncrazed. $5500-$7500

119 Rare Black Iris glaze vase with carved and electroplated copper overlay, painted with small yellow flowers by Kataro Shirayamadani in 1901. Marks on the base include the Rookwood logo, the date, shape number 911, W for white glaze and the artist's cypher. Height 4 inches. $5000-$7000

120 Sea Green glaze vase decorated with jonquils by Albert Valentien in 1895. Marks on the base include the Rookwood logo, the date, shape number 732 B, G for Sea Green glaze and a partial paper label from J.B. Hudson Jewelers 519 Nicollet Avenue Minneapolis. The artist's full name appears on the side of the vase. Height 10⅛ inches. Exhibitions: "Art Pottery of the Midwest" University Art Museum University of Minnesota, Minneapolis, 1988 -1989, Item 15, Figure 4 in the catalog, photo on page 5. $3000-$4000

121 Standard glaze vase decorated by Elizabeth Lincoln in 1899 with daisies. Marks on the base include the Rookwood logo, the date, shape number 808 and the artist's initials. Height 7½ inches. $400-$600

122 Standard glaze vase with Gorham silver overlay, decorated with daisies by Artus Van Briggle in 1888. Marks on the base include the Rookwood logo, the date, shape number 400, W for white clay, D for dark Standard glaze and the artist's initials. Marks on the silver include "Gorham Mfg. Co. S.1278. S." Height 5 inches. $3000-$4000

123 High glaze vase painted with two stylized angel fish by Carolyn Stegner in 1946. Marks on the base include the Rookwood logo, the date, shape number 356 E, the number 383 A and the artist's monogram. Height 6½ inches. $500-$700

124 Good Standard glaze vase with large areas of Goldstone effect, decorated with crayfish by Amelia Sprague in 1894. Marks on the base include the Rookwood logo, the date, shape number 568 C, R for red clay, M for Mohogany glaze and the artist's monogram. Height 6⅞ inches. Minor glaze dimple. $3000-$5000

125 Limoges style glaze handled gourd shaped jug, decorated by Martin Rettig circa 1886 with flying dragonflies. Marks on the base, all partly glazed over, include the Rookwood logo, the date, a shape number and the artist's initials. Height 12 inches. Exhibitions: "American Art Pottery 1873-1930" Delaware Museum of Art, 1978, Item 6 in the catalog with photo. $1000-$1500

126 Iris glaze vase with floral decoration, painted in 1901 by Carl Schmidt. Marks on the base include the Rookwood logo, the date, shape number 881 F, W for white glaze and the artist's monogram. Height 2⅞ inches. $500-$700

127   Unusual dull finish vase, decorated with buff colored applied leaves and stems and covered elsewhere with a $1500-$2000
speckled ground by Albert Valentien in 1884. Marks on the base include Rookwood in block letters, the date,
shape number 126 A, G for ginger clay and the artist's initials. Height 12 inches.

128   Standard glaze two handled vase painted in 1899 by Mary Nourse with jonquils. Marks on the base include the $500-$700
Rookwood logo, the date, shape number 604 C, L for light Standard glaze and the artist's initials. Height 9 inches.
Glaze scratches and underglaze flaws to two of the jonquils near the base.

129   Good Vellum glaze vase decorated in 1906 by Kataro Shirayamadani with three rooks flying through a winter $2500-$3500
woods. Marks on the base include the Rookwood logo, the date, shape number 935 D, V for Vellum glaze body
and the artist's cypher. Height 7⅝ inches.

130   Standard glaze vase showing much Goldstone and Tiger Eye effect, decorated with a dragon in 1894 by Amelia $2000-$3000
Sprague. Marks on the base include the Rookwood logo, the date, shape number 172 C, R for red clay, the artist's
monogram and a paper label which reads: "Rookwood Pottery Cincinnati, USA 1904 Louisiana Purchase
Exposition, St. Louis". Height 8⅜ inches.

131   Tall Bengal Brown glaze vase made at Rookwood in 1959. Marks on the base include the Rookwood logo, the $400-$600
date, shape number 6919 and Rookwood Cinti, O. Height 12⅛ inches.

132   Important Black Iris glaze vase by Carl Schmidt, painted with larger than life irises in 1903. Marks on the base $10000-$15000
      include the Rookwood logo, the date, shape number 904 B, W for white glaze and the artist's monogram. Height
      13½ inches. Neatly drilled. Future Exhibition: "Rookwood Pottery: The Glorious Gamble" The Cincinnati Art
      Museum 1991 -1993, NOTE: Although you may purchase this vase from its current owner and receive clear title,
      possession will not be granted until the Cincinnati Art Museum Exhibit ends sometime in October, 1993, after
      traveling to two additional museums in the United States. The exhibition catalog is in press and will credit current
      ownership.

133   Standard glaze vase loaded with Goldstone effect and decorated with several flying geese by Harriet Wilcox in 1894. Marks on the base include the Rookwood logo, the date, shape number 482, R for red clay and the artist's initials. Height 9¼ inches. Flake on rim and area of loose glaze near the base. Exhibited: "American Art Pottery 1875 - 1930" Delaware Art Museum, 1978, Item 15 in the catalog with photo. $1500-$2500

134   Vellum glaze plaque decorated with a portrait of Champion Elmcroft Coacher, painted by E.T. Hurley in 1942, a commission for Charles M. Williams, owner of Rookwood Pottery. The artist's initials appear in the lower left hand corner. Marks on the back include the Rookwood logo, the date and the numbers 8 x 10. Affixed to the frame is a complete pedigree of the famous Dalmatian, "Danny" and other pertinent information. Accompanying the plaque is an etching used by the Williams Family for Christmas cards which shows the dog in a similar pose. Size is approximate 8 x 10 inches. Uncrazed. $4000-$5000

135   Rare carved mat glaze lamp base, decorated with nasturtiums by Kataro Shirayamadani in 1905. Marks on the base include the Rookwood logo, the date, shape number 950 C and the artist's cypher. Height 10¼ inches. Crack in one of the reticulated legs. Exhibitions: "From Our Native Clay" The American Ceramic Arts Society, 1987, Item 148 in the catalog, Color plate on page 82. $2500-$3500

136   Mat glaze vase decorated with irises by Sallie Coyne in 1926. Marks on the base include the Rookwood logo, the date, shape number 2785 and the artist's initials. Height 13½ inches. Drilled $600-$800

137   Standard glaze vase decorated with autumn leaves by Constance Baker in 1899. Marks on the base include the Rookwood logo, the date, shape number 803 B, a Burley & Co. Chicago paper label and the artist's initials. Height 12¼ inches. $1200-$1800

138   Vellum glaze vase decorated with a blue, a red and a green tulip by E.T. Hurley in 1941. Marks on the base include the Rookwood logo, the date, shape number 6666 and the artist's initials. Height 6⅜ inches. Uncrazed. A few tiny glaze pits. $700-$900

139   Standard glaze vase with bright orange mums, decorated in 1903 by E.T. Hurley. Marks on the base include the Rookwood logo, the date, shape number 927 F and the artist's initials. Height 5⅜ inches. $400-$600

140   Vellum glaze vase decorated with fuscia by Elizabeth McDermott in 1919. Marks on the base include the Rookwood logo, the date, shape number 932 C, V for Vellum glaze body, a Glover Collection label, number 1176 and the artist's monogram. Height 12¼ inches. Small repair to lip and some minor abrasions. $800-$1200

141   Standard glaze ewer with a single turtle swimming through large passages of Goldstone effect. Decorated by M.A. Daly in 1886, the marks on the base include Rookwood in block letters, the date, shape number 26, a Glover Collection label, number 1097 and the artist's initials. Height 12¼ inches. $1500-$2000

142   Large and important carved mat glaze vase, decorated with cattails by Sallie Toohey in 1908. Marks on the base $5000-$7000
include the Rookwood logo, the date, shape number 900 A, V for Vellum glaze body and the artist's monogram.
Height 12⅝ inches. Exhibitions: "Ode to Nature: Flowers and Landscapes of the Rookwood Pottery 1880 -1940"
The Jordan-Volpe Gallery, 1980, Item 62 in the catalog. Future Exhibition: "Rookwood Pottery: The Glorious
Gamble" The Cincinnati Art Museum 1991-1993. NOTE: Although you may purchase this vase from its current
owner and receive clear title, possession will not be granted until the Cincinnati Art Museum Exhibit ends
sometime in October, 1993, after traveling to two additional museums in the United States. The exhibition
catalog is in press and will credit current ownership.

143   Standard glaze vase with leaf and berry decoration, painted in 1898 by Lenore Asbury. Marks on the base include $300-$500
the Rookwood logo, the date, shape number 566 C, a wheel ground x and the artist's initials. Height 8⅝ inches.
Glaze scratches.

144   High glaze vase with painted magnolia decoration, done in 1951 by Loretta Holtkamp. Marks on the base $600-$800
include the Rookwood logo, the date, shape number 2984 A and the artist's initials. Height 15½ inches. Drilled
and repaired. The artist's initials appear to have been added during the vase's repair, but the work is surely that of
Loretta Holtkamp, who with Earl Menzel were the last decorators employed by Rookwood in Cincinnati.

145   Commercial vase with molded poppies designed by Kataro Shirayamadani and hand tinted by Lenore Asbury in $1000-$1200
1929. Marks on the base include the Rookwood logo, the date, shape number 6006, V for Vellum glaze, a wheel
ground x and Asbury's initials. Height 11¾ inches. Some glaze bubbles are evident inside and outside the vase.

146   Good Vellum glaze vase with a colorful woodland scene painted by E.T. Hurley in 1942. Marks on the base $2500-$3500
include the Rookwood logo, the date, shape number 6840 and the artist's initials. Height 9¾ inches. Very minor
glaze dimples. Uncrazed. Illustrated: "Rookwood Pottery Potpourri" Virginia Raymond Cummins, Copyright
1991, Cincinnati Art Galleries, photo on page 89 shows this vase with medals won by Rookwood for developing
its Vellum glaze.

147   Vellum glaze plaque decorated and probably signed on the front by Charles McLaughlin in 1913. Marks on the $1000-$1500
back include the Rookwood logo, the date and V for Vellum glaze body. Affixed to the frame is an original label
with the title, "Down th........J. Mc Laughlin". Size 4¼ x 8⅛ inches.

148   Standard glaze vase decorated with incised leaves and berries in 1899 by Kataro Shirayamadani. Most of the $1500-$2500
glaze has a luminous Tiger Eye effect. Marks on the base include the Rookwood logo, the date, shape number
807, a Glover Collection Label with the number 1112 and the nearly obscured artist's cypher. Height 12½ inches.

149   Large and impressive Standard glaze vase with iris decoration, done by Mary Nourse in 1903. Marks on the base $2500-$3500
include the Rookwood logo, the date, shape number 904 B, L for light Standard glaze and the artist's initials.
Height 13⅜ inches.

150   High glaze vase with exotic foliage and a single peacock, done by E.T. Hurley in 1923. Marks on the base $500-$700
include the Rookwood logo, the date, shape number 2067, the partially obscured number 8070 and the artist's
initials. Height 7½ inches.

151   Iris glaze vase decorated with small blue flowers by Constance Baker in 1901. Marks on the base include the $400-$600
Rookwood logo, the date, shape number 919, a wheel ground x and the artist's initials. Height 3¾ inches. Minor
roughness on rim.

152   Standard glaze whiskey jug decorated with cherries by Luella Perkins in 1898. Marks on the base include the $400-$600
Rookwood logo, the date, shape number 733 C, a star shaped esoteric mark and the artist's initials. Height 7⅛
inches.

153   Standard glaze vase with peacock feather decoration, painted by Howard Altman in 1903. Marks on the base $500-$700
include the Rookwood logo, the date, shape number 915 E, a wheel ground x and the artist's initials. Height 5⅛
inches.

154   Vellum glaze vase decorated in an Arts and Crafts manner in 1915 with a woodland scene by Sallie Coyne. $1000-$1500
Marks on the base include the Rookwood logo, the date, shape number 2060, V for Vellum glaze body and the
artist's initials. Height 7¾ inches. Uncrazed.

155   Standard glaze vase decorated with thistles by Virginia Demarest in 1900. Marks on the base include the $500-$700
      Rookwood logo, the date, shape number 735 D and the artist's initials. Height 7 inches.

156   Dull finish lidded scent jar decorated with wild roses by Grace Young in 1889. Marks on the base include the $500-$700
      Rookwood logo, the date, shape number 479, W for white clay, S for dull finish (smear glaze) and the artist's
      monogram. Height 5⅞ inches. Firing separations in the body of the jar.

157   Iris glaze vase decorated with wild roses by Constance Baker in 1902. Marks on the base include the Rookwood $600-$800
      logo, the date, shape number 917 D and the artist's initials. Height 6½ inches.

158   Standard glaze vase with pansy decoration, painted in 1898 Carrie Steinle. Marks on the base include the $300-$400
      Rookwood logo, the date, shape number 162 D and the artist's monogram. Height 5⅛ inches.

159   Pink tinted high glaze lidded jar decorated with irises by Carl Schmidt in 1923. Marks on the base include the $2000-$3000
      Rookwood logo, the date, shape number 47 C and the artist's monogram. The lid also carries the artist's
      monogram. Height 6⅛ inches. Uncrazed

160 Standard glaze ribbed vase, painted with daisies and mums by Harriet Wilcox in 1893. Marks on the base include the Rookwood logo, the date, shape number 612 B, W for white clay and the artist's initials. Height 6¾ inches. $500-$700

161 High glaze vase decorated with blue flowers, green leaves and a single bird by Kay Ley in 1945. Marks on the base include the Rookwood logo, the date, shape number 6914, the number 4258 and the artist's last name. Height 5¼ inches. $500-$700

162 Unusual Vellum glaze scenic vase decorated with a mountain range and lowland lakes by Ed Diers in 1910. Marks on the base include the Rookwood logo, the date, shape number 940 D, V for Vellum glaze body, V for Vellum glaze, a wheel ground X and the artist's initials. Height 9⅞ inches. Very tight line at rim. $2000-$2500

163 Unusual Standard glaze tankard painted in 1896 with the portrait of a black woman shucking corn by Kataro Shirayamadani. Marks on the base include the Rookwood logo, the date, shape number 775, a wheel ground x and the artist's cypher. Height 7 inches. There is a tight dark line descending from the inside of the rim on the front of the piece and a long crack in the back. $2000-$3000

164 Mat glaze vase decorated with a single nude reclining among large abstract flowers, painted by Jens Jensen in 1933. Marks on the base include the Rookwood logo, the date, S for special shape, a wheel ground x, a Glover Collection label number 874 and the artist's monogram. Height 6½ inches. $2000-$3000

165   Vellum glaze vase decorated by Ed Diers in 1930, depicting a reflecting woodland scene. Marks on the base include the Rookwood logo, the date, shape number 904 D, V for Vellum glaze, a fan shaped esoteric mark, a wheel ground x and the artist's initials. Height 8⅜ inches. an old repair to the lip is evident. Uncrazed. $400-$600

166   Standard glaze creamer and sugar bowl decorated with clover by Marianne Mitchell in 1901. Marks on the base of both pieces include the Rookwood logo, the date, shape number 330 and the artist's initials. Height 2⅜ for the creamer and 2⅞ for the sugar bowl . Lip damage and old repair to the sugar. $200-$300

167   Vellum glaze scenic plaque decorated by Sara Sax in 1916. The artist's last name appears in the lower right hand corner. Marks on the back include the Rookwood logo, the date and V for Vellum glaze body. Affixed to the frame is an original Rookwood label with the title, "A Glimpse of the Sea Sarah (sic) Sax". Size is 9⅜ x 12⅜ inches. $3500-$5000

168   Rare Aerial Blue glaze vase decorated with a small boat in rough waters and several gulls by Harriet Strafer in 1894. Marks on the base include the Rookwood logo, the date, shape number 720 C, the number 273 bracketed with crescent moons, the letter L and the artist's initials. Height 3⅜ inches. Lip repair and some glaze scratches. $1500-$2500

169   Interesting high glaze vase decorated in 1945 with a Sun god figure and a Missouri Mule amid wild foliage by Jens Jensen. Marks on the base include the Rookwood logo, the date, shape number 604 D, the number 8004 and the artist's monogram. Height 7½ inches. $2000-$3000

170   Mat glaze vase decorated in 1924 with Virginia creepers by Elizabeth Lincoln. Marks on the base include the $500-$700
Rookwood logo, the date, shape number 614 D and the artist's initials. Height 10⅝ inches.

171   Good high glaze Venetian harbor scenic vase, decorated by Carl Schmidt in 1923. Marks on the base include the $5500-$7500
Rookwood logo, the date, shape number 1667, P for porcelain body and the artist's monogram. Height 10⅛
inches.

172   Standard glaze mug decorated with corn by Charles Dibowski in 1895. Marks on the base include the Rookwood $300-$500
logo, the date, shape number S 1220, L for light Standard glaze and the artist's monogram. Height 2⅞ inches. This
mug was designed to be fitted with a lid but appears to have never had one.

173   Iris glaze vase decorated with wild roses by Ed Diers in 1910. Marks on the base include the Rookwood logo, the $2000-$3000
date, shape number 951 C, W for white glaze and the artist's initials. Height 9⅝ inches.

174   Standard glaze vase with wild rose decoration, done in 1891 by William P. McDonald. Marks on the base $700-$1000
include the Rookwood logo, the date, shape number 606 B, W for white clay, L for light Standard glaze and the
artist's initials. Height 8¼ inches.

175   High glaze vase with applied chevron decoration, done in 1931 by Elizabeth Barrett. The interior of the vase is covered with Aventurine glaze. Marks on the base include the Rookwood logo, the date, shape number 6013, a fan shaped esoteric mark and the artist's monogram. Height 6½ inches. Minor roughness on the base. $700-$900

176   Unusual carved and painted mat glaze vase, decorated with wisteria by Sallie Toohey in 1930. Marks on the base include the Rookwood logo, the date, shape number 2918, a fan shaped esoteric mark and the artist's monogram impressed twice. Height 6½ inches. $600-$800

177   Standard glaze vase with iris decoration, painted by Elizabeth Lincoln in 1905. Marks on the base include the Rookwood logo, the date, shape number 950 D and the artist's initials. Height 8¼ inches. Minor underglaze flaws. $500-$700

178   Large high glaze vase decorated with mums and fruit blossoms by Kataro Shirayamadani in 1921. Marks on the base include the Rookwood logo, the date, shape number 2448 and the artist's cypher. Height 10¾ inches. Uncrazed. The Shape Record book shows this number with a lid and a relief border near the rim. $2500-$3500

179   Standard glaze vase decorated with yellow lilies by Albert Valentien in 1885. Marks on the base include Rookwood in block letters, the date, shape number 172 C, R for red clay and the artist's initials. Height 8½ inches. $800-$1200

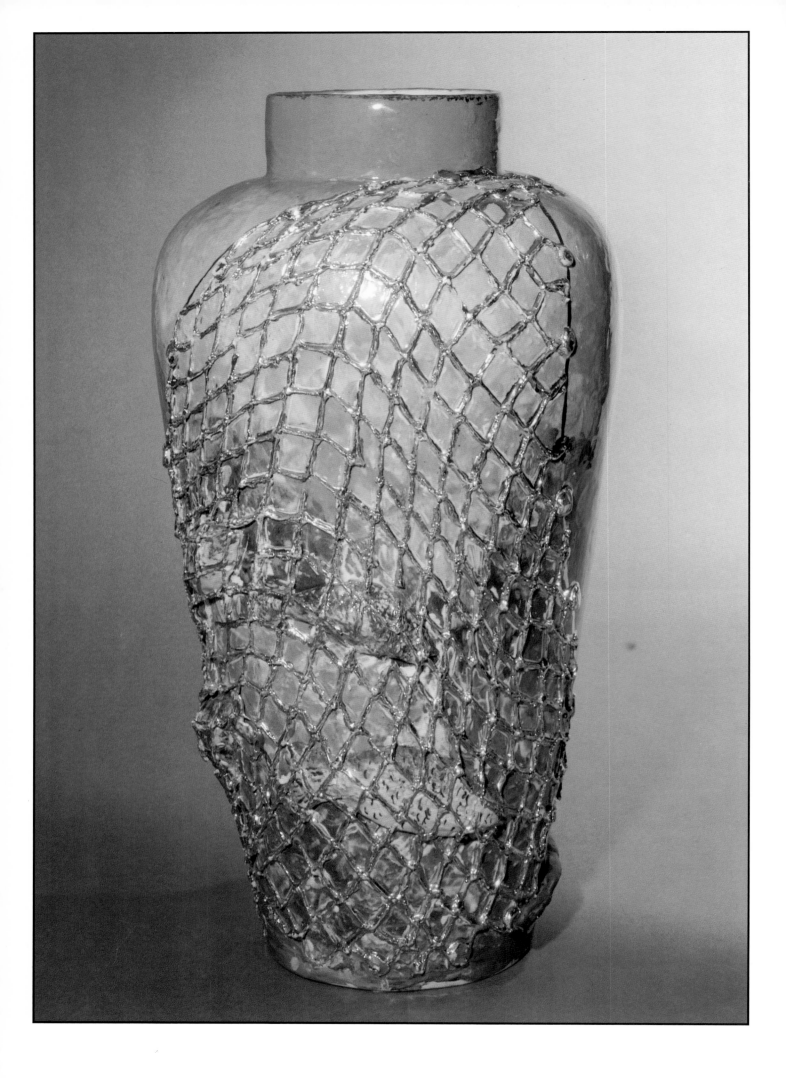

180   Monumental Limoges style glaze Aladdin vase, decorated circa 1880 with carved and painted fish entrapped in a $20000-$30000
      gold net and a single gecko pulling at the netting with his mouth, painted by Maria Longworth Nichols. There are
      no marks on the piece. Height 19⅜ inches. Typical minor damage to the gold netting. Exhibitions: "Fragile
      Blossoms, Enduring Earth" The Everson Museum of Art, 1989, Item 14 in the catalog, Color plate on page 19.
      "From Our Native Clay" The American Ceramic Arts Society, 1987, Item 80, Color plate on page 56.

181 Standard glaze two handled vase decorated with trumpet creepers by Mary Nourse in 1900. Marks on the base include the Rookwood logo, the date, shape number 581 E, L for light Standard glaze, a wheel ground x and the artist's initials. Height 8⅞ inches. One small glaze bubble. — $700-$900

182 Large and impressive high glaze vase decorated with birds and lush foliage by E.T. Hurley in 1928. Marks on the base include the Rookwood logo, the date, shape number 2984 and the artist's initials. Height 16 inches. Uncrazed. — $5000-$7000

183 Dull finish ewer decorated with grasses and a turtle by Martin Rettig in 1885. Marks on the base include Rookwood in block letters, the date, shape number 101 C, Y for yellow clay and the artist's initials. Height 8⅛ inches. Repairs on the body and the neck cover the loss of a handle. — $300-$500

184 Unusual Vellum glaze vase decorated in 1905 with two large swimming fish by E.T. Hurley. Marks on the base include the Rookwood logo, the date, shape number 939 B, V for Vellum glaze body, the die impressed number 294, a wheel ground X and the artist's full name. Height 10⅞ inches. Some glaze peppering, glaze drip and discoloration. — $1500-$2000

185 Unusually colorful and crisply decorated Vellum glaze vase, painted with a village on a lake seen through an autumn wood by Fred Rothenbusch in 1927. Marks on the base include the Rookwood logo, the date, shape number 1126 C, V for Vellum glaze and the artist's initials. Height 9⅜ inches. Uncrazed. — $2000-$3000

186 Standard glaze ewer decorated with holly by Jeannette Swing in 1900. Marks on the base include the Rookwood logo, the date, shape number 657 D and the artist's initials. Height 6⅛ inches. $350-$450

187 Iris glaze vase with clover decor, done by Ed Diers in 1903. Marks on the base include the Rookwood logo, the date, shape number 907 F, W for white glaze, a wheel ground x and the artist's initials. Height 7 inches. Glaze loss from rim. $300-$500

188 Vellum glaze plaque decorated in 1918 by Lenore Asbury. The artist's initials appear in the lower left hand corner. Marks on the back include the Rookwood logo and the date. Affixed to the frame is an original Rookwood paper label with the title, "The Banks of the River L. Asbury". Size 11 x 8½ inches. $4000-$6000

189 Standard glaze vase with two loop handles, decorated with autumn leaves by an unknown artist at Rookwood in 1897. Marks on the base include the Rookwood logo, the date and shape number 459 E. Height 3⅞ inches. Tiny flake on rim. $200-$300

190 Vellum glaze vase with crocus decoration, done in 1914 by Margaret McDonald. Marks on the base include the Rookwood logo, the date, shape number 2068, V for Vellum glaze body and the artist's monogram. Height 5½ inches. Moderate glaze peppering. $200-$400

191 Standard glaze pitcher decorated with wisteria by Charles Dibowski in 1893. Marks on the base include the Rookwood logo, the date, shape number 18 D, L for light Standard glaze, the number 261 bracketed by crescent moons and the artist's monogram. Height 5⅝ inches. Small chip on rim with old repair. The crescent moons represent a glaze experiment by Joseph Bailey. $200-$300

192   Standard glaze vase with swirled ribbing, decorated with nasturtiums by Sallie Toohey in 1891. Marks on the base include the Rookwood logo, the date, shape number 612 D, W for white clay, L for light Standard glaze and the artist's monogram. Height 4¾ inches. $400-$600

193   Vibrant high glaze vase decorated with cherries among blue and green leaves by Kataro Shirayamadani in 1924. Marks on the base include the Rookwood logo, the date, shape number 2040 E and the artist's cypher. Height 7⅜ inches. Uncrazed. $1500-$2500

194   High glaze vase with floral decoration, done in very heavy slip by Jens Jensen in 1943. Marks on the base include the Rookwood logo, the date, shape number 6183 F and the artist's monogram. Height 4⅛ inches. $500-$700

195   Limoges style glaze pitcher decorated with several flying insects among clouds and oriental grasses by Albert Valentien in 1882. Marks on the base include Rookwood in block letters, the date, an impressed anchor mark and the artist's initials. Height 7¼ inches. $800-$1000

196   Standard glaze pillow vase with leaf and berry decoration, painted by Jeannette Swing in 1904. Marks on the base include the Rookwood logo, the date, shape number 90 C and the artist's monogram. Height 3⅝ inches. $150-$250

197   Vellum glaze vase decorated with tulips by Edith Noonan in 1905. Marks on the base include the Rookwood logo, the date, shape number 932 E, V for Vellum glaze body, V for Vellum glaze, a wheel ground x and the artist's initials. Height 7½ inches. Glaze runs. $300-$400

198   Good Standard glaze vase decorated with the portrait of a Native American by Sturgis Laurence in 1900. Marks $3000-$4000
       on the base include the Rookwood logo, the date, shape number 786 C, a wheel ground X, the title "Sioux Brave"
       and the artist's initials. Height 10 inches.

199   High glaze vase decorated with trailing vines and flowers under a repeating border, painted by Arthur Conant in $1000-$1500
       1919. Marks on the base include the Rookwood logo, the date, shape number 2039 E, P for porcelain body, the
       number 2423 and the artist's monogram. Height 7 inches.

200   Iris glaze vase decorated with thistles by Carl Schmidt in 1907. Marks on the base include the Rookwood logo, $3000-$4000
       the date, shape number 909 BB, W for white glaze and the artist's monogram. Height 10 inches.

201   Standard glaze vase with violet decoration, done in 1893 by Mary Nourse. Marks on the base include the $300-$400
       Rookwood logo, the date, shape number 898 B, W for white clay, L for light Standard glaze and the mostly
       obscured artist's initials. Height 6⅛ inches. Very tight line at rim and roughness at base.

202   Unusual high glaze vase with lushly painted floral decoration, done by E.T. Hurley in 1922. Marks on the base $500-$700
       include the Rookwood logo, the date, shape number 940 C and the mostly obscured artist's initials. Height 11¼
       inches. Grinding chips on base and drilled.

203 Unusual polychromed high glaze bulldog, made at Rookwood in 1944. Marks on the base include the Rookwood logo and the date. Height 10¼ inches. $800-$1200

204 Large and handsome Vellum glaze scenic plaque decorated by Ed Diers in 1916. The artist's initials appear in the lower left hand corner. Marks on the back include the Rookwood logo, the date and V for Vellum glaze body. A silver plated brass plaque on the frame reads: Presented to George W. Cleveland by the Fire Underwriters Club of Cincinnati January 11-1917. Size 14⅝ x 9⅜ inches. A few very tiny glaze bubbles appear near the lower edge of the plaque. $5000-$7000

205 Standard glaze mug painted with the portrait of a Native American by Sturgis Laurence in 1896. Marks on the base include the Rookwood logo, the date, shape number 645 and the artist's initials. Height 4⅝ inches. A spider crack in the base extends up the sides in at least three places but does not involve the portrait. $400-$600

206 Vellum glaze scenic vase decorated in 1923 by Ed Diers. Marks on the base include the Rookwood logo, the date, shape number 2305, V for Vellum glaze, P for porcelain body, a wheel ground X and the artist's initials. Height 9⅜ inches. Several unobtrusive glaze dimples. Uncrazed. $1500-$2000

207 Unusual Iris glaze vase decorated with two Rooks flying through pine boughs, done by Sallie Coyne in 1906. Marks on the base include the Rookwood logo, the date, shape 909 BB, W for white glaze and the artist's initials. Height 9¾ inches. Uncrazed. $5000-$7000

208   Good Arts and Crafts mat glaze vase, decorated in 1906 with two carved panels, each showing different stands of $1500-$2000
       cattails by Alice Willitts. Marks on the base include the Rookwood logo, the date, shape number 925 C and the
       artist's monogram. Height 9½ inches.

209   Standard glaze vase with the profile portrait of a Native American, done in 1900 by Jeannette Swing. Marks on $1000-$1500
       the base include the Rookwood logo, the date, shape number 659 D, a wheel ground x and the artist's initials.
       Height 5 inches. Underglaze skip on handle and small spider in bottom.

210   Large mat glaze vase decorated with trumpet creepers by Kataro Shirayamadani in 1937. Marks on the base $1500-$2000
       include the Rookwood logo, the date, shape number 2918 B, a wheel ground X and the artist's cypher. Height
       11¼ inches. Minor glaze flaws.

211   Good Sea Green glaze vase decorated with several fish fighting through sea foam, painted by E.T. Hurley in $4000-$5000
       1901. Marks on the base include the Rookwood logo, the date, shape number 860, G for Sea Green glaze and
       the artist's initials. Height 6⅛ inches.

212   Vellum glaze vase painted with apple blossoms by Charles McLaughlin in 1916. Marks on the base include the $800-$1000
       Rookwood logo, the date, shape number 999 C, V for Vellum glaze body and the artist's initials. Height 9¼
       inches.

213   Dull finish Turkish coffee pot, decorated in 1884 with oriental grasses and a single flying bird by M.A. Daly. $500-$700
Marks on the base include Rookwood in block letters, the date, shape number 51, Y for yellow clay and the
artist's initials. Height 9½ inches. Lid missing.

214   Iris glaze vase decorated with trailing fruit blossoms by Sallie Coyne in 1911. Marks on the base include the $800-$1000
Rookwood logo, the date, shape number 1659 E, W for white glaze, a wheel ground x and the artist's monogram.
Height 7¼ inches.

215   Tall Limoges style glaze French crushed vase, decorated in 1882 very much in the manner of Maria Longworth $2500-$3500
Nichols, showing a nesting bird in a tree branch. Marks on the base include Rookwood in block letters and the
date. Height 14 ¾ inches.

216   Standard glaze ewer with floral decoration, painted by Sallie Toohey in 1891. Marks on the base include the $500-$700
Rookwood logo, the date, shape number 578 D, W for white clay, L for light Standard glaze and the artist's
monogram. Height 10⅜ inches. Some underglaze discoloration.

217   High glaze vase decorated in 1946, showing two birds perched in a lilac bush by Jens Jensen. Marks on the base $1500-$2000
include the Rookwood logo, the date, shape number 2785, the number 8589 and the artist's monogram. Height
13⅛ inches.

218 Unusually colorful Vellum glaze vase decorated with a woodland scene by Fred Rothenbusch in 1917. Marks on $2500-$3500
the base include the Rookwood logo, the date, shape number 838 B, V for Vellum glaze body and the artist's
initials. Height 13 inches. Tiny spot of underglaze color loss on rim.

219 Standard glaze vase decorated in 1902 with jonquils by Amelia Sprague. Marks on the base include the $600-$800
Rookwood logo, the date, shape number 786 C and the artist's monogram. Height 9⅞ inches.

220 Large and impressive Standard glaze vase decorated in 1890 with sharply painted fruit blossoms by Kataro $2500-$3500
Shirayamadani. Marks on the base include the Rookwood logo, the date, shape number 563 A, W for white clay,
L for light Standard glaze and the artist's cypher. Height 17⅞ inches. Drilled, a few small glaze blisters and a small
bruise at the base. Quality brass fittings, burner and font accompany the vase which was made into an oil lamp
early in its life.

221 Vellum glaze vase decorated with a misty woodland scene by Mary Grace Denzler in 1915. Marks on the base $1000-$1500
include the Rookwood logo, the date, shape number 1356 D, V for Vellum glaze body and the artist's monogram.
Height 8⅞ inches.

222 Large high glaze vase with floral decoration, made in 1924 by William Hentschel. Marks on the base include the $1000-$1500
Rookwood logo, the date, shape number 2640 C and the artist's monogram. Height 13⅜ inches. Grinding chips
around most of the base.

223　Rare and important Dull finish vase, delicately carved and lightly tinted in 1899 with a figure of Eve standing in a　$25000-$35000
field of poppies by Harriet Wilcox. The rim is surmounted by an electroplated copper collar with gold wash,
depicting the moon amongst clouds. Marks on the base include the Rookwood logo, the date, shape number 879
B, the partly obscured title, "Garden of Eden", Cincinnati Art Museum accession numbers .... : 06 and the artist's
initials. Height 14 3/4 inches. Drilled. Listed: S.G. Burt's book, "2,292 pieces of early Rookwood Pottery in the
Cincinnati Art Museum in 1916", as item 59 on page 136. Future Exhibition: "Rookwood Pottery: the Glorious
Gamble" The Cincinnati Art Museum 1991 -1993. Note: Although you may purchase this vase from its current
owner and receive clear title, possession will not be granted until the Cincinnati Art Museum Exhibit ends
sometime in October, 1993, after traveling to two additional museums in the United States. The exhibition
catalog is in press and will credit current ownership.

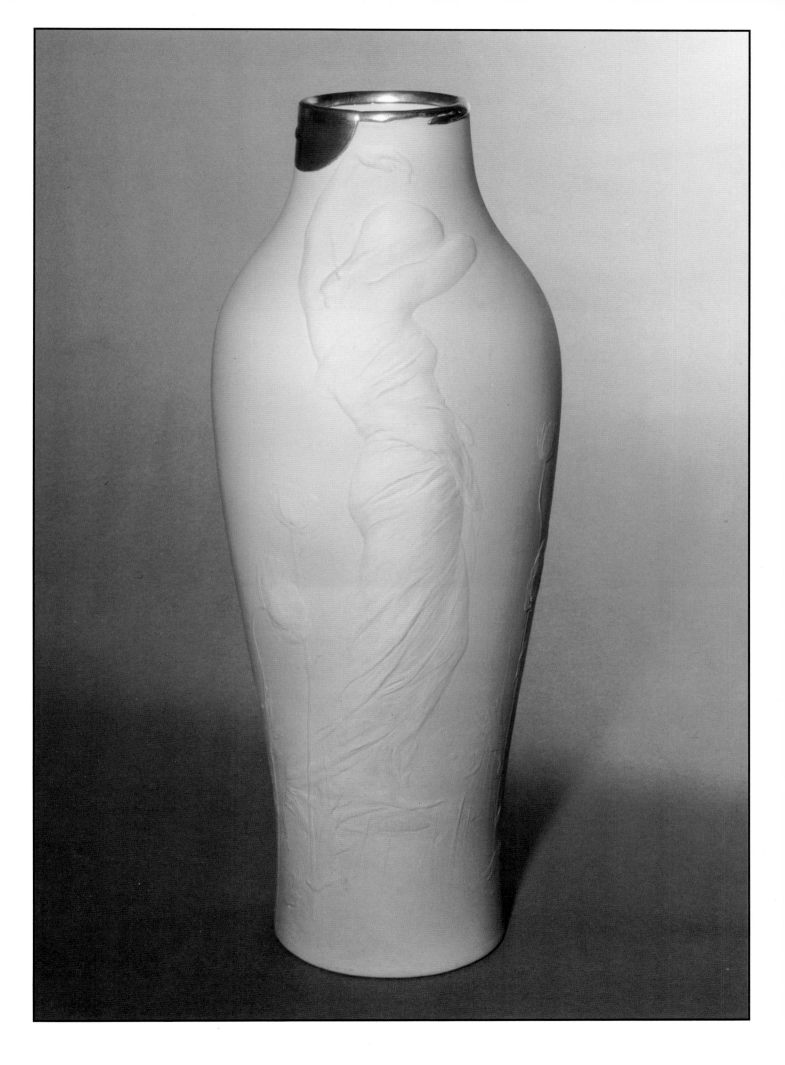

224 Rookwood mat glaze garden urn in classical form with two ram's head handles and lid. The body is made in two pieces which are bolted together. Marks on the base include the Rookwood Faience logo and the shape number 3042 Y. Marks inside the body include the Rookwood logo and shape number 3042 Y. Height 26 inches. Oral history indicates this vase once graced the chapel of Bob Jones University in Greenville, South Carolina. A few minor nicks and chips can be found on this otherwise remarkably clean vessel. $800-$1200

225 Rookwood mat glaze garden urn in classical form with two ram's head handles and lid. The body is made in two pieces which are bolted together. Marks on the base include the Rookwood Faience logo and the shape number 3042 Y. Marks inside the body include the Rookwood logo and shape number 3042 Y. Height 26 inches. Oral history indicates this vase once graced the chapel of Bob Jones University in Greenville, South Carolina. A few minor nicks and chips can be found on this otherwise remarkably clean vessel. $800-$1200

226 Three Architectural Faience tiles depicting an English Cottage setting, made at Rookwood circa 1915. Marks on the back include the Rookwood Faience logo, the number 1227 Y and the number 4 in a circle. The respective tiles are numbered left to right, 3,4 and 5 on the back and on the lower edge. Edge chips and surface chips on all tiles. Some inner edge chips have been repaired. Size of all three tiles is 16 x 48 inches. $3000-$5000

227   Mat glaze vase with a repeating band of incised and painted flowers, decorated by C.S. Todd in 1915. Marks on the base include the Rookwood logo, the date, shape number 942 C and the artist's initials. Height 7⅛ inches. $600-$800

228   Vellum glaze scenic vase depicting a twilight winter landscape, painted by Katherine Van Horne in 1912. Marks on the base include the Rookwood logo, the date, shape number 1871, V for Vellum glaze, V for Vellum glaze body and the artist's monogram. Height 6¼ inches. Uncrazed but with some glaze peppering. $700-$900

229   Vellum glaze bowl decorated with three repeating sprays of lily of the valley, painted in 1919 by E.T. Hurley. Marks on the base include the Rookwood logo, the date, shape number 957 C, V for Vellum glaze body and the artist's initials. Height 3⅜ inches. $400-$600

230   Large Vellum glaze plaque decorated in 1926 with a tree lined lake by Carl Schmidt. The artist's name appears in the lower right hand corner. Marks on the back include the Rookwood logo and the date. Size 9¼ x 14½ inches. Several small glaze bubbles but no crazing. $5000-$7000

231   Standard glaze vase with clover decoration, executed in 1898 by Ed Diers. Marks on the base include the Rookwood logo, the date, shape number 748 D, a star shaped esoteric mark and the artist's initials. Height 6 inches. $300-$400

232   Vellum glaze vase with colorful floral decoration, painted in 1928 by Fred Rothenbusch. Marks on the base include the Rookwood logo, the date, shape number 2191, V for Vellum glaze, a wheel ground x and the artist's initials. Height 5¼ inches. Glaze flaws at the rim and at the base. $200-$300

233 Standard glaze vase with floral decoration, painted in 1897 by Katherine Hickman. Marks on the base include the Rookwood logo, the date, shape number 743 C and the artist's monogram. Height 6⅝ inches. $250-$350

234 Mat glaze cabinet vase painted with apple blossoms in 1930 by Lenore Asbury. Marks on the base include the Rookwood logo, the date, shape number 6144, a fan shaped esoteric mark and the artist's initials. Height 2⅞ inches. $200-$300

235 Colorful high glaze vase with lush floral decoration, done in 1931 by Margaret McDonald. Marks on the base include the Rookwood logo, the date, shape number 2190, a fan shaped esoteric mark and the artist's monogram. Height 6¼ inches. $1200-$1500

236 Standard glaze vase with much Tiger Eye effect, decorated circa 1898 with at least one small frog by Albert Valentien. Slightly obscured marks on the base include the Rookwood logo, the date, shape number 568 B and the artist's initials. Height 4¼ inches. $100-$200

237 Banded Vellum glaze woodland scenic vase, decorated by Charles McLaughlin in 1914. Marks on the base include the Rookwood logo, the date, shape number 1278 F, V for Vellum glaze body and the artist's initials. Height 7⅜ inches. $800-$1200

238 Pink tinted high glaze vase with stylized fruit blossom decoration, painted by Harriet Wilcox in 1923. Marks on the base include the Rookwood logo, the date, shape number 357 F and the artist's initials. Height 6 inches. $400-$600

239   Standard glaze ewer decorated with holly by Amelia Sprague in 1899. Marks on the base include the Rookwood logo, the date, shape number 578 D, a wheel ground x and the artist's monogram. Height 10½ inches. $500-$700

240   Pink tinted high glaze vase decorated with a band of flowers on the shoulder by Sara Sax in 1927. Marks on the base include the Rookwood logo, the date, shape number 1927 and the artist's monogram. Height 4 inches   .$400-$600

241   Rare and unusual carved mat glaze charger, done in high relief with the face and headdress of a Native American by Anna Valentien in 1901. Marks on the base include the Rookwood logo, the date, shape number 369 Z and the artist's initials. Greatest distance across is 13½ inches. $3000-$4000

242   Standard glaze vase with swirled ribbing, painted with mums by Anna Valentien in 1892. Marks on the base include the Rookwood logo, the date, shape number 612 C, W for white clay, L for light Standard glaze and the artist's initials. Height 5¾ inches. $400-$600

243   Early Vellum glaze vase with Arts and Crafts decoration of Rooks flying through a winter forest, painted in 1905 by E.T. Hurley. Marks on the base include the Rookwood logo, the date, shape number 951 D, V for Vellum glaze body, V for Vellum glaze and the artist's initials. Height 8⅜ inches. Small, tight line descends ¼ inch from rim. $1500-$2000

244 High glaze vase decorated with flowers and fish by Jens Jensen in 1944. Marks on the base include the Rookwood logo, the date, shape number 6864 and the artist's monogram. Height 7⅜ inches. $1000-$1500

245 Standard glaze pitcher painted with multicolored pansies by Constance Baker circa 1895. Marks on the base include the Rookwood logo, the partially obscured date, shape number 259 D, W for white clay and the artist's initials. Height 4¼ inches. $400-$600

246 Vellum glaze scenic plaque decorated by E.T. Hurley in 1948. The artist's initials appear in the lower left hand corner. Marks on the back include the Rookwood logo, the date and the numbers 10 x 12. Size 9¾ x 11¾ inches. Uncrazed. $7000-$9000

247 Mat glaze vase with cherry decoration, done in 1925 by Sallie Coyne. Marks on the base include the Rookwood logo, the date, shape number 935 E and the artist's monogram. Height 6⅝ inches. $400-$600

248 Mat glaze decorated with a band of stylized flowers at the rim by Sallie Coyne in 1925. Marks on the base include the Rookwood logo, the date, shape number 1358 E and the artist's monogram. Height 7 inches. $300-$400

249 Standard glaze ewer with dogwood decoration, painted by E.T. Hurley in 1901. Marks on the base include the Rookwood logo, the date, shape number 868 and the artist's initials. Height 9 inches. $400-$600

250   Mat glaze vase with Art Deco leaf and berry decoration, done by William Hentschel in 1927. Marks on the base $500-$700
include the Rookwood logo, the date, shape number 2996, a Glover Collection label, number 681 and the artist's
monogram. Height 8¾ inches.

251   Limoges style glaze vase decorated with a large bird perched on a branch and several small birds in flight by $400-$600
Albert Valentien in 1883. Marks on the base include Rookwood in block letters, the date, G for ginger clay, a
small impressed kiln and the artist's initials. Height 11¾ inches. Line at rim and repaired chip at base.

252   Standard glaze lidded teapot painted in 1894 with wild roses by Emma Foertmeyer. Marks on the base include $300-$500
the Rookwood logo, the date, shape number 404, W for white clay and the artist's initials. Height 5⅛ inches.
Some glaze discoloration and a tiny nick on the under side of the handle.

253   Standard glaze vase with jonquil decoration, painted in 1896 by Albert Valentien. Marks on the base include the $800-$1200
Rookwood logo, the date, shape number 556 B, Y for yellow (Standard) glaze, a wheel ground x and the artist's
full name. Height 13⅛ inches.

254   Iris glaze vase with daisy decoration, painted in 1903 by Sara Sax. Marks on the base include the Rookwood $2000-$2500
logo, the date, shape number 917 B, W for white glaze, and the artist's monogram. Height 9⅛ inches.

255   Unusual mat glaze vase, made to be used as a lamp base, with overall hand carved leaf decoration, done in 1934 $500-$700
by Wilhelmine Rehm. Marks on the base include the Rookwood logo, the date and shape number 977. Marks on
the side of the vase include the Rookwood logo without flames and the artist's initials. Height 10⅜ inches. This
piece has a cast hole in the base.

256   Standard glaze mug decorated with corn and wheat by Carrie Steinle in 1899. Marks on the base include the $300-$500
Rookwood logo, the date, shape number 587 B and the artist's monogram. Height 5⅝ inches. Glaze scratches.

257   Vellum glaze vase decorated with a band of blue flowers near the rim by Sara Sax in 1915. Marks on the base $500-$700
include the Rookwood logo, the date, shape number 1023 C, V for Vellum glaze body, V for Vellum glaze and
the artist's monogram. Height 10⅝ inches. Some glaze peppering.

258   Standard glaze ewer decorated with nasturtiums by E.T. Hurley in 1898. Marks on the base include the $300-$400
Rookwood logo, the date, shape number 851 D and the artist's initials. Height 8½ inches. Crack in handle.

259   Mat glaze vase with morning glory decoration, painted by Margaret McDonald in 1930. Marks on the base $500-$700
include the Rookwood logo, the date, shape number 2745 and the artist's monogram. Height 9¼ inches.

260   Rare and monumental Vellum glaze vase, made as a presentation piece in 1925 and decorated with a school of $3000-$5000
      fish swimming beneath lotus blossoms and pads by Carl Schmidt. Marks on the base include the Rookwood logo,
      the date, shape number 944 A, the name William David Carrier, reportedly a famous pianist, V for Vellum glaze,
      the artist's monogram and the artist's full name. Height 17¾ inches. Some tight glaze fissures appear on the
      surface of the vase, probably occurring in the fire, due to the mass of the piece. Most of these lines occur only in
      the exterior glaze with one or two appearing inside.

261   Vellum glaze scenic plaque decorated in 1921 by Lenore Asbury. The artist's initials appear in the lower right $1250-$1750
      hand corner. Marks on the back include the Rookwood logo and the date. Affixed to the frame is an original
      Rookwood label with the title, "Early Twilight L. Asbury". Size is 4 x 7⅞ inches.

262   Commercial high glaze Art Deco lidded bowl, designed by Louise Abel and made at Rookwood in 1950. Marks $100-$200
      on the base include the Rookwood logo, the date, shape number 6286 and the artist's monogram. Height 5¼
      inches. Crack in base.

263   Large and impressive Standard glaze vase decorated in 1899 with several lifelike peacock feathers by Albert $600-$800
      Valentien. Marks on the base include the Rookwood logo, the date and shape number 856 A. The artist's full
      name appears near the base on the vase's side. Height 17½ inches. This vase shows evidence of old repairs to
      sides and base.

264   Large and important Sea Green glaze vase decorated in 1900 with swirling oriental designs and a three $30000-$40000
dimensional carved and electroplated copper dragon encircling the base by Kataro Shirayamadani. Electroplated
silver bands encircle the rim and an area just below the rim. Marks on the base include the Rookwood logo, the
date, shape number S 1578, G for Sea Green glaze and the artist's cypher. Height 17⅛ inches. The dragon's tail
has lost its copper covering and a small glaze line appears just under the dragon's head. A tiny chip occurs near
the end of the Dragon's tail. This vase is done in much the same fashion as item 241 in the Glover Collection.

265 Standard glaze vase decorated with nasturtium in 1905 by Alice Willitts. Marks on the base include the Rookwood logo, the date, shape number 604 E, a wheel ground x and the artist's monogram. Height 5¼ inches. — $300-$400

266 Incised and painted mat glaze bowl decorated in 1907 with leaves and berries by Cecil Duell. Marks on the base include the Rookwood logo, the date, shape number 1195, V for Vellum glaze body, a wheel ground x, a Glover Collection label, number 593 and the artist's initials. Diameter 7½ inches. Some minor glaze pitting. — $300-$400

267 Mat glaze vase painted in 1931 with multicolored flowers by Kataro Shirayamadani. Marks on the base include the Rookwood logo, the date, shape number 915 E and the artist's cypher. Height 5⅞ inches. — $800-$1200

268 Flat sided Standard glaze jug with leaf and berry decoration, done in 1894 by Bertha Cranch. Marks on the base include the Rookwood logo, the date, shape number 706, W for white clay, L for light Standard glaze and the artist's initials. Height 4½ inches. — $250-$350

269 Mat glaze vase incised with an asymmetrical band in a basket weave pattern by William Hentschel in 1912. Marks on the base include the Rookwood logo, the date, shape number 831 and the artist's monogram. Height 3 inches. — $150-$200

270 High glaze vase with magnolia decoration, done in 1944 by Jens Jensen. Marks on the base include the Rookwood logo, the date, shape number 6305 and the artist's monogram. Height 4⅞ inches. Uncrazed. — $400-$600

271 Unusual Standard glaze vase with overall Goldstone effect, decorated in 1894 with two bats flying through a $2000-$3000
grass field by Kataro Shirayamadani. Marks on the base include the Rookwood logo, the date, shape number 568
C, R for red clay and the artist's cypher. Height 6⅞ inches. A small glaze flake is missing from the rim and an area
of loose glaze exists on the back of the piece.

272 Mat glaze vase with violet decoration, painted in 1938 by Kataro Shirayamadani. Marks on the base include the $600-$800
Rookwood logo, the date, shape number 6660 F and the artist's cypher. Height 3½ inches.

273 Cameo glaze bowl with magnolia decoration, painted by an unknown artist in 1886. Marks on the base include $300-$500
the Rookwood logo, the date, shape number 305 and 3 W for a type of white clay. Diameter is 10¼ inches. There
are three areas of clay loss where the firing stilts attached to the base but these are glazed over and quite
unobtrusive. Some glaze scratches.

274 Standard glaze mug painted with the portrait of an African American child by Bruce Horsfall in 1895. Marks on $2000-$3000
the base include the Rookwood logo, the date, shape number 656 and the artist's monogram. Height 5 inches.

275 Vellum glaze vase decorated with small blue flowers by Lenore Asbury in 1931. Marks on the base include the $600-$800
Rookwood logo, the date, shape number 2721, V. for Vellum glaze, a fan shaped esoteric mark and the artist's
initials. Height 6⅛ inches. Uncrazed.

276   Sea Green glaze vase with pansy decoration, painted in 1903 by Constance Baker. Marks on the base include the $3000-$4000
Rookwood logo, the date, shape number 932 D, G for Sea Green glaze and the artist's initials. Height 8⅝ inches.
There is a 1/16 inch glaze nick on the side of the vase.

277   Mat glaze vase with floral decoration, painted by Katherine Jones in 1930. Marks on the base include the $400-$600
Rookwood logo, the date, shape number 2917 E, a fan shaped esoteric mark and the artist's initials. Height 6¼
inches.

278   Vellum glaze scenic plaque done in an Arts and Crafts style by Sallie Coyne in 1914. The artist's initials appear in $2500-$3500
the lower left hand corner. Marks on the back include the Rookwood logo and the date. Size approximately 9 x 5
inches.

279   Standard glaze bowl decorated with clover by Carrie Steinle in 1908. Marks on the base include the Rookwood $250-$350
logo, the date, shape nunmber 214 C and the artist's initials. Height 2¾ inches. Minor glaze scratches.

280   Vellum glaze vase with lily of the valley decoration, painted in 1912 by Elizabeth Lincoln. Marks on the base $500-$700
include the Rookwood logo, the date, shape number 1867, V for Vellum glaze body, V for Vellum glaze and the
artist's initials. Height 7½ inches.

281   Standard glaze vase with much Goldstone effect, decorated with five small birds in flight by M.A Daly in 1895. $500-$700
Marks on the base include the Rookwood logo, the date, shape number 534 C, R for red clay and the artist's
initials. Height 6¾ inches. A short crack descends from the rim with a slight loss of glaze and body.

282   Vellum glaze vase decorated with trailing apple blossoms by Sallie Coyne in 1908. Marks on the base include the Rookwood logo, the date, shape number 907 F, V for Vellum glaze body, V for Vellum glaze and the artist's monogram. Height 7½ inches. $500-$700

283   Limoges style glaze lidded pitcher decorated in 1885 with a sparrow flying over oriental grasses by an unknown artist. Marks on the base include Rookwood in block letters, the date, shape number 251 and R for red clay. Height 7½ inches. Chips to the lid and base and a small crack descends from the rim. $200-$300

284   Vellum glaze scenic plaque decorated by Carl Schmidt in 1920. The artist's name appears in the lower right hand corner. Marks on the back include the Rookwood logo and the date. An original Rookwood paper label with the title, "The Basin C. Schmidt" and an original paper Rookwood logo appear on the frame. Size 9 x 7 inches. $3000-$4000

285   Standard glaze creamer decorated with wild violets by Carl Schmidt in 1897. Marks on the base include the Rookwood logo, the date, shape number 330, a diamond shaped esoteric mark and the artist's monogram. Height 2⅝ inches. $200-$300

286   Mat glaze vase with stylized peacock feather decoration, painted by Elizabeth Lincoln in 1920. Marks on the base include the Rookwood logo, the date, shape number 2067, V for Vellum glaze body and the artist's initials. Height 7¾ inches. $300-$400

287   Crisp Standard glaze ewer with Gorham silver overlay, decorated in 1893 with leaves and berries by Olga Reed. Marks on the base include the Rookwood logo, the date, shape number 379, W for white clay and the artist's initials. Marks on the silver include Gorham Mfg. Co. and the number R. 1242. Height 8⅝ inches. Damage to the lip has been repaired and is not visible from the outside because of the silver overlay. $3500-$4500

288   Blue tinted high glaze vase with a border of repeating stylized floral designs painted around the shoulder by $600-$800
Charles McLaughlin in 1918. Marks on the base include the Rookwood logo, the date, shape number 553 C, P for
porcelain body, an old paper label with the notation # 30 and the artist's monogram. Height 10 inches.

289   Unusually clean and crisp Vellum glaze Venetian harbor scene, decorated by Carl Schmidt in 1924. Marks on the $4000-$6000
base include the Rookwood logo, the date, shape number 907 DD, V for Vellum glaze and the artist's monogram.
Height 10⅜ inches. Uncrazed.

290   Mat glaze vase carved and painted with a repeating leaf pattern by William Hentschel in 1914. Marks on the base $300-$400
include the Rookwood logo, the date, shape number 2082 and the artist's monogram. Height 3½ inches.

291   Iris glaze vase decorated with violets by Ed Diers in 1903. Marks on the base include the Rookwood logo, the $1000-$1200
date, shape number 907 E, W for white glaze, the number 85 and the artist's initials. Height 8⅜ inches.

292   Limoges style glaze ewer decorated with spiders and webs spun through a stand of daisies by an unknown artist $300-$500
in 1882. Marks on the base include Rookwood in block letters and the date. Height 12 inches.

293 Standard glaze vase with wild rose decoration, painted by an unknown artist in 1893. Marks on the base include the Rookwood logo, the date, shape number 468 BB, W for white clay and the artist's monogram. Height 9⅝ inches. $400-$600

294 Vellum glaze scenic vase decorated in 1939 by E.T. Hurley. Marks on the base include the Rookwood logo, the date, shape number 913 C, P for porcelain body and the artist's initials. Height 9 inches. $2000-$2500

295 Limoges style glaze bowl painted with bamboo and a single butterfly by Albert Valentien in 1882. Marks on the base include Rookwood in block letters, the date, shape number 121, G for ginger clay and the artist's initials. Height 4 inches. Some glaze bubbles inside the bowl. This piece is from Rookwood Pottery's Museum, descending in the family of one of Rookwood's last owners and has never been offered for sale until now. $600-$800

296 Bizarre Limoges style glaze ewer completely covered with oriental designs, symbols and images by an unknown artist in 1882. Marks on the base include Rookwood in block letters, the date twice and the initials, A.E.W. Height 11⅝ inches. Repaired handle. $200-$300

297 Standard glaze vase with pansy decoration, painted in 1891 by Artus Van Briggle. Marks on the base include the Rookwood logo, the date, shape number 589 E, W for white clay, L for light Standard glaze and the artist's initials. Height 8⅛ inches. $400-$600

298   Vellum glaze vase painted with a band of hanging branches and flowers by Margaret McDonald in 1913. Marks on the base include the Rookwood logo, the date, shape number 1873, V for Vellum glaze body, a wheel ground x and the artist's monogram. Height 5⅜ inches. $250-$350

299   Standard glaze vase decorated with wild roses by Grace Young in 1889. Marks on the base, which are all incised by hand, include the Rookwood logo, the date, shape number 509, W for white clay, L for light Standard glaze and the artist's monogram. Height 5⅛ inches. Chip off rim. $200-$300

300   High glaze vase decorated with bleeding hearts and partially covered with a drip glaze, painted by E.T. Hurley in 1922. Marks on the base include the Rookwood logo, the date, shape number 112 and the artist's initials. Height 6⅞ inches. $1200-$1400

301   Standard glaze lidded teapot with floral decoration, painted in 1894 by Sallie Toohey. Marks on the base include the Rookwood logo, the date, shape number 615, W for white clay and the artist's monogram. Height 6 inches. $500-$700

302   Vellum glaze vase with cherry blossom decoration by Laura Lindeman, painted in 1907. Marks on the base include the Rookwood logo, the date, shape number 939 D, V for Vellum glaze body, V for Vellum glaze and the artist's initials. Height 7⅝ inches. $500-$700

303   Mat glaze vase decorated with abstract flowers by Wilhelmine Rehm in 1929. Marks on the base include the $300-$500
        Rookwood logo, the date, shape number 356 D and the artist's monogram. Height 8⅛ inches.

304   Standard glaze ewer with daisy decoration painted by Olga Reed in 1891. Marks on the base include the $100-$200
        Rookwood logo, the date, shape number 584 C, W for white clay, L for light Standard glaze and the artist's
        initials. Height 5½ inches. Handle broken and glued and chip at base.

305   Black Opal glaze vase with morning glory decoration, painted by Harriet Wilcox in 1924. Marks on the base $300-$300
        include the Rookwood logo, the date, shape number 923 and the artist's initials. Height 2⅜ inches.

306   Dull finish ewer decorated with honeysuckle in heavy slip by Sallie Toohey in 1888. Marks on the base include $500-$700
        the Rookwood logo, the date, shape number 62 B, W for white clay, S for smear (dull) glaze and the artist's
        monogram. Height 7¼ inches.

307   Standard glaze lidded humidor painted in 1899 with pipes, cigars, matches and foliage by Carl Schmidt. Marks $800-$1000
        on the base include the Rookwood logo, the date, shape number 683, a paper label which reads, "F.C. Coe
        China Glass Jacksonville Ill." and the artist's monogram. The lid is also marked with the artist's monogram.
        Height 6⅛ inches.

308 High glaze vase decorated in 1930 with repeating geometric designs by Sara Sax. Marks on the base include the Rookwood logo, the date, shape number 6175, a fan shaped esoteric mark, a wheel ground x and the artist's monogram. Height 7 inches. $400-$600

309 Standard glaze lidded cracker jar painted with nasturtiums by Albert Valentien in 1885. Marks on the base include Rookwood in block letters, the date, shape number 240, S inside an incised circle for sage green clay and the artist's initials. Height 9 inches. The lid is cracked about half way through. $500-$700

310 Standard glaze inkwell with floral decoration, done in 1899 by Edith Felten. Marks on the base include the Rookwood logo, the date, shape number 501 B and the artist's initials. Height 2½ inches. Missing inner well. The lid is marked with the monogram of Sara Sax but may be a reproduction. $200-$400

311 Vellum glaze vase with cherry blossom decoration, done by Kataro Shirayamadani in 1941. Marks on the base include the Rookwood logo, the date, shape number 80 C and both the artist's initials and cypher. Height 6⅞ inches. Uncrazed. $700-$900

312 Mat glaze vase with crystaline inclusions, decorated with stylized floral designs by William Hentschel in 1926. Marks on the base include the Rookwood logo, the date, shape number 2618 D and the artist's monogram. Height 8½ inches. $300-$400

313   Vellum glaze vase decorated with a woodland scene by E.T. Hurley in 1909. Marks on the base include the $1500-$2000
       Rookwood logo, the date, shape number 922 C, V for Vellum glaze body, V for Vellum glaze and the artist's
       initials. Height 9 inches.

314   Limoges style glaze pillow vase painted in 1882 with a bird nesting with her brood in a grassy swamp, possibly $600-$800
       by E.G. Leonard. The decoration is enhanced with much fired on gold. Marks on the base include Rookwood in
       block letters and the date. Marks on the back side of the vase include what appear to be the initials E.G.L and the
       date, Dec 1st 1882. Minor roughness on rim and base.

315   High glaze demonstration vase, thrown and signed on the side by Anton Lang on a visit to the Pottery in 1924. $300-$400
       Marks on the base include the Rookwood logo, the date, the letter M in grease pencil and a paper label with # 12
       written in pen. Height 4⅜ inches. This piece is from the Rookwood Pottery's Museum, descending in the family of
       one of Rookwood's last owners and has never been offered for sale until now.

316   High glaze vase with magnolia decoration, done by Jens Jensen in 1944. Marks on the base include the $800-$1200
       Rookwood logo, the date, shape number 614 E and the artist's monogram. Height 8¼ inches.

317   Cameo glaze pitcher with floral decoration, painted by Amelia Sprague in 1889. Marks on the base include the $500-$700
       Rookwood logo, the date, shape number 251, W for white clay, W for white glaze and the artist's initials. Height
       8⅝ inches.

318   Dull finish story mug decorated in 1886 showing a group of people ministering to a very sick, bed ridden fellow, $200-$300
painted by E.P. Cranch. Marks on the base include Rookwood in block letters, the date, shape number 260, S for
sage green clay, the title, "Isaac Abbott. sh. ser. 10" and the artist's initials. Beneath the scene is inscribed, "But
this made Isaac much more sick, And wonderful soon he gave his last kick. ...derful soon he gave his last kick."
Height 6 inches. Handle broken and repaired.

319   Mat glaze vase with stylized floral decoration, done in 1930 by Wilhelmine Rehm. Marks on the base include the $400-$600
Rookwood logo, the date, shape number 900 C, a fan shaped esoteric mark and the artist's initials. Height 8⅝
inches. Small grinding chips on base.

320   Standard glaze vase with wild rose decoration, painted by Charles Dibowski in 1895. Marks on the base include $300-$500
the Rookwood logo, the date, shape number 717, L for light Standard glaze and the artist's monogram. Height 5
inches.

321   Standard glaze vase with pine cone decoration, done in 1902 by Lenore Asbury. Marks on the base include the $400-$600
Rookwood logo, the date, shape number 888 C, a wheel ground x and the artist's initials. Height 9¾ inches.
Minor glaze scratches.

322   High glaze vase decorated in 1919 with small blue flowers on a white ground by Lorinda Epply. Marks on the $800-$1200
base include the Rookwood logo, the date, shape number 2347 and the artist's monogram. Height 7⅛ inches.

323   Unusual Iris glaze vase decorated in 1902 with several gulls flying over a series of incoming waves by Sturgis Laurence. Marks on the base include the Rookwood logo, the date, shape number 939 C, W for white glaze, a wheel ground x and the artist's initials. Height 8 inches. Tiny flake off rim. $2000-$3000

324   Mat glaze vase with abstract floral decoration, painted in 1924 by Margaret McDonald. Marks on the base include the Rookwood logo, the date, shape number 170 and the artist's monogram. Height 11½ inches. Some glaze peppering. $200-$300

325   Standard glaze inkwell decorated in 1896 with grasses and yellow butterflies by Lenore Asbury. Marks on the base include the Rookwood logo, the date, shape number 418 B and the artist's initials. Height 2⅛ inches. Missing lid. $300-$500

326   Banded Vellum glaze vase with floral decoration, done in 1916 by Carrie Steinle. Marks on the base include the Rookwood logo, the date, shape number 1124 E, a wheel ground x and the artist's monogram. Height 7⅛ inches. Drilled, glaze loss from rim and glaze peppering. $150-$200

327   Limoges style glaze horn pitcher decorated in 1882 with grasses and dragonflies by Albert Valentien. Marks on the base include Rookwood in block letters, the date, shape number 116, G for ginger clay, an impressed anchor mark and the artist's initials. Height 6⅜ inches. This piece is from Rookwood Pottery's Museum, descending in the family of one of Rookwood's last owners and has never been offered for sale until now. $800-$1200

328 Early mat glaze stoppered whiskey jug, decorated with incised Arts and Crafts designs by Earl Menzel in 1901. $500-$700
Marks on the base include the Rookwood logo, the date, shape number 274 Z and the artist's initials. Height 7
inches.

329 Architectural Faience tile made at Rookwood circa 1915, showing two geese done in an Arts and Crafts green $1000-$1500
mat glaze. Marks on the back include the Rookwood Faience logo, the number 1220 Y and the number 2 in a
circle. Size 8 x 8 inches.

330 Limoges style glaze bowl and saucer decorated with a panel containing the name Hazyp and flowers outlined in $200-$300
fired on gold, painted in 1889 by an unknown artist. The base of the bowl is marked, R.L.C. ap. 1889. Marks on
the base of the saucer include the Rookwood logo, the date and shape number 87. Both pieces are marked with a
G for ginger clay. Height 4 inches. Minor rim roughness.

331 Unusual carved Sea Green glaze vase decorated with hyacinths by Sallie Toohey in 1900. Marks on the base $1200-$1500
include the Rookwood logo, the date, shape number 614 E, G for Sea Green Glaze and the artist's monogram.
Height 8⅛ inches.

332   Standard glaze syrup pitcher decorated with small yellow flowers by an unknown artist in 1886. Marks on the base include the Rookwood logo, the date, shape number 239 and S for sage green clay. Height 7 inches. Tiny nick inside rim. $200-$300

333   Colorful Vellum glaze plaque painted by Fred Rothenbusch in 1922. The artist's monogram appears in the lower right hand corner. Marks on the back include the Rookwood logo, the date and P for porcelain body. Size 8 7/8 x 5 inches. Minor glaze run near the top and some small pits. Uncrazed. $2500-$3500

334   Mat glaze charger decorated with three seahorses clinging to sea weed, painted in 1903 by Sallie Toohey. Faint marks on the back inlcude the Rookwood logo, the date, shape number 678 Z and the artist's monogram. Diameter 11 inches. $400-$600

335   High glaze tankard with several embossed cherubs, done at Rookwood, circa 1886. Marks on the base include the Rookwood logo and 2 W for a type of white clay. Height 7⅜ inches. $200-$400

336   Standard glaze vase with wild rose decoration, painted in 1897 by Sallie Coyne. Marks on the base include the Rookwood logo, the date, shape number 611 D, a trianglular esoteric mark and the artist's initials. Height 8⅛ inches. Minor glaze scratches. $300-$400

337   Standard glaze pillow vase with grape decoration, painted in 1896, possibly by John Dee Wareham. Marks on the base include the Rookwood logo, the date, shape number 90 A and what appear to be the initials of Wareham. Height 7 inches. $400-$600

338   Limoges style glaze plate decorated in 1885, showing oriental grasses and a single butterfly by Anna Bookprinter. Marks on the base include Rookwood in block letters, the date, shape number 87, G for ginger clay impressed twice and the artist's initials. Diameter 6⅜ inches. Possible small repair inside bowl. $150-$250

339   Architectural Faience tile made at Rookwood circa 1925, showing a bird perched on a flower pod. Marks on the back include the numbers E 353, 3169 Y 1, 345 and the Rookwood logo. Size 5⅞ inches square. $400-$500

340   Vellum glaze scenic vase, painted by Fred Rothenbusch in 1920. Marks on the base include the Rookwood logo, the date, shape number 900 D, V for Vellum glaze body and the artist's initials. Height 7 inches. $1000-$1500

341   Standard glaze vase decorated with Art Nouveau flowers by Adeliza Sehon in 1902. Marks on the base include the Rookwood logo, the date, shape number 765 D and the artist's initials. Height 8 inches. $400-$600

342 Mat glaze four footed bud vase with floral decoration, painted by Louise Abel in 1923. Marks on the base include the Rookwood logo, the date, shape number 2015 and the artist's monogram. Height 8⅛ inches. $350-$450

343 Standard glaze vase painted in 1901 with day lilies by Lenore Asbury. Marks on the base include the Rookwood logo, the date, shape number 901 C and the artist's initials. Height 8⅞ inches. $400-$600

344 High glaze bowl decorated inside with repeating leaves by Elizabeth Barrett in 1944. Marks on the base include the Rookwood logo, the date, shape number 6313 and the artist's initials. Height 3 inches. Some glaze scratches and grinding chips on the base. $250-$350

345 Vellum glaze vase with dogwood decoration, painted in 1905 by Lenore Asbury. Marks on the base include the Rookwood logo, the date, shape number 913 D, V for Vellum glaze, V for Vellum glaze body, a wheel ground x and the artist's initials. Height 7½ inches. Glaze flaws. $250-$350

346 Mat glaze vase with floral decoration by Jens Jensen, painted in 1930. Marks on the base include the Rookwood logo, the date, shape number 6180, a fan shaped esoteric mark and the artist's monogram. Height 5⅞ inches. $800-$1000

347   Monumental dull finish ewer decorated with pink roses by Albert Valentien in 1887. Marks on the base include $3000-$5000
      the Rookwood logo, the date, shape number 308 A, 7 W for a type of white clay, S for smear (dull) glaze and the
      artist's initials. Height 22⅞ inches. Minor glaze discolorations and a slight warping of the neck.

348   Large and impressive Standard glaze vase decorated in 1901 with the portrait of Native American by Grace $12000-$15000
      Young. Marks on the base include the Rookwood logo, the date, shape number 787 C, the title, "Susie Shot in the
      Eye, Sioux" and the artist's monogram. Height 11⅛ inches. Pictured: "Art Pottery of the United States" Paul Evans,
      1987, Second Edition, Feingold and Lewis Publishing Corp. Color plate 35.

349   Tall and impressive Vellum glaze winter scene vase, decorated in 1919 by Sallie Coyne. Marks on the base $4000-$6000
      include the Rookwood logo, the date, shape number 2441, V for Vellum glaze body and the artist's initials.
      Height 14¼ inches. Two very tight lines appear inside the rim but can not be felt or seen on the outside.

350   Large Standard glaze vase decorated with beech leaves by Albert Valentien in 1895. Marks on the base include $800-$1200
the Rookwood logo, the date and shape number 581 C. The vase is signed with the artist's full name on the side
near the base. Height 13¼ inches. Drilled and minor roughness on base.

351   Impressive Sea Green glaze vase decorated with tulips by Sallie Coyne in 1903. Marks on the base include the $3500-$4500
Rookwood logo, the date, shape number 902 C, G for Sea Green glaze and the artist's initials. Height 9 inches.
Minor glaze abrasion.

352   Large mat glaze lamp base, painted in 1902 with parrot tulips by John Dee Wareham. Marks on the base include $3000-$4000
the Rookwood logo, the date and shape number 426 Z. The artist's full name appears rather faintly on the side of
the vessel near the base. Height with ceramic cap in place, 19¾ inches. A tight firing crack encircles the base and
another runs up from the base about six inches.

353 Standard glaze whiskey jug decorated with hops by Elizabeth Lincoln in 1896. Marks on the base include the Rookwood logo, the date, shape number 767 and the artist's initials. Height 5⅝ inches. — $300-$400

354 Unusual mat glaze bowl decorated with the Rookwood logo and one flame mark in the bottom of the bowl and 14 flames encircling the shoulder of the piece, painted in 1901 by M.A. Daly. Marks on the base include the Rookwood logo, the date, shape number 29 Z and the artist's full name. Height 2½ inches. Glaze separations. — $200-$300

355 Large Commercial centuar figure, designed by William McDonald and made at Rookwood in 1931. Marks on the base include the Rookwood logo, the date, shape number 6210 and a fan shaped esoteric mark. The artist's name is cast into the side of the base. Height 14½ inches. Some tight firing lines appear in the base. — $800-$1200

356 Commercial mat glaze trivet designed by Sallie Toohey and cast at Rookwood in 1920. Marks on the back include the Rookwood logo, the date and shape number 2350. Diameter is 6 inches. — $150-$250

357 Standard glaze vase with two strap handles painted with small yellow flowers by Ed Abel in 1891. Marks on the base include the Rookwood logo, the date, shape number 604 D, W for white clay, L for light Standard glaze and the artist's initials. Height 6⅜ inches. The rim has been damaged and repaired. — $200-$300

358   Iris glaze vase painted with white irises by Carrie Steinle in 1911. Marks on the base include the Rookwood logo, the date, shape 907 F, W for white glaze and the artist's monogram. Height 7⅛ inches. $1200-$1500

359   Unusual dull finish ewer decorated with a scene of lions and lambs, incised and highlighted in black by an unknown artist in 1882. Marks on the base include Rookwood in block letters, the date, what appears to be an incised G possibly for ginger clay and the conjoined initials of the artist which appear to be some combination of B F C. Height 7⅝ inches. $1250-$1750

360   Architectural Faience tile depicting a sailing ship, made at Rookwood circa 1910. Marks on the back include the Rookwood Faience logo and the numbers 1251 Y 3. Size 12 x 12 inches. $1000-$1500

361   Standard glaze pitcher painted with nasturtiums by Jeanette Swing in 1899. Marks on the base include the Rookwood logo, the date, shape number 788 and the artist's monogram. Height 3½ inches. $200-$300

362   Standard glaze vase decorated with fruit blossoms by Anna Bookprinter in 1886. The glaze is completely saturated with Goldstone and Tiger Eye effect. Marks on the base include the Rookwood logo, the date, shape number 244, R for red clay and the artist's initials. Height 5¼ inches. Small grinding chips off the base. $500-$700

363 Yellow tinted high glaze lidded jar decorated with prunus blossoms by Arthur Conant in 1922. Marks on the base include the Rookwood logo, the date, shape number 2301 E and the artist's monogram. Height 9⅜ inches. The purchasher of this lot will be given the option of purchasing lot 368 at the same price. $2000-$3000

364 Unique Iris glaze cane handle decorated with a single dragonfly, undoubtedly the work of Carl Schmidt while at Rookwood, circa 1905. The piece is unmarked but comes from the Estate of Schmidt's daughter. Height 3⅜ inches. $300-$500

365 Pink tinted high glaze vase with floral decoration, painted by Fred Rothenbusch in 1923. Marks on the base include the Rookwood logo, the date, shape number 1343, P for Porcelain body, P possibly for pink glaze and the artist's initials. Height 4⅞ inches. $700-$900

366 Standard glaze lidded humidor decorated with bamboo, pipes, matches and cigars by Ed Diers in 1899. Marks on the base include the Rookwood logo, the date, shape number 801 and the artist's initials. The artist's initials are also found on the underside of the lid. Height 6⅝ inches. Minor glaze scratches. $700-$900

367 High glaze vase with applied holly decoration, done by an unknown artist in 1882. Marks on the base include Rookwood in block letters, the date and the artist's initials, S.S.S. Height 3⅝ inches. Tight crack descends from the rim. $150-$250

368 Yellow tinted high glaze lidded jar decorated with yellow lilies by Arthur Conant in 1922. Marks on the base include the Rookwood logo, the date, shape number 2301 E and the artist's monogram. Height 9⅜ inches. The purchasher of lot 363 will be given the option of purchasing this lot at the same price. $2000-$3000

369   Cameo glaze pitcher with floral decoration painted by Luella Perkins in 1887. Marks on the base include the Rookwood logo, the date, shape number 13, W for white clay, W for white glaze and the artist's initials. Height 6 inches. $300-$500

370   High glaze vase with floral decoration, painted by Jens Jensen in 1944. Marks on the base include the Rookwood logo, the date, shape number 2194 and the artist's monogram. Height 9⅜ inches. $800-$1000

371   Pink tinted high glaze vase, painted with trailing leaves and berries by Fred Rothenbusch in 1923. Marks on the base include the Rookwood logo, the date, shape number 1356 E, P marked twice, probably for pink glaze, and the artist's monogram. Height 7⅛ inches. $700-$900

372   Original Rookwood high glaze lamp decorated in 1952 with magnolia, very much in the style of Loretta Holtkamp. Marks on the base include the Rookwood logo, the date, a cast hole for electrical fittings and shape number 925 B. An original Rookwood paper label is affixed to the side of the vase. Height of ceramic portion is 13¼ inches. Rookwood made many lamps in the late 40's and early 50's using fittings from the Crest Lamp Company. $400-$600

373   Standard glaze portrait of a Saint Bernard, painted by E.T. Hurley in 1899. Marks on the base include the Rookwood logo, the date, shape number 512 B and the artist's initials. Height 9⅝ inches. $1000-$1500

374   Aventurine glaze vase signed by Carl Schmidt and dated 1910. Marks on the base include the Rookwood logo, $500-$700
       the date, shape number 932 F, V for Vellum glaze body and the artist's monogram. Height 6¼ inches. Minor
       grinding chips on the base. Rookwood's experiments with Aventurine glaze seem to begin about 1918 and it is
       possible that this piece was reglazed at the Pottery several years after it was first fired.

375   Vellum glaze vase decorated with a wooded landscape in a rainstorm by Ed Diers in 1917. Marks on the base $1200-$1800
       include the Rookwood logo, the date, shape number 589 E and the artist's initials. Height 9 inches. Uncrazed.

376   Standard glaze basket decorated with fall leaves by Amelia Sprague in 1893. Marks on the base include the $200-$400
       Rookwood logo, the date, shape number 337, W for white clay and the artist's monogram. Greatest distance
       across is 9¼ inches. Minor glaze scratches.

377   Single Commercial blackbird bookend with an unusual polychromed glaze, made at Rookwood in 1923. Marks $200-$300
       on the base include the Rookwood logo, the date and shape number 2658. Height 5¼ inches.

378   Mat glaze vase with floral decoration, painted in 1924 by Vera Tischler. Marks on the base include the $300-$400
       Rookwood logo, the date, shape number 2268 E and the artist's initials. Height 5¼ inches.

379 Blue tinted high glaze Commercial vase with multicolored background, made at Rookwood in 1945. Marks on the base include the Rookwood logo, the date, shape number 6761 and the number 59. Height 6⅛ inches. Minor grinding chips on base and small dark line at rim. $200-$300

380 Lightly crystaline mat glaze vase with Art Deco leaf decoration, painted in heavy slip by Elizabeth Barrett in 1930. Marks on the base include the Rookwood logo, the date, shape number 130, a fan shaped esoteric mark and the artist's monogram. Height 6⅛ inches. $400-$600

381 Standard glaze tile decorated with dogwood by Lenore Asbury in 1898. The artist's initials appear in the lower right hand corner. Marks on the back include the Rookwood logo, the date and shape number X 421 X. Affixed to the frame is a paper label from Traxel and Maas, Art Dealers, 206 W. Fourth Street, Cincinnati, O. Size 6 x 6 inches. A burst glaze bubble and several minor scratches appear on the surface. $700-$900

382 Mat glaze vase with incised stylized floral decoration, done in 1912 by William Hentschel. Marks on the base include the Rookwood logo, the date, shape number 1358 D and the artist's monogram. Height 8½ inches. $300-$500

383 Vellum glaze vase with a lakeside woodland scene painted by Carl Schmidt in 1917. Marks on the base include the Rookwood logo, the date, shape number 2102, V for Vellum glaze and the artist's initials. Height 6⅝ inches. $1000-$1250

384   Vellum glaze vase, decorated with a twilight woodland scene by Lenore Asbury in 1919. Marks on the base include the Rookwood logo, the date, shape number 922 C, V for Vellum glaze body and the artist's initials. Height 9½ inches. $1200-$1500

385   Standard glaze flower boat decorated with crisply painted flowers by Albert Valentien in 1889. Marks on the base include the Rookwood logo, the date, shape number 369, W for white clay, L for light Standard glaze and the artist's initials. Height 9⅛ inches. $900-$1200

386   Architectural Faience tile depicting a spanish moss covered tree, made at Rookwood circa 1915. Marks on the back include the Rookwood Faience logo, the numbers 3027 Y 4 and the number 6 in a circle. Size 12 x 12 inches. Minor edge chips. $1000-$1500

387   Unusual painted and incised mat glaze vase, decorated in 1921 with stylized lilies by Elizabeth Lincoln. Marks on the base include the Rookwood logo, the date, the partially obscured shape number 904 C and the artist's initials. Height 12⅛ inches. Drilled. $600-$800

388   Iris glaze vase depicting a group of geese taking flight, painted in 1896 by Olga Reed. Marks on the base include the Rookwood logo, the date, shape number 808, W for white glaze and the artist's initials. Height 7½ inches. $2000-$3000

389   Standard glaze pitcher painted with leaves and berries by Katherine Hickman in 1896. Marks on the base include the Rookwood logo, the date, shape number 607 C and the artist's initials. Height 4⅞ inches. $300-$400

390   Dull finish Spanish water jug decorated in 1883 with a spider, several flying bats and a large crescent moon by an unknown artist. Marks on the base include Rookwood in block letters, the date, shape number 41, Y for yellow clay and an impressed kiln. Height 9⅛ inches. $400-$600

391   Standard glaze four footed basket decorated with wild roses, painted in 1888 by Artus Van Briggle. Marks on the base include the Rookwood logo, the date, shape number 45 C, S for sage green clay, L for light Standard glaze and the artist's initials. Height 5 inches. Small chip on one foot. $400-$600

392   High glaze vase with iris decoration, painted in 1946 by Jens Jensen. Marks on the base include the Rookwood logo, the date, shape number 2194, an obscured group of numbers and the artist's monogram. Height 9¼ inches. $700-$900

393   High glaze Commercial vase designed with irises in relief by Harriet Wilcox and cast at Rookwood in 1930. Marks on the base include the Rookwood logo, the date, shape number 6171, a fan shaped esoteric mark and the cast initials of the artist. Height 15¾ inches. Minor grinding chips on the base. $250-$350

394   Iris glaze vase decorated with blue irises by Sallie Coyne in 1905. Marks on the base include the Rookwood logo, the date, shape number 907 D, W for white glaze, a wheel ground x and the artist's monogram. Height 11⅛ inches. Small burst glaze bubble near rim and minor underglaze slip separation. $2000-$3000

395   Standard glaze ewer with jonquil decoration, painted in 1902 by Virginia Demarest. Marks on the base include the Rookwood logo, the date, shape number 496 B, a wheel ground x and the artist's initials. Height 11¼ inches. Old repairs to the lip and handle. $400-$600

396   Yellow tinted high glaze vase with floral decoration, done in 1938 by Margaret McDonald. Marks on the base include the Rookwood logo, the date, S for special shape, a large triangular shaped esoteric mark and the artist's monogram. Height 4⅝ inches. $400-$600

397   Lightly crystaline mat glaze vase decorated in heavy slip with Art Deco patterns by Elizabeth Barrett in 1927. Marks on the base include the Rookwood logo, the date, shape number 6013 and the artist's monogram. Height 6¾ inches. $900-$1100

398   Unusual Standard glaze vase decorated with apple blossoms growing from a thick branch, painted in 1895 by Charles Dibowski. Marks on the base include the Rookwood logo, the date, shape number 716 C, W for white clay, L for light Standard glaze and the artist's monogram. Height 9¼ inches. Minor glaze scratches and a small burst bubble. $600-$800

399　Iris glaze vase with daisy decoration, painted by Edith Noonan in 1904. Marks on the base include the Rookwood logo, the date, shape number 935 E, W for white glaze and the artist's initials. Height 6¼ inches. ⟶ $400-$600

400　Standard glaze ewer painted with chrysanthemums by Amelia Sprague in 1888. Marks on the base include the Rookwood logo, the date, shape number 101 D, R for red clay, D for dark Standard glaze and the artist's initials. Height 6½ inches. Some minor glaze blisters and a small flake off the rim. ⟶ $200-$300

401　Standard glaze creamer with leaf and berry decoration, painted by Katherine Hickman in 1899. Marks on the base include the Rookwood logo, the date, shape number 43 and the artist's monogram. Height 2 inches. ⟶ $150-$200

402　Vellum glaze scenic plaque decorated with a reflected woodland scene by Carl Schmidt in 1915. The artist's name appears in the lower right hand corner. Marks on the back include the Rookwood logo, the date and V for Vellum glaze body. Size is 5 x 9¼ inches. Several glaze blisters on the surface. ⟶ $1750-$2250

403　Unusual Mat glaze vase decorated with peonies on a black ground by Kataro Shirayamadani in 1934. Marks on the base include the Rookwood logo, the date, S for special shape and the artist's cypher. Height 5⅞ inches. ⟶ $800-$1200

404　Standard glaze vase with passages of Tiger Eye, decorated with wild roses by Luelle Perkins in 1888. Marks on the base include the Rookwood logo, the date, shape number 535 E, Y for yellow clay, L for light Standard glaze and the artist's monogram. Height 6⅜ inches. Minor roughness on rim. ⟶ $300-$500

405   Standard glaze vase decorated with poppies by Ed Diers in 1901. Marks on the base include the Rookwood logo, the date, shape number 900 C and the artist's initials. Height 8 inches. One burst glaze bubble on the side of the vase. $500-$700

406   High glaze cigarette lighter and ash tray, decorated respectively in 1946 with a Dalmation and an Airdale by Flora King. Marks on the bases of both pieces include the Rookwood logo, the date and the artist's initials. The cigarette lighter is marked with shape number 6922 and the numbers 221 and 65 while the ash tray is marked with shape number 6922 A and the number 215. Height of the lighter is 3¾ inches. $250-$350

407   Cameo glaze plate decorated with daisies by Olga Reed in 1891. Marks on the base include the Rookwood logo, the date, shape number 284, W for white clay, W for white glaze and the artist's initials. Diameter is 7⅝ inches. $200-$300

408   Limoges style glaze perfume jug, decorated in 1884 by an unknown artist with oriental grasses and a single butterfly. Marks on the base include Rookwood in block letters, the date, shape number 60 and G for ginger clay. Height 4½ inches. Chip off base. $125-$175

409   Early vellum glaze vase with mistletoe decoration, painted for the Louisiana Purchase Exposition in 1904 by Lenore Asbury. Marks on the base include the Rookwood logo, the date, shape number 33 EZ, V for Vellum glaze body, a paper label which reads, "Rookwood Pottery, Cincinnati, U.S.A. 1904 Louisiana Purchase Exposition, St. Louis" and the artist's initials. Height 5⅛ inches. $400-$600

410   Vellum glaze vase decorated with a band of apple blossoms by Lenore Asbury in 1913. Marks on the base $300-$400
include the Rookwood logo, the date, shape number 1917, V for Vellum glaze body, V for Vellum glaze and the
artist's initials. Height 6 inches. Small glaze flaw at shoulder.

411   Standard glaze mug decorated with poppies by Ed Diers in 1898. Marks on the base include the Rookwood logo, $300-$400
the date, shape number S 1445 and the artist's initials. Height 4 inches. Minor glaze scratches.

412   Standard glaze vase decorated by Amelia Sprague in 1895 with Virginia creepers. Marks on the base include the $500-$700
Rookwood logo, the date, shape number 433 B and the artist's monogram. Height 7⅞ inches.

413   High glaze mug decorated by E.P. Cranch in 1892 with a panorama of the evils of drinking and carousing which $500-$700
lead to punishment and ultimately death. Marks on the base include the Rookwood logo, the date, shape number
587, W for white clay, the date incised and the artist's initials. Height 4¼ inches. According to Edwin J. Kircher,
Cranch was the Grandma Moses of Rookwood. Mr. Kircher is possibly the real Grandpa Moses.

414   Vellum glaze vase decorated by Carl Schmidt in 1917 with crisply painted lilies of the valley. Marks on the base $1000-$1500
include the Rookwood logo, the date, shape number 904 E, V for Vellum glaze and the artist's monogram. Height
7⅜ inches.

415 Standard glaze pitcher with fruit blossom decoration, painted in 1889 by Harriet Wilcox. Marks on the base include the Rookwood logo, the date, shape number 259, S for sage green clay and the artist's initials. Height 5¼ inches. $400-$600

416 Mat glaze vase with pine cone decoration, done in 1928 by Elizabeth Lincoln. Marks on the base include the Rookwood logo, the date, shape number 915 C and the artist's initials. Height 7⅞ inches. $500-$700

417 Unmatched cup and saucer, made by Haviland & Company and decorated by Mary Louise McLaughlin in 1888 and 1890. Marks on the cup include the Haviland logo, the artist's initials and the date, 1888. Marks on the saucer include the Haviland logo, the artist's initials and the date, 1890. Height 2⅜ inches. A similar cup and saucer appear as item 33 in the 1989 Everson Museum of Art catalog, "Fragile Blossoms, Enduring Earth". $300-$500

418 Standard glaze vase with tulip decoration, painted in 1900 by Virginia Demarest. Marks on the base include the Rookwood logo, the date, shape number 817 and the artist's initials. Height 7⅞ inches. $400-$600

419 High glaze porcelain bodied vase painted with a band of pink blossoms on a trellis, done in 1918 by Harriet Wilcox. Marks on the base include the Rookwood logo, the date, shape number 1278 F, P for porcelain body, the number 2416 and the artist's initials. Height 7⅛ inches. Uncrazed $600-$800

420   Rare and unusual Aventurine glaze vase decorated with three incised and painted stylized irises by Sara Sax in 1922. Marks on the base include the Rookwood logo, the date, shape number 1779 and the artist's monogram. Height 7½ inches. Grinding chip on base. $2000-$3000

421   Standard glaze three handled mug painted with the portrait of a Native American by Adeliza Sehon in 1901. Marks on the base include the Rookwood logo, the date, shape number 659 C, a wheel ground x, the inscription, "Three Fingers - Cheyennes (sic)" and the artist's initials. Height 6 inches. Minor glaze scratches. $2000-$3000

422   Standard glaze vase painted by Kataro Shirayamadani in 1894 with four cranes standing in a grassy marsh. Marks on the base include the Rookwood logo, the date, shape number 750 C, W for white clay and the artist's cypher. Height 5¼ inches. Very minor glaze pooling and glaze scratches. $3000-$4000

423   Yellow tinted high glaze vase decorated with a repeating band of stylized flowers on the shoulder by Arthur Conant in 1921. Marks on the base include the Rookwood logo, the date, shape number 614 F, a wheel ground x and the artist's monogram. Height 6¼ inches. A tight five inch vertical crack is visible in the middle of the body. $300-$500

424   Standard glaze vase with extremely intricate silver overlay, painted in 1895 by Elizabeth Lincoln with small yellow flowers. Marks on the base include the Rookwood logo, the date, shape number 551 and the artist's initials. Height 6 inches. $2500-$3500

END OF SATURDAY SESSION

SUNDAY
MAY 31th
1992
LOTS 425-853

425   High glaze vase with repeating geometric patterns, decorated by Lorinda Epply circa 1944. The interior of the vase is covered with a Bengal Brown type glaze. Marks on the base include the Rookwood logo, the partially obscured date, shape number 6305 and the artist's monogram. Height 4⅞ inches. $400-$600

426   Cameo glaze cup and saucer painted with daisies by Ed Abel in 1891. Marks on the base of both pieces include the Rookwood logo, the date, shape number 291, W for white clay, W for white glaze and the artist's initials. Height 2¼ inches. $200-$300

427   Standard glaze whiskey jug with corn decor, painted in 1896 by Anna Valentien. Marks on the base include the Rookwood logo, the date, shape number 677, a small triangular shaped esoteric mark and the artist's initials. A wheel ground V appears on the side of the piece near the base, a variation on the usual "x". Height 9⅜ inches. Several glaze blisters in the decoration. $200-$300

428   Unusual potpourri jar with a dull finish over a hammered clay ground, decorated with fruit blossoms and a small butterfly by Laura Fry in 1883. Marks on the base include Rookwood in block letters, the date, Y for yellow clay, two small impressed kiln marks and the artist's monogram. Height 3¾ inches. This piece is from Rookwood Pottery's Museum, descending in the family of one of Rookwood's last owners and has never been offered for sale until now. $500-$700

429   Standard glaze vase decorated with small yellow flowers by Mattie Foglesong in 1898. Marks on the base include the Rookwood logo, the date, shape number 162 D, a small star shaped esoteric mark and the artist's monogram. Height 5⅛ inches. $200-$300

430   Commercial vase with some hand outlining, possibly by a Junior Decorator, done at Rookwood in 1946. Marks on the base include the Rookwood logo, the date, shape number 6455 and what may be an artist's initials. Height 6¼ inches. $200-$300

431   Standard glaze whiskey jug with crisp floral decoration, painted in 1893 by Olga Reed. Marks on the base include the Rookwood logo, the date, shape number 694 and the artist's initials. Height 6⅜ inches. $500-$700

432 Vellum glaze vase with a band of fruit blossoms, decorated by E.T. Hurley in 1927. Marks on the base include the Rookwood logo, the date, shape number 363, V for Vellum glaze and the artist's initials. Height 6 inches. Uncrazed. $500-$700

433 Limoges style glaze lidded chocolate pot painted in 1884 with grasses and a single butterfly by an unknown artist. Marks on the base include Rookwood in block letters, the date, shape number 80 A and R for red clay. Height 8⅛ inches. $700-$900

434 Cameo glaze creamer with floral decoration, painted in 1888 by Amelia Sprague. Marks on the base include the Rookwood logo, the date, shape number 455, W for white clay, W for white glaze and the artist's initials. Height 2⅜ inches. $100-$150

435 Standard glaze vase decorated with exotic orange flowers by Albert Valentien in 1894. Marks on the base include the Rookwood logo, the date, shape number 640, a partial Rookwood Salesroom label and the artist's initials. Height 10¼ inches. Firing cracks in the base. $700-$1000

436 Standard glaze vase with floral decoration, painted in 1902 by Grace Hall. Marks on the base include the Rookwood logo, the date, shape number 913 E and the artist's initials. Height 5⅞ inches. $300-$400

437 High glaze vase with floral decor, done in 1946 by Jens Jensen. Marks on the base include the Rookwood logo, the date, S for special shape number, the number 8787 and the artist's monogram. Height 7⅛ inches. Uncrazed. $400-$600

438 Mat glaze vase with two handles, painted with hanging fruit blossoms by Elizabeth Lincoln in 1923. Marks on the base include the Rookwood logo, the date, shape number 2708 and the artist's initials. Height 8 inches. $300-$500

439   Standard glaze whiskey jug painted with poppies and wheat by Virginia Demarest in 1900. Marks on the base $600-$800
include the Rookwood logo, the date, shape number S 1664 and the artist's initials. Height 8½ inches.

440   Vellum glaze vase with floral decoration, painted in 1917 by Carrie Steinle. Marks on the base include the $700-$900
Rookwood logo, the date, shape number 1872 and the artist's initials. Height 7⅞ inches. Uncrazed.

441   Cameo glaze plate with floral decoration, painted in 1886 by M.A. Daly. Marks on the back include the $300-$400
Rookwood logo, the date, shape number 317, R for red clay and the artist's initials. Greatest distance across is
10¼ inches. Glaze scratches.

442   Early carved Vellum glaze bowl, decorated with oak leaves and acorns by Kataro Shirayamadani in 1904. Marks $500-$700
on the base include the Rookwood logo, the date, shape number 100 Z, a leaf shaped esoteric mark, a wheel
ground x and the artist's cypher. Height 3¼ inches. Glaze flaw in side of bowl.

443   Limoges style glaze pitcher decorated with birds, bats, grasses, a crescent moon and an owl by E.G. Winslow in $400-$600
1882. Marks on the base include Rookwood in block letters, the date and the artist's initials. Height 7⅜ inches.
Flake on rim has been repaired.

444   Unusual mat glaze advertising paperweight made at Rookwood in 1940. Marks on the back include the $150-$250
Rookwood logo, the date and the title, "Potter At The Wheel Rookwood Cincinnati Ohio". Diameter is 3⅜ inches.

445   Standard glaze vase decorated by M.A. Daly in 1897 with three cranes resting in a grassy area. Marks on the base $2000-$3000
include the Rookwood logo, the date, shape number 589 D, a diamond shaped esoteric mark and the artist's
initials. Height 7⅛ inches. Minor roughness on base.

446   Colorful Vellum glaze scenic vase, decorated in 1925 by E.T. Hurley. Marks on the base include the Rookwood $2500-$3000
logo, the date, shape number 1126 C, V for Vellum glaze and the artist's initials. Height 9¼ inches. Minor glaze
bubbles and slight glaze roughness at base. Uncrazed.

447   Standard glaze candle holder, decorated with wild roses by Caroline Bonsall in 1903. Marks on the base include $300-$500
the Rookwood logo, the date, shape number 635 and the artist's initials. Height 2¾ inches.

448   Large and unusual Rookwood water cooler decorated with a group of polar bears discussing the fate of an $600-$800
unfortunate fish, painted circa 1881, possibly by Edward P. Cranch. There are no marks on the piece but a similar
example decorated by Cranch is pictured in Herbert Peck's "The Second Book of Rookwood Pottery" on page 6.
Height 19⅝ inches. One handle is broken and glued, several chips exist inside the rim and a spider crack can be
seen in the base.

449   Large carved and painted mat glaze vase, decorated by William Hentschel with repeating patterns and emblems $700-$900
in 1914. Marks on the base include the Rookwood logo, the date, shape number 1369 C and the artist's
monogram. Height 11⅛ inches.

450   Rookwood high glaze double sided advertising sign, made in 1947. Marks on the base include the Rookwood $500-$700
logo, the date, shape number 2788 and the number 5. Height 3¾ inches.

451   Unusual drip glaze vase made at Rookwood circa 1945. Marks on the base include the Rookwood logo, the $150-$250
obscured date, an inscribed circle and shape number 2634. Height 9⅞ inches. Minor grinding roughness on base.

452 Mat glaze vase with four incised and painted dragonflies, decorated by Sallie Coyne in 1906. Marks on the base $800-$1200
     include the Rookwood logo, the date, shape number 942 C, V for Vellum glaze body and the artist's initials.
     Height 6⅛ inches. Tiny glaze flake at edge of one dragonfly wing.

453 Limoges style glaze perfume jug painted by William McDonald in 1883 with swallows in flight. Marks on the $300-$500
     base include Rookwood in block letters, the date, shape number 60, G for ginger clay, an impressed kiln mark,
     an impressed anchor mark and the artist's initials. Height 4½ inches. This piece is from Rookwood Pottery's
     Museum, descending in the family of one of Rookwood's last owners and has never been offered for sale until
     now.

454 Vellum glaze plaque decorated with a view of Point Loma, near San Diego, California, painted in 1916 by Lenore $1250-$1750
     Asbury. The artist's initials appear in the lower left hand corner. Marks on the back include the Rookwood logo,
     the date and V for Vellum glaze body. Affixed to the frame is an original Rookwood label with the title, "Point
     Loma, San Diego, Cal. L. Asbury". Size 5⅛ x 8⅛ inches. Accompanying the plaque is a postcard from 1915
     showing the same view of Point Loma.

455 Standard glaze bowl with leaf and berry decoration, done in 1894 by Bertha Cranch. Marks on the base include $300-$400
     the Rookwood logo, the date, shape number 703 C, W for white clay, L for light Standard glaze and the artist's
     initials. Height 2 inches.

456 Rare Losanti oval porcelain portrait plaque, decorated with the profile of a young woman by Mary Louise $500-$700
     McLaughlin. The artist's monogram appears at the right center edge. Marks on the back include Losanti, the
     number 406 and the artist's monogram. Losanti pieces were produced between 1898 and 1906. Height 3¼
     inches.

457 Blue tinted high glaze vase with cross hatch design decorated by Loretta Holtkamp and Earl Menzel in 1953. $400-$600
     Marks on the base include the Rookwood logo, the date, S for special shape, Earl Menzel's whorl signature and
     the initials of both artist's. Height 7⅛ inches.

458 Standard glaze vase with lily of the valley decoration, painted by Carl Schmidt in 1900. Marks on the base $400-$600
     include the Rookwood logo, the date, shape number 882 and the artist's monogram. Height 5 inches.

459   Multicolor drip glaze vase made at Rookwood in 1932. Marks on the base include the Rookwood logo, the date $250-$350
       and S for special shape. Height 6¼ inches.

460   Limoges style glaze perfume jug decorated with several swallows in flight by Martin Rettig in 1883. Marks on the $300-$400
       base include Rookwood in block letters, the date, shape number 61, G for ginger clay, a small kiln and the artist's
       initials. Height 4⅛ inches. Tiny flake off base.

461   Standard glaze bowl with pansy decoration, painted in 1899 by Carrie Steinle. Marks on the base include the $400-$600
       Rookwood logo, the date, shape number 494 B and the artist's monogram. Height 3¾ inches.

462   Standard glaze ewer with hops decoration, done in 1902 by Marianne Mitchell. Marks on the base include the $300-$400
       Rookwood logo, the date, shape number 498 D and the artist's initials. Height 4¼ inches

463   Unusual Vellum glaze vase decorated with stylized crocus bulbs and flowers, painted in 1905 by Anna Valentien. $800-$1000
       Marks on the base include the Rookwood logo, the date, shape number 950 E, V for Vellum glaze body and the
       artist's initials. Height 6¾ inches.

464 Cameo glaze pitcher decorated with wild roses by Amelia Sprague in 1889. Marks on the base include the Rookwood logo, the date, shape number 343, G for ginger clay, W for white glaze and the artist's initials. Height 7¼ inches. This piece may have originally come with a lid. $300-$500

465 Mat glaze vase decorated with roses by Elizabeth Lincoln in 1925. Marks on the base include the Rookwood logo, the date, shape number 614 E and the artist's initials. Height 8⅜ inches. $400-$600

466 Standard glaze plate decorated with dancing mice by Anna Valentien in 1890. Marks on the back include the Rookwood logo, the date, shape number 59 P, W for white clay, L for light Standard glaze and the artist's initials. Diameter is 7 inches. Moderate glaze scratches. $400-$600

467 Vellum glaze vase with apple blossom decoration, painted by Lenore Asbury in 1905. Marks on the base include the Rookwood logo, the date, shape number 925 D, V for Vellum glaze body, a wheel ground X and the artist's initials. Height 8⅛ inches. Minor glaze peppering. $400-$600

468 Rare decorated Aventurine glaze vase, painted with a band of stylized flowers by Lorinda Epply in 1922. Marks on the base include the Rookwood logo, the date, shape number 1926 and the artist's monogram. Height 6⅛ inches. $700-$900

469 Good Standard glaze tankard decorated with the portrait of actor, Joe Jefferson in the role of Caleb Plummer, $2500-$3500
painted by his friend Sturgis Laurence in 1897. Marks on the base include the Rookwood logo, the date, shape
number 820, a small triangular esoteric mark and the inscription, "Jos. Jefferson as 'Caleb Plummer' Sturgis
Laurence — June, 1897". Height 8⅛ inches. Pictured: "Rookwood Its Golden Era of Art Pottery 1880 -1929"
Published by Edwin J. Kircher and Barbara and Joseph Agranoff, 1969. Color photo on Plate 4, Item 1, Middle
Row.

470 Cameo glaze vase decorated with small white flowers and Victorian patterns by Kataro Shirayamadani in 1887. $700-$900
Marks on the base include the Rookwood logo, the date, shape number 30 C, W for white clay, W for white
glaze, a Glover Collection label, number 1107 and the early mark of the artist. Height 6 inches. A two inch line
descends from the rim.

471 Unusual high glaze bowl decorated with abstract flowers by Jens Jensen in 1945. Marks on the base include the $600-$800
Rookwood logo, the date, shape number 6313, the number 8352 and the artist's monogram. Diameter is 8½
inches.

472 Standard glaze vase decorated in 1900 with small orange flowers by Howard Altman. Marks on the base include $250-$350
the Rookwood logo, the date, shape number 785 E and the artist's initials. Height 6⅜ inches.

473 Iris glaze vase in shades of blue, possibly a test piece, done in 1906 by Carl Schmidt. Marks on the base include $300-$500
the Rookwood logo, the date, shape number 821 F, a series of four dots in a line and the artist's monogram.
Height 5⅛ inches.

474 Iris glaze vase decorated with orchids by Carl Schmidt in 1903. Marks on the base include the Rookwood logo, the date, shape number S 1756 and the artist's logo. Height 7¾ inches. $2500-$3500

475 Standard glaze pitcher with floral decoration, painted in 1894 by Bertha Cranch. Marks on the base include the Rookwood logo, the date, shape number 692, W for white clay and the artist's initials. Height 3⅝ inches. Tight line in handle. $200-$300

476 Large Vellum glaze scenic plaque painted in 1919 by Sallie Coyne. The artist's monogram appears in the lower left hand corner. Marks on the back include the Rookwood logo and the date. Size 9⅜ x 14⅝ inches. $6000-$8000

477 Limoges style glaze perfume jug decorated by Martin Rettig in 1883 with bamboo and a single butterfly. Marks on the base include Roowkood in block letters, the date, shape number 60, G for ginger clay, a small impressed kiln mark and the artist's initials. Height 4⅞ inches. Burst glaze bubble and small flake off base. $200-$400

478 High glaze rectangular vase decorated with carved and painted orchids by Kataro Shirayamadani in 1946. Marks on the base include the Rookwood logo, the date, shape number 6292 C, a wheel ground x, the number 6346 and the artist's initials. Height 7⅜ inches. $800-$1000

479   Standard glaze vase decorated with nasturtium by Edith Noonan in 1903. Marks on the base include the Rookwood logo, the date, shape number 80 B and the artist's initials. Height 6¾ inches. Small glaze flake off the base and some glaze scratches. $300-$500

480   Dull glaze perfume jug decorated with incised and fired on gold floral motifs by Harriet Wenderoth in 1883. Marks on the base include Rookwood in block letters, the date, shape number 61, R for red clay, a small impressed kiln mark and the artist's initials. Height 4⅝ inches. This piece appears to have been made without a handle. $200-$300

481   Iris glaze vase decorated with grapes by Irene Bishop in 1903. Marks on the base include the Rookwood logo, the date, shape number 942 C, W for white glaze, a circular paper label which reads, "Davis Collamore & Co. Ltd. Fifth Ave. and 37th St. New York" and the artist's initials. Height 6¼ inches. Some glaze scratches. $800-$1000

482   Good Standard glaze vase decorated with a dragon by M.A. Daly in 1894. The glaze shows large passages of Goldstone. Marks on the base include the Rookwood logo, the date, shape number 763 C, R for red clay, D for dark Standard glaze and the artist's initials. Height 5⅝ inches. Small area of slightly loose glaze on back. $3000-$5000

483   Vellum glaze vase decorated in 1907 by Elizabeth Lincoln with white poppies. Marks on the base include the Rookwood logo, the date, shape number 932 E, V for Vellum glaze body, V for Vellum glaze and the artist's initials. Height 7¾ inches. $500-$800

484   Standard glaze oil lamp with early brass fittings, painted in 1891 with lilacs by Albert Valentien. Marks on the $600-$800
base include the Rookwood logo, the date, shape number 576 C, W for white clay and the artist's initials. Height
of ceramic portion is 12 inches. Drilled for fittings and scratched near the base. The fittings are old but probably
did not originate at Rookwood.

485   Commercial high glaze lidded jar designed by Arthur Conant with intricate repeating patterns of flowers and $700-$900
rabbits and made at Rookwood in 1920. Marks on the base include the Rookwood logo, the date, shape number
2450 and the molded monogram of the designer. Height 13¾ inches.

486   Commercial vase with Aventurine glaze, made at Rookwood in 1959. Marks on the base include the Rookwood $250-$350
logo, the date, shape number S 2180 and the words, "Rookwood Cinti, O.". Height 6¼ inches.

487   Vellum glaze vase decorated with vining flowers by Harriet Wilcox in 1925. Marks on the base include the $1200-$1800
Rookwood logo, the date, shape number 2785 and the artist's initials. Height 13½ inches.

488   Standard glaze vase with tulip decoration, painted in 1903 by Carrie Steinle. Marks on the base include the $400-$600
Rookwood logo, the date, shape number 932 D and the artist's initials. Height 8⅝ inches.

489 Monumental and rare Limoges style glaze vase decorated with a heavily carved and painted dragon, done by $40000-$60000
Maria Longworth Nichols in 1881. Marks incised in the base include Rookwood Pottery Cin O and the date,
1881. Height 15 inches. Small firing cracks in the base and some minor chips on the surface. Exhibitions: "Fragile
Blossoms, Enduring Earth" The Everson Museum of Art, 1989, Item 58 in the catalog, Color plate on page 79.
"From Our Native Clay" The American Ceramics Art Society, 1987, Item 79 in the catalog, Color plate on page
56.

490   Standard glaze vase decorated by Carl Schmidt in 1898 with mushrooms. Marks on the base include the $250-$350
         Rookwood logo, the date, shape number 534 C and the artist's monogram. Height 6⅞ inches. A loose crack
         descends from the rim.

491   Rare Losanti vase done by Mary Louise McLaughlin with flowing glaze of green, black and red over white. Marks $2000-$3000
         on the base include the name Losanti and the artist's monogram. Losanti pieces were produced between 1898
         and 1906. Height 3 inches.

492   Rare Iris glaze vase with dandelion decoration, carved and painted in 1900 by John Dee Wareham. Marks on the $2000-$3000
         base include the Rookwood logo, the date, shape number S 1531 A, a wheel ground x, and the artist's initials.
         Affixed to the base is most of an original Rookwood paper label from the Paris International Exposition in 1900.
         (See Peck, "The Book of Rookwood Pottery", photo on page 159). Height 7⅜ inches. Very minor pits and glaze
         discolorations.

493   High glaze perfume jug decorated by an unknown artist with incised flowers in 1882. Marks on the base include $250-$350
         Rookwood in block letters, the date and Y for yellow clay. Height 5 inches. Minor underglaze flaws.

494   Vellum glaze vase decorated with a woodland scene by E.T. Hurley in 1921. Marks on the base include the $900-$1100
         Rookwood logo, the date, shape number 925 E, V for Vellum glaze body and the artist's initials. Height 7¼
         inches. Minor glaze bubbles.

495   Standard glaze pitcher decorated with mums by Harriette Strafer in 1892. Marks on the base include the $300-$400
Rookwood logo, the date, shape number 607, W for white clay, L for light Standard glaze and the artist's
monogram. Height 4¼ inches.

496   Coromandel glaze vase made at Rookwood in 1932. Marks on the base include the Rookwood logo, the date and $400-$600
shape number 635. Height 6¼ inches.

497   Mat glaze vase with abstract floral decoration, painted in 1921 by C.S. Todd. Marks on the base include the $150-$200
Rookwood logo, the date, shape number 2105 and the artist's initials. Height 4⅜ inches. Tiny flake off rim and
chip off base.

498   Standard glaze basket decorated with a spray of yellow flowers by Grace Young in 1886. Marks on the base $100-$150
include Rookwood in block letters, the date, shape number 228 E, S for sage green clay and the artist's
monogram. Size 3½ inches square.

499   Pair of Rook bookends, made at Rookwood in 1945 with an unusual red and green mottled glaze. Marks on the $300-$500
base include the Rookwood logo, the date and shape number 2275. Height of each, 5 inches. Minor grinding
chips on the bases.

500   Standard glaze vase with daisy decoration, done by Elizabeth Lincoln in 1904. Marks on the base include the Rookwood logo, the date, shape number 901 C and the artist's initials. Height 8⅜ inches. $500-$700

501   Standard glaze vase with nicely painted small yellow flowers, done in 1900 by Katherine Hickman. Marks on the base include the Rookwood logo, the date, shape number 816 E and the artist's monogram. Height 6⅛ inches. Minor glaze scratches. $300-$500

502   Vellum glaze scenic plaque decorated by Carl Schmidt in 1916. The artist's name appears in the lower right hand corner. Marks on the back include the Rookwood logo, the date and V for Vellum glaze body. Size 11 x 8⅜ inches. $3000-$5000

503   Bengal Brown glaze vase made at Rookwood in 1957. Marks on the base include the Rookwood logo, the date, shape number 6514 E and the words, "ROOKWOOD CINTI, O.". Height 3½ inches. $100-$200

504   Rare and impressive Iris glaze vase with peacock feather decoration, done in 1911 by Carl Schmidt. Marks on the base include the Rookwood logo, the date, shape number 30 D, W for white glaze, a wheel ground x and the artist's monogram. Height 9⅜ inches. A repair covers some problem at the rim, possibly a technical flaw which caused the piece to be xed. $3000-$4000

505   Nacreous glaze vase done in 1915 by Sara Sax. Marks on the base include the Rookwood logo, the date, shape number 2182, the letter Y and the artist's monogram. Height 4¾ inches. $500-$700

506   Commercial vase with unusual flat black crystaline glaze and maroon interior, done at Rookwood in 1922. Marks on the base include the Rookwood logo, the date and shape number 1123. Height 6 inches. $200-$300

507   Unusual hand painted china tea service consisting of creamer, sugar bowl and tray, decorated in the Dresden pattern by Clara Chipman Newton circa 1880. The creamer and sugar bowl are marked T & V France and the tray is marked Leonard Vienna Austria. All three pieces are signed Clara Chipman Newton Cincinnati. Height of tallest piece is 3¼ inches. $400-$600

508   Standard glaze two handled vase decorated with wild roses by Amelia Sprague in 1898. Marks on the base include the Rookwood logo, the date, shape number 800 C, a wheel ground x and the artist's monogram. Height 8⅞ inches. Minor glaze scratches and flaws. $400-$600

509   Rare and exotic glaze vase, decorated by Maria Longworth Nichols Storer in 1896 with a single honey bee. Marks on the base include the Rookwood logo, the date and the artist's initials. Height 5⅛ inches. Although very similar to another Storer piece in the sale, item 680, this work bears the Rookwood logo as well as Mrs. Storer's own marks. The glazing on both pieces is quite unlike anything done commercially at Rookwood, making it seem likely that Mrs. Storer carried on private experiments in her studio at Rookwood. Illustrated: Art and Antiques, July - August 1980, page 79. $1000-$1500

510 Standard glaze potpourri jar with areas of Tiger Eye effect, decorated with oriental floral patterns by M.A. Daly in 1888. Marks on the base include the Rookwood logo, the date, shape number 400, R for red clay, L for light Standard glaze and the artist's initials. Height 6 inches. Some roughness on the rim and a few small burst glaze bubbles. — $500-$700

511 Mat glaze commercial reticulated bowl made at Rookwood in 1910 with ferns encircling the rim. Marks on the base include the Rookwood logo, the date and shape number 1388. Height 2¾ inches. — $200-$300

512 Aerial Blue plate decorated by William McDonald in 1895 with the portrait of Aesop, after Velasquez. Marks on the base include the Rookwood logo, the date, shape number T 1022 B and the artist's initials. While experimenting with new glazes in the mid 1890's, Rookwood incorporated a blue clay body into their test of Aerial Blue. This piece, listed as item 54 on page 116, in S.G. Burt's book, "2,292 pieces of early Rookwood Pottery in the Cincinnati Art Museum in 1916" is described as "blue clay no glaze". Burt list two other pieces on the same page as being Aerial Blue clay or biscuit. Greatest distance across is 11⅜ inches. — $3000-$5000

513 Vellum glaze scenic vase, decorated by Lorinda Epply in 1916. Marks on the base include the Rookwood logo, the date, shape number 1661, V for Vellum glaze body, a wheel ground x and the artist's monogram. Height 8½ inches. Glaze peppering and a small bruise on the rim. — $800-$1200

514 Standard glaze vase with wild rose decoration, painted by Charles J. Dibowski in 1894. Marks on the base include the Rookwood logo, the date, shape number 595 B, W for white clay, L for light Standard glaze and the artist's initials. Height 4⅜ inches. Shape 595 is shown with a long neck and flared rim in the Shape Record Book. This piece has lost its neck but appears to have been finished off at the factory. — $300-$500

515 Rare and impressive Iris glaze vase decorated with a pair of finely detailed cranes in flight by Albert Valentien in 1905. Marks on the base include the Rookwood logo, the date, shape number 952 C, W for white glaze and the artist's full name. Height 10⅜ inches. The vase appears to be uncrazed. $5000-$7000

516 Mat glaze vase with floral decoration, done in 1934 by Kataro Shirayamadani. Marks on the base include the Rookwood logo, the date, S for special shape and the artist's cypher. Height 6¼ inches. $700-$900

517 Dull finish vase decorated by Anna Bookprinter in 1886 with grasses and a small bird. Marks on the base include Rookwood in block letters, the date, shape number 238 C, Y for yellow clay and the artist's initials. Height 10⅝ inches. There is a small chip on the rim. $400-$600

518 Pink tinted high glaze vase decorated with irises by Carl Schmidt in 1924. Marks on the base include the Rookwood logo, the date, shape number 1358 E and the artist's monogram. Height 7¼ inches. Uncrazed. $2000-$3000

519 High glaze vase with abstract floral designs, painted by Lorinda Epply in 1928. Marks on the base include the Rookwood logo, the date, shape number 2640 C and the artist's monogram. Height 13⅛ inches. One or two glaze bubbles are present. $1200-$1400

520   High glaze lidded potpourri jar, decorated with exotic flowers and birds by E.T. Hurley in 1924. Marks on the base include the Rookwood logo, the date, shape number 2582 and the artist's initials. Height 14½ inches. $4000-$6000

521   Vellum glaze scenic plaque, decorated by Fred Rothenbusch in 1927. The artist's monogram appears in the lower right hand corner. Marks on the back include the Rookwood logo and the date. Affixed to the frame are an original Rookwood paper logo and an original label with the title "Across the Lake, F. Rothenbusch. Size 6 x 7⅞ inches. Uncrazed. $2000-$3000

522   Standard glaze ewer with cherry decoration, painted in 1902 by Leona Van Briggle. Marks on the base include the Rookwood logo, the date, shape number 461 and the artist's initials. Height 3¾ inches. $350-$550

523   Large Standard glaze ewer decorated with Virginia creepers by Sallie Toohey in 1900. Marks on the base include the Rookwood logo, the date, shape number 496 X, a wheel ground x and the artist's monogram. Height 19½ inches. A few glaze bubbles and minor scratches are present. $1250-$1750

524 Coromandel glaze ribbed vase made at Rookwood in 1932. Marks on the base include the Rookwood logo, the date and S for special shape. Height 5¾ inches. Tiny grinding chips on base. $200-$250

525 Vellum glaze scenic vase, painted in 1916 by Lenore Asbury. Marks on the base include the Rookwood logo, the date, shape number 1661, V for Vellum glaze body and the artist's initials. Height 8⅝ inches. Faint discoloration in the sky. $700-$900

526 Standard glaze creamer with crocus decoration, painted in 1900 by Eliza Lawrence. Marks on the base include the Rookwood logo, the date, shape number 770 and the artist's initials. Height 2¼ inches. $150-$250

527 Vellum glaze vase decorated with trailing fruit blossoms by Lenore Asbury in 1925. Marks on the base include the Rookwood logo, the date, shape number 925 E, V for Vellum glaze body and the artist's initials. Height 7⅛ inches. Uncrazed. $700-$900

528 Standard glaze vase with floral decoration, painted in 1901 by William Klemm. Marks on the base include the Rookwood logo, the date, shape number 614 F, a wheel ground x and the artist's initials. Height 6⅛ inches. $300-$500

529   Standard glaze lidded sugar bowl and creamer decorated in 1901 with small yellow flowers by Jeanette Swing. $400-$600
Marks on both bases include the Rookwood logo, the date, shape number 832 and the artist's monogram. The lid
is also monogrammed by Swing. Height of sugar bowl is 3¾ inches and height of creamer is 2¼ inches.

530   Large mat glaze vase decorated with morning glories by Margaret McDonald in 1926. Marks on the base include $700-$900
the Rookwood logo, the date, shape number 424 B and the artist's monogram. Height 13¾ inches.

531   Standard glaze vase with wild rose decoration, painted in 1905 by Irene Bishop. Marks on the base include the $250-$450
Rookwood logo, the date, shape number 922 E and the artist's initials. Height 5½ inches.

532   Mat glaze floral vase, painted in 1925 by Katherine Jones. Marks on the base include the Rookwood logo, the $300-$400
date, shape number 295 E, a wheel ground x and the artist's initials. Height 7¼ inches.

533   Dull finish perfume jug made for a member of the Cincinnati Commercial Club in 1883 by an unknown artist. $300-$500
Marks on the base include Rookwood in block letters, the date, shape number 61 and R for red clay. On the side
of the piece is the logo of the Club and the following inscription, "Earl W. Stimson Oct 13th 1883". Height 4
inches.

534   Vellum glaze vase painted with trailing fruit blossoms by Ed Diers in 1913. Marks on the base include the $500-$700
Rookwood logo, the date, shape number 901 D, V for Vellum glaze body, V for Vellum glaze and the artist's
initials. Height 7½ inches.

535   Standard glaze vase with Gorham silver overlay, decorated with daisies by Lenore Asbury in 1902. Marks on the $3000-$4000
base include the Rookwood logo, the date, shape number 901 C and the artist's initials. Marks on the silver
include the initials, E.H.C. and the Gorham hall marks. Height 9 inches. Glaze discoloration, glaze scratches and
one loose leaf in the silver.

536   Pair of Standard glaze portrait mugs showing dancing children, a boy with a trumpet and a girl with a mirror, $1000-$1250
painted in 1891 by Artus Van Briggle. Marks on both bases include the Rookwood logo, the date, shape number
587, W for white clay, L for light Standard glaze and the artist's initials. Height of each is 4⅛ inches. The portrait
of the young girl is badly cracked through the decoration.

537   Handsome high glaze vase with life size iris decoration, done in 1925 by Carl Schmidt. Marks on the base $1500-$2000
include the Rookwood logo, the date, the partially obscured shape number 1369 C, a wheel ground x and the
artist's monogram. Height 11⅛ inches. There is an area of bad glaze about 1 x 5 inches on one side near the rim
and the piece is drilled. A firing crack is visible on the inside of the vase and a craze line outside the vase follows
the path of the crack.

                                                                                                    $800-$1200

538   High glaze vase decorated with repeating border by Arthur Conant in 1917. Marks on the base include the
Rookwood logo, the date, shape number 2240, P for porcelain body and the artist's monogram. Height 6¼ inches.
Uncrazed.

539   Vellum glaze vase decorated with several swimming fish by Edith Noonan in 1908. Marks on the base include $800-$1000
the Rookwood logo, the date, shape number 1358 E, V for Vellum glaze body, V for Vellum glaze, possibly a
wheel ground x and the faint initials of the artist. Height 6⅞ inches. A small glaze bump in the side may have
caused the piece to be xed and someone has defaced much of the base, possibly to hide the x.

540   Iris glaze vase with wisteria decoration, painted in 1902 by an unknown decorator. Marks on the base include the $1200-$1500
Rookwood logo, the date and W for white glaze. A drill hole obliterates the shape number and most of the artist's
initials. Height 9⅜ inches. Drilled, glaze flaw near base, two inch chip off rim and tight fisures in base due to
drilling.

541   Standard glaze stoppered whiskey jug decorated with corn by Laura Lindeman in 1907. Marks on the base $250-$350
include the Rookwood logo, the date, shape number 747 C, a wheel ground x and the artist's initials. Height 7¼
inches. Several small glaze bubbles near the base.

542   Mat glaze water jug with some crystaline effect, made at Rookwood in 1922. Marks on the base include the $100-$200
Rookwood logo, the date and shape number 2644. Height 7⅜ inches.

543   Standard glaze ewer with floral decoration, painted in 1894 by Anna Valentien. Marks on the base include the $500-$700
Rookwood logo, the date, shape number 657 C, W for white clay and the artist's initials. Height 8⅜ inches.

544 Unusual Sea Green glaze vase, decorated in 1898 by E.T. Hurley with a lobster amongst undulating sea grasses. Marks on the base include the Rookwood logo, the date, shape number 745 B, G for Sea Green glaze, a star shaped esoteric mark and the artist's initials. Height 7¼ inches. — $5000-$7000

545 Unusual high glaze vase painted in 1930 with repeating patterns of interlocking triangles and exotic fruit by Sara Sax. Marks on the base include the Rookwood logo, the date, shape number 2746, a fan shaped esoteric mark and the artist's monogram. Height 9¼ inches. — $2000-$3000

546 Good Standard glaze mug decorated with the portrait of a Native American, painted in 1900 by Adeliza Sehon. Marks on the base include the Rookwood logo, the date, shape number 587 C, the title "Armstrong Arapahoe" and the artist's initials. Height 4⅜ inches. Tight spider crack in base and one burst glaze bubble. — $1250-$1750

547 Dull finish vase decorated by Artus Van Briggle in 1888 with small white flowers. Marks on the base include the Rookwood logo, the date, shape number 402, W for white clay, S for smear (dull) finish and the artist's initials. Height 5⅜ inches. — $450-$650

548 Standard glaze vase decorated by Ed Diers in 1897 with small yellow flowers. Marks on the base include the Rookwood logo, the date, shape number 735 DD, two parallel lines under the artist's initials and the artist's initials. Height 7 inches. Glaze scratches. — $500-$700

549   Standard glaze vase decorated with small yellow flowers by Constance Baker in 1894. Marks on the base include the Rookwood logo, the date, shape number 80 B and the artist's initials. Height 6¼ inches. $300-$400

550   Vellum glaze vase with fruit blossom decor, painted by Lenore Asbury in 1925. Marks on the base include the Rookwood logo, the date, shape number 2831 and the artist's initials. Height 5½ inches. Small flake on the base glazed over at factory. $300-$400

551   Vellum glaze plaque decorated by Ed Diers in 1919. The artist's initials appear in the lower right hand corner. Marks on the back include the Rookwood logo and the date. On the frame is an original paper label with the title, "Pasture Scene. E. Diers". Size 6¼ x 8⅛ inches. $1500-$2000

552   Vellum glaze vase with floral decoration, done in 1914 by Helen Lyons. Marks on the base include the Rookwood logo, the date, shape number 1356 E, V for Vellum glaze body and the artist's monogram. Height 7¼ inches. Glaze peppering. $300-$400

553   Standard glaze vase with chestnut decoration, painted in 1901 by Lenore Asbury. Marks on the base include the Rookwood logo, the date, shape number 874 and the artist's initials. Height 8½ inches. $300-$400

554 Standard glaze vase decorated with palm fronds by Mary Nourse in 1902. Marks on the base include the Rookwood logo, the date, shape number 939 B, L for light Standard glaze, a wheel ground x and the artist's initials. Height 9¾ inches. Minor glaze scratches. $300-$500

555 Coromandel glaze vase made at Rookwood in 1932. Marks on the base include the Rookwood logo, the date and shape number 6319 D. Height 4⅜ inches. $300-$400

556 Vellum glaze Venetian harbor scene, decorated by Carl Schmidt in 1919. Marks on the base include the Rookwood logo, the date, shape number 1882, V for Vellum glaze body, V for Vellum glaze and the artist's monogram. Height 9¾ inches. $3000-$4000

557 Limoges style glaze vase with two handles, possibly made at Cincinnati Art Pottery circa 1881, decorated with painted and incised flowers by an artist with the initials S.L. Marks on the base include the artist's initials and the letter c. Height 3¾ inches. $300-$400

558 Standard glaze ewer with wild rose deocration by Artus Van Briggle, painted in 1890. Marks on the base include the Rookwood logo, the date, shape number 537 E, L for light Standard glaze and the artist's initials. Height 10⅛ inches. Moderate flaws in the background color. $250-$350

559   Unusual Commercial vase with a band of repeating fish under a slightly crystaline glaze, made at Rookwood in 1910. Marks on the base include the Rookwood logo, the date and a triangular shaped esoteric mark. Height 8¼ inches. $200-$300

560   Standard glaze mug decorated by E.T. Hurley with the head of a dog in 1899. Marks on the base include the Rookwood logo, the date, shape number 656, a wheel ground x and the artist's initials. Height 4¾ inches. Moderate underglaze flaws. $200-$300

561   Vellum glaze vase with several small buildings visible behind a grove of trees, decorated by Fred Rothenbusch in 1928. Marks on the base include the Rookwood logo, the date, shape number 900 B, V for Vellum glaze and the artist's initials. Height 10½ inches. Uncrazed. $2500-$3500

562   Unusual speckled mat glaze vase made at Rookwood in 1924. Marks on the base include the Rookwood logo, the date and shape number 2111. Height 6⅛ inches. $100-$200

563   Standard glaze vase decorated with hydrangia by Amelia Sprague in 1897. Marks on the base include the Rookwood logo, the date, shape number 216, a small triangular shaped esoteric mark and the artist's monogram. Height 12⅛ inches. Tiny rough spot on rim. $500-$700

564 High glaze vase decorated with blue flowers, green leaves and a single bird by Kay Ley in 1945. Marks on the base include the Rookwood logo, the date, shape number 6914, the number 4258 and the artist's last name. Height 5¼ inches. $500-$700

565 Mat glaze Arts and Crafts jardiniere, decorated with incised repeating patterns by Albert Munson in 1901. Marks on the base include the Rookwood logo, the date, shape number 47 BZ and the artist's monogram. Height 8½ inches. Cracked. $200-$300

566 Pair of unusual polychromed Rook bookends in the large size, made at Rookwood in 1926. Marks on the base include the Rookwood logo, the date and shape number 2274. Height 6¼ inches. The tail of one Rook has been damaged and professionally repaired. $300-$500

567 Large Standard glaze two handled vase decorated with trumpet creepers by Kataro Shirayamadani in 1899. Marks on the base include the Rookwood logo, the date, shape number 339 B and the artist's cypher. Height 12⅝ inches. $2000-$3000

568 Large four handled Commercial vase with a crystaline mat glaze, made at Rookwood in 1913. Marks on the base include the Rookwood logo, the date and shape number 463 C. Height 13 inches. $300-$400

569	Drip glaze vase made at Rookwood in 1932. Marks on the base include the Rookwood logo, the date and shape number 6306. Height 7 inches.	$300-$400
570	Standard glaze vase with Goldstone effect, decorated with a small flower by Anna Bookprinter in 1887. Marks on the base include the Rookwood logo, the date, shape number 76 and the partially obscured artist's initials. Height 2½ inches.	$200-$400
571	Limoges style glaze plate painted by an unknown artist in 1885 with grasses and a small bird. Marks on the back include Rookwood in block letters, the date, shape number 87 and G for ginger clay. Diameter 6⅛ inches.	$75-$100
572	High glaze perfume jug with incised shamrock decoration, done by Harriet Wenderoth in 1884. Marks on the base include Rookwood in block letters, the date, shape number 61, W for white clay and the artist's initials. Height 4⅜ inches. Tiny chip off handle.	$250-$350
573	High glaze vase with wisteria decoration, painted by E.T. Hurley in 1924. Marks on the base include the Rookwood logo, the date, shape number 2790, a wheel ground x and the artist's initials. Height 11½ inches. Grinding chips on the base and some glaze unevenness.	$700-$900

574   Early dull finish vase with incised floral decoration, done by Harriet Wenderoth in 1881. Marks incised in the base include Rookwood Pottery Cin O 1881 and the artist's initials. Height 7 inches. $200-$300

575   Mat glaze vase with floral decoration by Sallie Coyne, painted in 1929. Marks on the base include the Rookwood logo, the date, shape number 2066 and the artist's monogram. Height 7½ inches. $300-$400

576   Standard glaze lidded box decorated in 1899 by Virginia Demarest with pansies. Marks on the base include the Rookwood logo, the date, shape number 591 and the artist's initials. The lid is also marked with the artist's initials. Height 1¾ inches. $200-$300

577   Standard glaze ewer with clover decoration by Clara Lindeman, painted in 1900. Marks on the base include the Rookwood logo, the date, shape number 639 D and the artist's initials. Height 6¼ inches. $300-$500

578   Rare carved mat glaze bowl in the form of a lotus blossom laying on a lotus pad, done in 1901 by Anna Valentien. Marks on the base include the Rookwood logo, the date, shape number 353 Z and the artist's initials. Diameter 9¼ inches. Small glaze dimple. $700-$900

579   Standard glaze vase with floral decoration, done in 1894 by Kate Matchette. Marks on the base include the Rookwood logo, the date, shape number 162 D, W for white clay and the artist's initials. Height 4⅞ inches. $250-$450

580 Standard glaze lidded chocolate pot, painted in 1904 by Elizabeth Lincoln with jonquils. Marks on the base $500-$700
include the Rookwood logo, the date, shape number 771 B, a wheel ground x and the artist's initials. Height 9⅜
inches.

581 Standard glaze vase with Gorham silver overlay, decorated with beech leaves and nuts by Lenore Asbury in $3000-$4000
1897. Marks on the base include the Rookwood logo, the date, shape number 531 E, a small diamond shaped
esoteric mark and the artist's initials. Marks on the silver include the Gorham hall marks and notation, "D 110
999/1000 Fine". Height 5⅝ inches.

582 Very clean Vellum glaze plaque decorated with several houses in a woodland setting by Fred Rothenbusch in $4500-$5500
1929. The artist's monogram appears in the lower left hand corner. Marks on the back include the Rookwood
logo and the date. Affixed to the frame are an original Rookwood paper logo and an original Rookwood paper
label with the title, "Autumn F. Rothenbusch". Size is approximately 7 x 11½ inches. Uncrazed

583 Standard glaze vase with much Tiger Eye effect, decorated circa 1885 by Albert Valentien with a winged dragon. $1000-$2000
Marks on the base which are partially obscured by the glaze include Rookwood in block letters, the date, shape
number 28 C and the artist's initials. Height 6⅜ inches.

584 Iris glaze vase decorated with fruit blossoms by Sara Sax in 1899. Marks on the base include the Rookwood logo, $1500-$2000
the date, shape number 589 E, W for white glaze and the artist's monogram. Height 8⅜ inches. Uncrazed.

585 Vellum glaze vase decorated in 1914 by Sallie Coyne with three small sailboats at sea. Marks on the base include the Rookwood logo, the date, shape number 1369 E, V for Vellum glaze body and the artist's monogram. Height 7¼ inches. A tight two inch line descends from the rim. — $750-$1000

586 Dull finish Spanish water jug with decoration of grasses and butterflies, done in 1884 by Martin Rettig. Marks on the base include Rookwood in block letters, the date, shape number 41, Y for yellow clay and the artist's initials. Height 9¼ inches. Spout has been chipped and ground down. — $500-$700

587 Standard glaze lidded teapot, decorated with small yellow flowers by Katherine Hickman in 1899. Marks on the base include the Rookwood logo, the date, shape number 832 and the artist's monogram. The lid also carries the artist's monogram. Height 4⅜ inches. — $350-$550

588 Vellum glaze vase painted with carnations by Fred Rothenbusch in 1908. Marks on the base include the Rookwood logo, the date, shape number 904 D, V for Vellum glaze and the artist's monogram. Height 8½ inches. — $800-$1200

589 Yellow tinted high glaze vase with floral decoration done by Sara Sax in 1923. Marks on the base include the Rookwood logo, the date, shape number 1096 and the artist's monogram. Height 4¾ inches. — $500-$700

590   Unusual Vellum glaze scenic vase, decorated with stylized flowering trees by Kate Curry in 1917. Marks on the base include the Rookwood logo, the date, shape number 901 C, a wheel ground x and the artist's monogram. Height 9¾ inches. There is a tiny flake off the rim. $1000-$1500

591   Blue Tinted high glaze vase with lush floral decoration and repeating borders, painted by Sara Sax in 1923. Marks on the base include the Rookwood logo, the date, shape number 904 C and the artist's monogram. Height 12⅜ inches. $2000-$3000

592   Standard glaze creamer and sugar bowl decorated with mistletoe in 1900 by Elizabeth Lincoln. Marks on both bases include the Rookwood logo, the date, shape number 831 and the artist's initials. Height of tallest piece is 2⅝ inches. $300-$500

593   Standard glaze ewer decorated in 1891 with beech leaves by Artus Van Briggle. Marks on the base include the Rookwood logo, the date, shape number 578 C, W for white clay, L for light Standard glaze and the artist's initials. Height 12½ inches. $800-$1200

594   Iris glaze vase decorated in 1906 with apple blossoms by Clara Lindeman. Marks on the base include the Rookwood logo, the date, shape number 941 D, W for white glaze and the artist's initials. Height 7⅝ inches. Uncrazed. $1500-$2000

595   Vellum glaze scenic vase painted by Fred Rothenbusch in 1927. Marks on the base include the Rookwood logo, the date, shape number 1667, V for Vellum glaze and the artist's monogram. Height 10¼ inches. Uncrazed. $2000-$2500

596   Standard glaze ewer decorated with holly by Lenore Asbury in 1898. Marks on the base include the Rookwood logo, the date, shape number 566 C and the artist's initials. Height 8¾ inches. $400-$600

597   Large and impressive Iris glaze vase painted with life size irises by Carl Schmidt in 1903. Marks on the base include the Rookwood logo, the date, shape number 943 B, a wheel ground x and the artist's monogram. Height 11¾ inches. $5000-$7000

598   Black tinted high glaze vase decorated with red and white fruit blossoms by Harriet Wilcox in 1923. Marks on the base include the Rookwood logo, the date, shape number 2306 and the artist's initials. Height 6⅞ inches. Uncrazed. $900-$1100

599   Standard glaze ewer crisply decorated with leaves and flowers by M.A. Daly in 1891. Marks on the base include the Rookwood logo, the date, shape number 496 A, W for white clay and the artist's initials. Height 12⅞ inches. $1200-$1500

600   Large and important Black Iris glaze vase depicting two groups of ducks on a moonlight lakeside walk beneath $25000-$35000
the cover of a dense evergreen wood, painted in 1909 by Kataro Shirayamadani. Marks on the base include the
Rookwood logo, the date, shape number 1358 B, W for white glaze and the artist's cypher. Height 12¾ inches.
Minor glaze scratches. Pictured: "Rookwood Pottery Potpourri" Virginia Raymond Cummins, Copyright 1991,
Cincinnati Art Galleries, Color plate on page 124. Exhibitions: "Ode to Nature: Flowers and Landscapes of the
Rookwood Pottery 1840 -1940" The Jordan - Volpe Gallery, 1980, Item 84 in the catalog, Color plate 6.

601 High glaze vase with Art Deco horses and leaves, painted with very heavy slip in 1929 by William Hentschel. Marks on the base include the Rookwood logo, the date, shape number 6080 and the artist's monogram. Height 12⅞ inches. $3000-$5000

602 Limoges style glaze lidded tea jar decorated with grasses and two birds in flight by Albert Valentien in 1885. Marks on the base include Rookwood in block letters, the date, shape number 142 B, R for red clay and the artist's initials. Height 6⅝ inches. $500-$700

603 Iris glaze vase painted in 1908 with water lilies and pads by Lenore Asbury. Marks on the base include the Rookwood logo, the date, shape number 917 C, W for white glaze and the artist's initials. Height 7¼ inches. $1200-$1500

604 Tall Standard glaze vase decorated with red poppies by Lenore Asbury in 1902. Marks on the base include the Rookwood logo, the date, shape number 216 and the artist's initials. Height 12⅜ inches. $800-$1000

605 Crisp mat glaze vase decorated in 1939 with Virginia creepers by Margaret McDonald. Marks on the base include the Rookwood logo, the date, shape number 6194 D and the artist's monogram. Height 6⅛ inches. $400-$600

606   Nacreous glaze vase made at Rookwood in 1915. Marks on the base include the Rookwood logo, the date, shape number 47 C and P for porcelain body. Height 5¼ inches. $200-$300

607   Standard glaze pillow vase with nasturtium decoration, painted in 1895 by Carrie Steinle. Marks on the base include the Rookwood logo, the date, shape number 707 C and the artist's monogram. Height 3⅜ inches. $200-$400

608   Limoges style glaze plate painted with grasses and a small bird by Anna Bookprinter in 1886. Marks on the base include Rookwood in block letters, the date, shape number 87, G for ginger clay and the artist's initials. Diameter 6⅜ inches. $150-$200

609   Blue tinted high glaze vase with maple leaf decoration, painted in 1925 by Kataro Shirayamadani. Marks on the base include the Rookwood logo, the date, shape number 389, a wheel ground x and the artist's cypher. Height 3½ inches. Glaze burn on the lower portion of the piece. $800-$1200

610   Standard glaze mug decorated with a dancing couple by Bruce Horsfall in 1894. Marks on the base include the Rookwood logo, the date, shape number 587 D, W for white clay and the artist's monogram. Height 5½ inches. $800-$1200

611 Vellum glaze scenic vase decorated by Lenore Asbury in 1918. Marks on the base include the Rookwood logo, the date, shape number 271 C, a wheel ground x and the artist's initials. Height 9 inches. Small chips on the base have been repaired. $600-$800

612 Standard glaze vase with floral decoration, done in 1896 by Katherine Hickman. Marks on the base include the Rookwood logo, the date, what may be shape number 19, a crescent moon, the letter "N", a shield with the number 110 inside and the artist's initials. Height 4⅛ inches. $300-$500

613 Standard glaze vase painted by E.T. Hurley in 1903 with nasturtiums. Marks on the base include the Rookwood logo, the date, shape number 909 BB and the artist's initials. Height 9⅝ inches. Small bruise at the base. $200-$300

614 Carved and painted mat glaze vase with repeating abstract designs, decorated in 1915 by C.S. Todd. Marks on the base include the Rookwood logo, the date, shape number 964, a wheel ground x and the artist's initials. Height 3¾ inches. Pin head size rim flake. $200-$300

615 Unusual Spanish water jug decorated with stylized flowers and highlighted with fired on gold by an unknown artist in 1882. Marks on the base include Rookwood in block letters and the date. Height 9 inches. $400-$500

616 Standard glaze vase with jonquil decoration, painted in 1897 by Fred Rothenbusch. Marks on the base include the Rookwood logo, the date, shape number 734 DD and the artist's initials. Height 6¾ inches. Minor glaze scratches. $300-$400

617   Vellum glaze mug designed by Sara Sax and Kataro Shirayamadani for an unknown organization and made at $300-$500
Rookwood in 1907. Marks on the base include the Rookwood logo, the date, shape number S 1798, V for Vellum
glaze, V for Vellum glaze body and the monogram and cypher of the respective artists. Height 6⅞ inches.

618   Vellum glaze vase painted by Ed Diers in 1905 with Art Nouveau daisies. Marks on the base include the $700-$900
Rookwood logo, the date, shape number 907 E, V for Vellum glaze body, V for Vellum glaze and the artist's
initials. Height 9 inches.

619   Vellum glaze plaque decorated by Ed Diers in 1921. The artist's initials appear in the lower left hand corner. $3000-$4000
Marks on the back include the Rookwood logo and the date. Affixed to the frame is an original paper title,
"Kentucky Woodland, E. Diers". Size 8¾ x 11⅞ inches.

620   Standard glaze pillow vase painted by Carrie Steinle in 1902 with nasturtiums. Marks on the base include the $250-$350
Rookwood logo, the date, shape number 707 B and the artist's monogram. Height 5⅝ inches.

621   Standard glaze three footed bowl with floral decoration, done in 1886 by Laura Fry. Marks on the base include $300-$500
the Rookwood logo, the date, shape number 11, R for red clay and the artist's monogram. Height 5½ inches. A
few tiny glaze bubbles appear on the rim and shoulder.

622   Dull finish ewer decorated by an unknown artist in 1886 with oriental grasses and a small flying bird. Marks on the base include the Rookwood logo, the date, shape number 101 A, Y for yellow clay and a paper label from Duhme & Company Jewelers, Cincinnati. Height 11 1/2 inches. Some restoration to the lip. $300-$400

623   Unusual vase decorated in 1924 by Sara Sax with abstract patterns and covered with Black Opal glaze. Marks on the base include the Rookwood logo, the date, shape number 216 and the artist's monogram. Height 12¾ inches. $2000-$2500

624   Standard glaze vase with wild violet decoration, painted in 1897 by Katherine Hickman. Marks on the base include the Rookwood logo, the date, shape number 625 and the artist's monogram. Height 5¼ inches. $300-$500

625   Standard glaze tankard decorated in 1891 by Anna Valentien with irises. Marks on the base include the Rookwood logo, the date, shape number 564 C, W for white clay, L for light Standard glaze and the artist's initials. Height 9¼ inches. Some glaze blisters and glaze discoloration. Roughness on the rim. $400-$600

626   Standard glaze puzzle mug painted by Harriet Wilcox in 1895 with hops. Marks on the base include the Rookwood logo, the date, shape number 711 and the artist's initials. Height 4¾ inches. Some minor glaze scratches. $300-$400

627   Tall high glaze vase decorated with magnolia blossoms, painted in 1946 by Kataro Shirayamadani. Marks on the base include the Rookwood logo, the date, shape number 6925, the number 6638 and the artist's initials. Height 12⅛ inches. $1250-$1750

628   Slightly crystaline mat glaze vase decorated with Art Deco impala by Elizabeth Barrett in 1946. Marks on the base include the Rookwood logo, the date, shape number 925 B, the number 3429, a cast hole and the artist's monogram. Height 12¾ inches. $1000-$1500

629   Standard glaze tray with floral decoration, painted by Amelia Sprague in 1887. Marks on the base include the Rookwood logo, the date, shape number 228 D, W 7 for a type of white clay, L for light Standard glaze and the artist's initials. Greatest distance across is 6¾ inches. $150-$250

630   Standard glaze ewer with crisp clover decoration by Anna Valentien, painted in 1893. Marks on the base include the Rookwood logo, the date, shape number 537 D, W for white clay, L for light Standard glaze and the artist's initials. Height 9⅝ inches. $500-$700

631   Vellum glaze scenic vase decorated by Mary Grace Denzler in 1916. Marks on the base include the Rookwood logo, the date, shape number 949 D and the artist's monogram. Height 9⅜ inches. $1250-$1750

632   Large and unusual painted and carved vase, done in 1900 by John Dee Wareham with floral decor and covered with what may be Flowing Glaze. Marks on the base include the Rookwood logo, the date, shape number 857, a wheel ground x and the artist's initials. The initials of William McDonald are crudely scratched in the base, presumably by someone unable to see the faint signature of Wareham and wishing to have a "signed" vase. Height 14⅞ inches. Some burst glaze bubbles and glaze flaws. For another example of what may be Flowing Glaze, see item 706 in this catalog. $4000-$6000

633   Vellum glaze plaque showing a snowy pine forest at dusk, decorated in 1919 by Elizabeth McDermott. The artist's name appears in the lower left hand corner. Marks on the back include the Rookwood logo and the date. An original Rookwood paper label is affixed to the frame and carries the title, "Winter Evening E.F. McDermott". Size 7 x 9 inches. Several pits in the glaze. $2500-$3500

634   Unusual Rook ashtray covered with Bengal Brown glaze, done at Rookwood in 1949. Marks on the base include the Rookwood logo, the date and the shape number 1139. Height 4 inches. $200-$300

635   High glaze vase with jonquil decoration, done in 1948 by Jens Jensen. Marks on the base include the Rookwood logo, the date, shape number 6184 C, a Glover Collection label, number 605 and the artist's monogram. Height 9¾ inches. $900-$1200

636 Large and unusual Standard glaze Presentation pitcher with silver overlayed rim and handle, decorated with an elk by E.T. Hurley in 1904. Marks on the base include the Rookwood logo, the date, shape number 837, a wheel ground x, the inscription "Presented to Chairman August Herrmann by Members of the Elks' Reunion Committee 1904 Cincinnati Ohio" and the artist's initials. Height 12 inches. Glaze scratches and small chips on the lower end of the handle. $2000-$2500

637 Large and impressive Iris glaze vase with showy white lily decoration, painted circa 1903 by Carl Schmidt. Marks on the base include shape number 907 B, W for white glaze, a wheel ground x and the artist's monogram. The Rookwood logo and date have been drilled through. Uncrazed. Height 16¼ inches. There is a tiny flake off the rim. $6000-$8000

638 Large Limoges style glaze vase decorated with sea creatures entrapped in a gold net, painted by Maria Longworth Nichols in 1882. Marks on the base include Rookwood in block letters, the date and the artist's initials. Height 13⅝ inches. Spider cracks in base and repair to lip. Minor damage to the fired on gold netting. $7000-$9000

639   Standard glaze vase with pansy decoration, painted in 1906 by Alice Willitts. Marks on the base include the Rookwood logo, the date, shape number 881 E and the artist's monogram. Height 4⅛ inches. $300-$500

640   Limoges style glaze lamp decorated in 1883 by Albert Valentien with grasses and swallows in flight. Marks on the base include Rookwood in block letters, the date, shape number 225, G for ginger clay, an impressed anchor mark, a cast hole and the artist's initials. Height of ceramic portion is 7½ inches. Original Duplex burner and brass fittings. $800-$1200

641   Standard glaze creamer, decorated with pansies by Olga Reed in 1891. Marks on the base include the Rookwood logo, the date, shape number 329, W for white clay, L for light Standard glaze and the artist's initials. Height 2¼ inches. $150-$250

642   Unusual Standard glaze vase decorated with flowers and oriental ribbons and medallions by Artus Van Briggle in 1888. A few areas of Goldstone effect are seen under the glaze. Marks on the base include the Rookwood logo, the date, shape number 707 S, L for light Standard glaze, S for sage green clay and the artist's initials. Height 12⅝ inches. $800-$1200

643   Standard glaze match holder decorated 1898 with forget me nots, matches and cigarettes by Carl Schmidt. Marks on the base include the Rookwood logo, the date, shape number 855 and the artist's monogram. Height 1¾ inches. $300-$500

644   Vellum glaze vase with wild rose decoration, done in 1924 by Ed Diers. Marks on the base include the Rookwood logo, the date, shape number 1369 F, V for Vellum glaze and the artist's initials. Height 6⅛ inches. Uncrazed. $600-$800

645   Standard glaze two handled vase painted in 1898 by Mary Nourse with palm fronds. Marks on the base include the Rookwood logo, the date, shape number 583 D, L for light Standard glaze and the artist's initials. Height 8½ inches. $500-$700

646   Rare Yellow Vellum glaze vase with crisp fruit blossom decoration, painted in 1924 by Lenore Asbury. Marks on the base include the Rookwood logo, the date, shape number 1927, Y.V. for Yellow Vellum and the artist's initials. Height 4 inches. Uncrazed. $800-$1000

647   Cameo glaze pitcher decorated with wild roses by M.A. Daly in 1887. Marks on the base include the Rookwood logo, the date, shape number 182, W for white clay, W for white glaze and the artist's initials. Height 7 inches. $300-$400

648   Standard glaze vase decorated with orange tulips by Constance Baker in 1903. Marks on the base include the Rookwood logo, the date, shape number 939 B, a wheel ground x and the artist's initials. Height 9⅞ inches. Minor glaze scratches. $600-$800

649   Vellum glaze vase with floral decoration, painted in 1907 by Lorinda Epply. Marks on the base include the Rookwood logo, the date, shape number 900 D, V for Vellum glaze body, V for Vellum glaze and the artist's monogram. Height 6¾ inches. Small chip near base. $200-$400

650 Standard glaze vase with the portrait of a young man, done in 1901 by Grace Young. Marks on the base include the Rookwood logo, the date, shape number 80 B, the inscription, "after Gerard Don" and the artist's monogram. Height 6⅞ inches. $1750-$2250

651 Standard glaze vase with holly decoration, done in 1903 by Elizabeth Lincoln. Marks on the base include the Rookwood logo, the date, shape number 531 E and the artist's initials. Height 5⅜ inches. $300-$500

652 Vellum glaze scenic plaque decorated in 1916 by Ed Diers. The artist's initials appear in the lower left hand corner. Marks on the back include the Rookwood logo, the date and V for Vellum glaze body. Size 8¾ x 10⅞ inches. Small glaze bubble in sky. $3000-$4000

653 Standard glaze vase with silver overlay by Gorham, decorated with fruit blossoms by Josephine Zettel in 1897. Marks on the base include the Rookwood logo, the date, shape number 733 C, the artist's monogram and two parallel lines underlining the artist's monogram. Marks on the base of the silver overlay include Gorham's hallmarks, 999/1000 Fine and the number R 2512. Glaze scratches inside the rim and some glaze discoloration. $2500-$3500

654 Vellum glaze vase with a colorful woodland scene, painted in 1915 by Ed Diers. Marks on the base include the Rookwood logo, the date, shape number 949 D, V for Vellum glaze body, a wheel ground x and the artist's initials. Height 9⅛ inches. Glaze skip on rim and peppering in the glaze. $500-$700

655 Iris glaze vase with goldenrod decoration, painted in 1903 by Ed Diers. Marks on the base include the Rookwood logo, the date, shape number 917 C, W for white glaze and the artist's initials. Height 7⅜ inches. $900-$1200

656 Tall Standard glaze vase with wild rose decoration, done circa 1887 by Laura Fry. Marks on the base include the Rookwood logo, the almost obscured date, shape number 216, W 2 for a type of white clay and the artist's monogram. Height 12⅛ inches. A small scratch, some tiny glaze bubbles and a short firing separation are present in the vase.
$500-$700

657 Standard glaze vase with grape decoration by Edith Felten, painted in 1903. Marks on the base include the Rookwood logo, the date, shape number 904 D and the artist's initials. Height 8 inches. Tiny flake off base.
$300-$400

658 Large and impressive dull finish jardiniere, decorated with magnolia by Albert Valentien in 1886. The collar is die stamped and colored with fired on gold. Marks on the base include Rookwood in block letters, the date, shape number 276, Y for yellow clay and the artist's initials. Height 9¾ inches.
$3000-$5000

659 Standard glaze vase with four small feet, painted with small yellow flowers by Adeliza Sehon in 1898. Marks on the base include the Rookwood logo, the date, shape number 688 and the artist's initials. Height 2⅝ inches.
$200-$300

660 Rare Black Opal glaze vase decorated with three repeating views of painted and incised birds perched in a fruit tree, done by Sara Sax in 1925. Marks on the base include the Rookwood logo, the date, shape number 1126 C and the artist's monogram. Height 9¼ inches. A long loose crack descends from the rim.
$1000-$1500

661   Pleasant Vellum glaze woodland scenic vase decorated by E.T. Hurley in 1931. Marks on the base include the $1500-$1800
Rookwood logo, the date, shape number 892 C and the artist's initials. Height 8⅞ inches. Uncrazed.

662   Standard glaze ewer decorated by Eliza Lawrence in 1901 with dogwood. Marks on the base include the $300-$500
Rookwood logo, the date, shape number 725 E and the artist's initials. Height 5¼ inches. Minor glaze
discoloration.

663   Tall Iris glaze vase decorated by Albert Valentien in 1902 with fiddlehead ferns. Marks on the base include the $2000-$2500
Rookwood logo, the date, shape number 816 B, a wheel ground x and the artist's full name. Height 14 inches.
Minor glaze flaws.

664   Early Limoges style glaze pitcher decorated with small blue flowers by Albert Valentien in 1881. Marks incised on $700-$900
the base include the following, "Rookwood Pottery. A.R.V. 1881. Cin. O." and a paper label which reads,
"Rookwood Pottery and the Arts & Crafts Movement 1880 - 1915 October 16, 1987 - January 31, 1988
Milwaukee Art Museum". Height 8⅞ inches. Exhibited: Milwaukee Art Museum as noted above.

665   Standard glaze vase decorated with chestnuts by Sallie Coyne in 1900. Marks on the base include the Rookwood $500-$700
logo, the date, shape number 846 B, a wheel ground x and the artist's monogram. Height 12¼ inches. Minor area
of glaze discoloration.

666 Oxblood glaze vase made at Rookwood in 1924. Marks on the base include the Rookwood logo, the date and shape number 356 E. Height 6½ inches. $400-$600

667 Colorful high glaze covered urn decorated with wisteria and butterflies by E.T. Hurley in 1922. Marks on the base include the Rookwood logo, the date, shape number 2582 and the artist's initials. The inner lid and outer lid are both marked with Hurley's initials. Height 14¼ inches. The outer lid had a small crack and chip which have been repaired. $3000-$4000

668 Two handled mat glaze vase with abstract floral decoration, painted in 1930 by Elizabeth Lincoln. Marks on the base include the Rookwood logo, the date, shape number 2078, a fan shaped esoteric mark and the artist's initials. Height 4¾ inches. Moderate glaze peppering. $200-$300

669 Rare high glaze scenic plaque, decorated by E.T. Hurley in 1941. The artist's initials appear in the lower right hand corner. Marks on the back include the Rookwood logo, the date and the numbers, 6 x 8. Size is 8 x 6 inches. $3000-$4000

670 Standard glaze vase with nasturtium decoration, painted by Constance Baker in 1902. Marks on the base include the Rookwood logo, the date, shape number 900 C and the artist's initials. Height 7⅞ inches. A few tiny glaze bubbles and one small area of glaze discoloration. $550-$650

671   Vellum glaze scenic vase, painted in 1920 by Elizabeth McDermott. Marks on the base include the Rookwood logo, the date, shape number 951 F, V for Vellum glaze body and the artist's initials. Height 6¼ inches. $600-$800

672   Tall mat glaze vase with some crystaline effect, designed by Louise Abel with several classical figures and made at Rookwood in 1925. Marks on the base include the Rookwood logo, the date, shape number 2543 and the cast monogram of the artist. Height 13⅛ inches. $250-$350

673   Standard glaze creamer with floral decoration by Howard Altman, painted in 1901. Marks on the base include the Rookwood logo, the date, shape number 547 and the artist's monogram. Height 2⅞ inches. $150-$250

674   Early Limoges style glaze vase decorated with flying birds, flowers and faux oriental calligraphy in the style of Maria Longworth Nichols, circa 1880. The base is indistinctly incised, Rookwood Pottery. Height 10¼ inches. Exhibitions: "Fragile Blossoms, Enduring Earth" The Everson Museum of Art, 1989, Item 42 in the Catalog, Color plate on page 74. $1500-$2500

675   Vellum glaze vase with woodland scene, painted by Lenore Asbury in 1920. Marks on the base include the Rookwood logo, the date, shape number 951 F, V for Vellum glaze body and the artist's initials. Height 6¼ inches. Tight ½ inch line descends from rim. $400-$600

676   Standard glaze ewer decorated by Clara Lindeman in 1901 with wild violets. Marks on the base include the Rookwood logo, the date, shape number 715 D and the artist's initials. Height 6¾ inches. $300-$500

677　Rare and important Sea Green glaze vase with electroplated copper foliage, decorated with lotus blossoms and　$12000-$15000
　　　pads by John Dee Wareham in 1900. Marks on the base include the Rookwood logo, the date, shape number T
　　　1239, G for Sea Green glaze and the artist's initials. Listed: S.G. Burt's book, "2,292 Pieces of early Rookwood
　　　Pottery in the Cincinnati Art Museum in 1916", as item 114 on page 142. Height 4⅞ inches.

678　Fine Black Iris glaze scenic vase, decorated in 1909 by Ed Diers with a banded view of several sailing ships at　$5000-$7000
　　　dockside. Marks on the base include the Rookwood logo, the date, shape number 1654 D, W for white glaze and
　　　the artist's initials. Height 9 inches. Uncrazed.

679　Unusual mat glaze vase with carved lotus blossoms and leaves, done in 1903 by Kataro Shirayamadani. Marks on　$1250-$1500
　　　the base include the Rookwood logo, the date, shape number 207 Z and the artist's cypher. Height 6 inches.
　　　Damage to some of the leaf tips and flowers has been repaired.

680　Rare and exotically glazed vase, decorated with swimming tadpoles by Maria Longworth Nichols Storer in　$2000-$3000
　　　1895. Marks on the base include the date, the artist's initials, W inside a circle and an Oriental cypher in red.
　　　Height 7½ inches. Crack at base. Although not marked Rookwood, this vase is very typical of Mrs. Storer's
　　　personal work, done in her own studio at the pottery. See item 509 in this sale for a similar example. The cypher
　　　in red has not been identified.

681   Commercial mat glaze vase with embossed poppies, made at Rookwood in 1929. Marks on the base include the $300-$400
       Rookwood logo, the date and shape number 6006. Height 11⅜ inches.

682   Standard glaze vase decorated by Luelle Perkins in 1896 with small flowers and berries. Marks on the base $400-$600
       include the Rookwood logo, the date, shape number 740 and the artist's initials. Height 7⅜ inches. A small glazed
       over flake at the base is in the making.

683   Unusual Art Deco mat glaze vase by William Hentschel, decorated with bands of applied cabachons in 1929. $500-$700
       Marks on the base include the Rookwood logo, the date, shape number 2969 and the artist's monogram. Height
       7½ inches.

684   Standard glaze ewer with wild grape decoration, painted in 1898 by Josephine Zettel. Marks on the base include $300-$500
       the Rookwood logo, the date, shape number 851 D and the artist's initials. Height 8¾ inches.

685   Vellum glaze mug designed by Sara Sax and Kataro Shirayamadani for an unknown organization and made at $150-$250
       Rookwood in 1907. Marks on the base include the Rookwood logo, the date, shape number S 1798, V for Vellum
       glaze; V for Vellum glaze body, a wheel ground x and the monogram and cypher of the respective artists. Height
       6⅞ inches. A tight crack descends form the rim.

686   Rare and important Carved Iris glaze lamp base, modeled and painted with hyacinths by Kataro Shirayamadani in $10000-$15000
1903. Marks on the base include the Rookwood logo, the date, shape number S 1744, W for white glaze, a wheel
ground x and the artist's cypher. Height 16⅜ inches. Damage and repair to some areas of the reticulated feet.

687 Rare Standard glaze tankard decorated with sculpted and painted nasturtiums by Mary Nourse in 1899. Marks on the base include the Rookwood logo, the date, shape number 564 C, L for light Standard glaze and the artist's initials. Height 10 inches. Some firing separations and clay loss in the sculpted areas and some minor scratches. $400-$600

688 Standard glaze ewer decorated with thistles by Anna Valentien in 1898. Marks on the base include the Rookwood logo, the date, shape number 495 B and the artist's initials. Height 8⅜ inches. $700-$900

689 Standard glaze pocket vase decorated with daisies by an unknown artist in 1886. Marks on the base include the Rookwood logo, the date, shape number 90 C and 2 W for a type of white clay. Height 3¼ inches. Minor roughness on feet and small spot in glaze. $150-$200

690 Vellum glaze vase with an evening woodland scene, painted by Carl Schmidt in 1915. Marks on the base include the Rookwood logo, the date, shape number 2033 D, V for Vellum glaze and the artist's monogram. Height 10 inches. Drilled. $2000-$3000

691 Tall Standard glaze vase painted in 1900 with irises, possibly by Sallie Toohey. Marks on the base include the Rookwood logo, the date, shape number 538 C, a wheel ground x and an indistinct mark that resembles the monogram of Sallie Toohey. Height 12 inches. $600-$800

692 Blue tinted high glaze vase decorated with stylized flowers by William Hentschel in 1921. Marks on the base $300-$400
include the Rookwood logo, the date, shape number 924 and the artist's monogram. Height 6 inches. Grinding
roughness on base.

693 Large mat glaze vase decorated by squeeze bag with repeating Art Deco patterns by Elizabeth Barrett in 1928. $800-$1200
Marks on the base include the Rookwood logo, the date, shape number 2917 B, an original Rookwood
Showroom label and the artist's monogram. Height 10⅜ inches. A ½ inch long flake off one of the applied lines is
very difficult to find. The Rookwood label describes the piece as "Decorated Mat" and the price in 1928 was $35.

694 Rookwood mat glaze advertising sign, made at the Pottery in 1945. Marks on the base include the Rookwood $600-$800
logo, the date, shape number 2788, the number 38 and in pencil, the notation, "Not for Sale". Height 3¾ inches.

695 Large and showy Vellum glaze vase decorated with water lilies by Sallie Coyne in 1922. Marks on the base $2500-$3500
include the Rookwood logo, the date, shape number 2441, V for Vellum glaze body and the artist's initials.
Height 14⅛ inches.

696 Black high glaze two handled vase made at Rookwood in 1925. Marks on the base include the Rookwood logo, $200-$300
the date and shape number 2923 A. Height 16⅜ inches.

697 Standard glaze four footed pocket vase painted with the stern visage of a bearded man wearing a tam and earrings, possibly standing in front of several sailboats. The work was done by Sturgis Laurence in 1898. Marks on the base include the Rookwood logo, the date, shape number 90 A, a wheel ground x, part of an old paper label with the word "sailor" still visible and the artist's last name. Tiny burst glaze bubble on lip. Height 6⅞ inches. $800-$1200

698 Standard glaze ewer with clover decoration, done by Laura Lindeman in 1902. Marks on the base include the Rookwood logo, the date, shape number 584 C and the artist's initials. Height 5½ inches. $400-$600

699 Mat glaze vase decorated with showy red poppies by Elizabeth Lincoln in 1922. Marks on the base include the Rookwood logo, the date, shape number 940 C and the artist's initials. Height 11⅛ inches. Drilled $700-$900

700 Mat glaze vase with poppy decoration, done in 1940 by Kataro Shirayamadani. Marks on the base include the Rookwood logo, the date, shape number 80 C, a wheel ground x and the artist's initials. Height 6¾ inches. Minor glaze flaws. $600-$800

701 Standard glaze bowl decorated with oriental flowers and designs by Kataro Shirayamadani in 1887. Marks on the base include the Rookwood logo, the date, shape number 244 A, S for sage green clay, L for light Standard glaze and the rare "chop" signature of the artist. Height 6¾ inches. Large grinding chip off the base and a crack descends from the rim. $200-$300

702   Standard glaze vase decorated with apple blossoms and branches by Clara Lindeman in 1906. Marks on the base $400-$600
include the Rookwood logo, the date, shape number 907 DD and the artist's initials. Height 9⅜ inches. Small
flake on rim.

703   Handsome Sea Green vase decorated with yellow jonquils by Sallie Toohey in 1898. Marks on the base include $2000-$3000
the Rookwood logo, the date, shape number 589 D, G for Sea Green glaze and the artist's monogram. Height
11¼ inches.

704   Vellum glaze plaque painted by Ed Diers in 1921. The artist's initials appear in the lower right hand corner. $2000-$3000
Marks on the back include the Rookwood logo and the date. Size 7⅞ x 9⅞ inches.

705   Standard glaze vase with Gorham silver overlay, decorated with wild roses by Laura Lindeman in 1903. Marks on $2500-$3500
the base include the Rookwood logo, the date, shape number 488 E and the artist's initials. Marks on the silver
include the initials G.N.T. and the Gorham hall marks. Height 6⅜ inches.

706   Unusual carved and painted vase decorated by M.A. Daly in 1901 with orchids and covered with what may be $1500-$2500
Flowing Glaze. Marks on the base include the Rookwood logo, the date, shape 905 C and the artist's full name.
Height 9⅜ inches. This vase has descended in the family of Carl Schmidt. Schmidt always described the piece to
his daughter as "Flowing Glaze", perhaps the first evidence of this elusive line. For another example of what may
be Flowing Glaze, see item 632.

707   Mat glaze vase by C.S. Todd, decorated in 1921 with painted and incised trailing flowers and vines. Marks on the base include the Rookwood logo, the date, shape number 1918 and the artist's initials. Height 8⅝ inches. $500-$700

708   Vellum glaze bowl with apple blossom decoration, done in 1916 by Charles McLaughlin. Marks on the base include the Rookwood logo, the date, shape number 957 D, V for Vellum glaze body and the artist's monogram. Height 2⅞ inches. Uncrazed. $350-$550

709   Rare Standard glaze plaque, painted in 1902 by Grace Young with a portrait of a cavalier. Marks on the back include the Rookwood logo and the date. Inscribed on the left hand edge of the plaque are the artist's monogram and the title, "Portrait after Jan di Bray". Size 8⅞ x 7⅛ inches. Minor glaze bubbles and some discoloration in the glaze. $3000-$4000

710   Vellum glaze vase with crisp decoration of carnations, done in 1925 by Ed Diers. Marks on the base include the Rookwood logo, the date, shape number 2544, V for Vellum glaze, a wheel ground x and the artist's initials. Height 8 inches. One or two very minor glaze bubbles. Uncrazed. $800-$1200

711   Standard glaze ewer with floral decoration, painted in 1899 by Jeanette Swing. Marks on the base include the Rookwood logo, the date, shape number 851 E and the artist's monogram. Height 7½ inches. $300-$500

712 Historically important Cincinnati Limoges glaze vase, decorated with flowers by Louise McLaughlin in 1878. $300-$500
Marks on the base include the artist's initials, the date, the number 108 in a circle and the word, "Cincinnati".
Height 9⅜ inches. Chips to the rim have been repaired, minor roughness on the base.

713 Standard glaze whiskey jug with corn and wheat decoration, painted in 1896 by Sallie Toohey. Marks on the $500-$700
base include the Rookwood logo, the date, shape number 676 and the artist's monogram. Height 5⅞ inches.

714 Mat glaze vase with floral decoration, painted in 1925 by Katherine Jones. Marks on the base include the $300-$400
Rookwood logo, the date, shape number 295 E and the artist's initials. Height 7¼ inches. Tiny chip on rim and
kiln kiss on base.

715 Standard glaze ewer decorated in 1896 by John Dee Wareham with chestnuts. Marks on the base include the $400-$600
Rookwood logo, the date, shape number 746 C and the artist's monogram. Height 7⅞ inches.

716 Vellum glaze vase with fruit blossom decoration, painted in 1905 by Sallie Coyne. Marks on the base include the $200-$300
Rookwood logo, the date, shape number 913 E, V for Vellum glaze body, V for Vellum glaze and the artist's
monogram. Height 6 inches. Some glaze pooling beneath the rim.

717   Standard glaze vase with wild rose decoration, painted in 1899 by Katherine Hickman. Marks on the base $300-$500
include the Rookwood logo, the date, shape number 172 C and the artist's monogram. Height 8⅜ inches.

718   Modern style Commercial vase covered with Bengal Brown glaze, made at Rookwood in 1960. Marks on the $300-$400
base include the Rookwood logo, the date, shape number 7073 and the words, "ROOKWOOD CINTI, O.".
Height 7⅞ inches.

719   High glaze vase with apple decoration, painted by Jens Jensen in 1948. Marks on the base include the Rookwood $600-$800
logo, the date, shape number S 2180 and the artist's monogram. Height 6½ inches.

720   Standard glaze vase with poppy decoration, done in 1900 by Lenore Asbury. Marks on the base include the $500-$700
Rookwood logo, the date, shape number 900 B and the artist's initials. Height 9⅛ inches.

721   Limoges style glaze vase decorated with swallows and oriental grasses by Hattie Horton in 1883. Marks on the $400-$600
base include Rookwood in block letters, the date, shape number 126, G for ginger clay, an impressed kiln mark
and the artist's initials. Height 8¾ inches.

722   Iris glaze vase decorated by Sara Sax in 1903 with parrot tulips. Marks on the base include the Rookwood logo, $5000-$7000
the date, shape number 926 B, W for white glaze and the artist's monogram. Height 10⅜ inches. Some glaze
bubbles at the base. Uncrazed.

723   Rare and impressive Vellum glaze vase decorated in 1910 by Kataro Shirayamadani with five cranes taking flight $5000-$7000
over a lake in a pine forest. Marks on the base include the Rookwood logo, the date, shape number 1660 B, V for
Vellum glaze body and the artist's cypher. Height 13¼ inches. Drilled.

724   Good carved mat glaze vase with flowering cactus decoration, done in 1905 by Kataro Shirayamadani. Marks on $2500-$3500
the base include the Rookwood logo, the date, shape number 907 D and the artist's cypher. Height 11¼ inches.
Grinding chips on the base.

725   Good Sea Green vase with iris decoration, painted in 1904 by Mary Nourse. Marks on the base include the $5500-$7500
Rookwood logo, the date, shape number 907 DD, G for Sea Green glaze and the artist's initials. Height 10½
inches. Exhibitions: "From Our Native Clay" The American Ceramic Arts Society, 1987, Item 41 in the catalog,
color plate on page 42.

726   Dull finish Spanish water jug decorated in an oriental manner by M.A. Daly in 1885 with a large bird perched on a spray of prunus blossoms. The shoulder is encircled with a die cut border, enhanced with fired on gold. Marks on the base include Rookwood in block letters, the date, shape number 41, Y for yellow clay and the artist's initials. Height 9 inches. A tiny chip off the base is barely visible. $2000-$3000

727   Large tonalistic landscape vase, painted in 1915 by E.T. Hurley and covered with Vellum glaze. Marks on the base include the Rookwood logo, the date, shape number 271 A, V for Vellum glaze body and the artist's initials. Height 14 inches. Some glaze peppering. $2000-$3000

728   Mat glaze bust of a small boy, made at Rookwood in 1913. Marks inside the piece include the Rookwood logo, the date, shape number 1849 and a wheel ground x. Height 9¾ inches. $600-$800

729   Unusual mat glaze vase with water lily and leaping frog decoration, painted by Jens Jensen in 1944. Marks on the base include the Rookwood logo, the date, shape number 2190 and the artist's monogram. Height 6⅛ inches. A ½ inch chip in the rim has been repaired. $800-$1200

730   Unusual Standard glaze pocket vase painted with flowering grasses and berry vines by Marie Rauchfuss in 1896. $300-$500
Marks on the base include the Rookwood logo, the date, shape number 90 C and the artist's initials. Height 3¾
inches.

731   Standard glaze vase with lotus decoration, done in 1902 by Sallie Coyne. Marks on the base include the $600-$800
Rookwood logo, the date, shape number 916 B and the artist's monogram. Height 9⅛ inches. Minor glaze
discoloration and slight scratch.

732   Green tinted high glaze plate with formal fruit compote decoration done by Arthur Conant circa 1920. Marks on $300-$500
the base include the Rookwood logo (reversed R and P with no flames), a Glover Collection label, number 746
and the artist's monogram. Diameter 10 inches.

733   Rare Aventurine glaze vase decorated with repeating floral patterns by Sara Sax in 1920. Marks on the base $1000-$1500
include the Rookwood logo, the date, shape number 1091 D and the artist's monogram. Height 6⅜ inches. Minor
grinding flakes off the base.

734   Standard glaze cracker jar decorated with prunus blossoms by M.A. Daly in 1885. Marks on the base include $200-$300
Rookwood in block letters, the date, shape number 240, R for red clay and the artist's initials. Height 7⅛ inches.
Lid missing, roughness on base and rim.

735　Standard glaze vase with jonquil decor, painted in 1899 by Sallie Coyne. Marks on the base include the Rookwood logo, the date, shape number 568 C and the artist's monogram. Height 6⅞ inches. Minor scratches.　　$250-$300

736　High glaze bowl with stylized floral decor, painted in 1929 by Lorinda Epply. Marks on the base include the Rookwood logo, the date, shape number 6033 and the artist's monogram. Height 3½ inches. Grinding chip at base.　　$300-$500

737　Architectural Faience tile with a woodland scene, made at Rookwood circa 1915. Marks on the back include the Rookwood Faience logo, the numbers 1981 YC 1 and the number 6 in a circle. Size is 12 x 12 inches. Minor edge chips.　　$800-$1200

738　Standard glaze pocket vase decorated with clover by William Klemm in 1901. Marks on the base include the Rookwood logo, the date, shape number 90 C and the artist's monogram. Height 3¾ inches.　　$200-$300

739　Unusual Arts and Crafts vase with repeating incised patterns under a very organic green glaze, executed in 1904 by Elizabeth Lincoln. Marks on the base include the Rookwood logo, the date, shape number 299 CZ and the artist's initials. Height 10⅛ inches. Unobtrusive grinding chip on base.　　$1200-$1800

740 Standard glaze two handled vase with poppy decoration, done in 1902 by Irene Bishop. Marks on the base include the Rookwood logo, the date, shape number 604 D and the artist's initials. Height 7 inches. A tight line descends from the rim. — $250-$350

741 Vellum glaze vase with landscape decorated by Fred Rothenbusch in 1916. Marks on the base include the Rookwood logo, the date, shape number 900 D, V for Vellum glaze body and the artist's initials. Height 7 inches. Peppering in the glaze and two lines descending from the rim. — $200-$400

742 Large Limoges style glaze jardiniere with applied and painted leaves and flowers, decorated by an unknown artist in 1882. Marks on the base include Rookwood in block letters, the date and G for ginger clay impressed twice. Height 13¼ inches. Some chips and losses to the applied foliage. — $500-$700

743 High glaze vase with incised grass decoration, done in 1882 by Harriet Wenderoth. Marks on the base include Rookwood in block letters, the date, Cincinnati Art Museum accession numbers 26:99 and the artist's initials. Height 8¼ inches. — $300-$500

744 Vellum glaze vase decorated with a woodland scene by Ed Diers in 1916. Marks on the base include the Rookwood logo, the date, shape number 900 D, V for Vellum glaze body and the artist's initials. Height 7 inches. Some peppering in the glaze. Uncrazed. — $800-$1200

745   Monumental Standard glaze jardiniere decorated with two carved and electroplated copper dragons, done in $15000-$25000
       1899 and unquestionably the work of Kataro Shirayamadani. The dragons are also painted and incised in the
design on the side of the piece, appearing to emerge from clouds before reaching the rim. Marks on the base
include the Rookwood logo, the date and shape number S 1476. Height 11¼ inches. Areas of glaze loss near each
dragon have been repaired and some glaze loss is evident near the base and on the base.

746   Standard glaze ewer decorated in 1900 by Josephine Zettel with tulips. Marks on the base include the Rookwood logo, the date, shape number 496 B and the artist's monogram. Height 11⅛ inches. $700-$900

747   High glaze vase with stylized deer decor, painted by Wilhelmine Rehm in 1944. Marks on the base include the Rookwood logo, the date, shape number 614 E and the artist's initials. Height 8⅜ inches. Minor grinding chips on base. $300-$500

748   Standard glaze whiskey jug decorated with the portrait of a cavalier by Harriet Wilcox in 1896. Marks on the base include the Rookwood logo, the date, shape number 747 C and the artist's initials. Height 5¾ inches. Handle broken and repaired and some minor glaze scratches. $600-$800

749   Large Standard glaze vase decorated in 1898 by Anna Valentien with goldenrod. Marks on the base include the Rookwood logo, the date, shape 531 C and the artist's initials. Height 10⅝ inches. $1350-$1750

750   Mat glaze vase with stylized floral decoration by Wilhelmine Rehm, painted in 1927. Marks on the base include the Rookwood logo, the date, shape number 912 and the artist's monogram. Height 6⅛ inches. $400-$600

751 Large and showy mat glaze vase decorated with repeating Art Deco patterns of stylized flowers by C.S. Todd in 1920. Marks on the base include the Rookwood logo, the date, shape number 614 B, V for Vellum glaze body and the artist's initials. Height 14⅞ inches. $2500-$3500

752 Large Architectural Faience circular plaque depicting what may be one of Columbus's vessels, cast in high relief at Rookwood in 1926. Marks on the back include the Rookwood logo twice, the date, shape number 3242 Y, the numbers 1 through 8 and the number 0484 both impressed and incised. On the face of the plaque, below the crashing sea can be found the signature of William P. McDonald, the designer of the piece. Diameter is 25⅞ inches. Some minor nicks on the surface and a 5 x 1½ inch chunk broken from the outer rim and crudely reattached. $2000-$3000

753 Standard glaze vase decorated with nasturtiums by Clara Lindeman in 1901. Marks on the base include the Rookwood logo, the date, shape number 531 E and the artist's initials. Height 5½ inches. $300-$500

754 Mat glaze two handled vase decorated by Katherine Jones in 1927 with fruit blossoms. Marks on the base include the Rookwood logo, the date, shape number 2077 and the artist's initials. Height 6⅛ inches. $400-$600

755 Standard glaze vase with jonquil decoration, painted in 1902 by M.A. Daly. Marks on the base include the Rookwood logo, the date, shape number 901 B, Y for yellow (Standard) glaze and the artist's full name. Height 11⅜ inches. $1400-$1800

756   Standard glaze vase decorated with wild grapes by Leona Van Briggle in 1901. Marks on the base include the Rookwood logo, the date, shape number 916 D and the artist's initials. Height 5½ inches. $300-$400

757   Standard glaze dish decorated with three cheese stealing mice who have just knocked over a bottle of milk, painted in 1892 by Kataro Shirayamadani. Marks on the base include the Rookwood logo, the date, shape number 59 P, W for white clay and the artist's cypher. Diameter 7¼ inches. Crack in rim. The large yellow area above the mice is purposeful, depicting milk spilled from the bottle. $200-$400

758   Arts and Crafts style Vellum glaze plaque decorated by E.T. Hurley in 1912. The artist's initials appear in the lower right corner. Marks on the back include the Rookwood logo, the date, V for Vellum glaze body and the artist's initials. Size 10⅜ x 8¼ inches $3000-$4000

759   Mat glaze vase decorated with poppies in 1939 by Kataro Shirayamadani. Marks on the base include the Rookwood logo, the date, shape number 6194 D and the artist's cypher. Height 6⅛ inches. $700-$900

760   Standard glaze ewer with wild rose decoration, painted in 1896 by M.A. Daly. Marks on the base include the Rookwood logo, the date, shape number 495 A and the artist's initials. Height 9⅛ inches. $800-$1200

761   Arts and Crafts mat glaze vase decorated with incised and painted stylized flowers and leaves by Elizabeth Lincoln in 1920. Marks on the base include the Rookwood logo, the date, shape number 1358 C and the artist's initials. Height 11⅛ inches. $600-$800

762   Dull finish vase decorated with blue flowers and a single dragonfly by Albert Valentien in 1883. The collar and base are encircled with a variety of die impressed patterns, all covered with fired on gold. Marks on the base include Rookwood in block letters, the date, shape number 162 B, Y for yellow clay, an impressed kiln mark and the artist's initials. Height 10½ inches. $1500-$2000

763   Cameo glaze bowl decorated with clover in 1889, possibly by Sallie Toohey. Marks on the base include the Rookwood logo, the date, shape number 520 and what appears to be Toohey's monogram. Diameter is 9¼ inches. $300-$500

764   Vellum glaze plaque decorated by Sallie Coyne in 1916. The artist's monogram appears in the lower right hand corner. Marks on the back include the Rookwood logo, the date and V for Vellum glaze body. Affixed to the frame is an original Rookwood paper logo and an original paper label with the title, "A Summer Morning S.E. Coyne". Size 5¼ x 8¼. $1750-$2250

765   Standard glaze vase decorated with lilies of the valley by Irene Bishop in 1902. Marks on the base include the Rookwood logo, the date, shape number 30 F and the artist's initials. Height 6 inches. $300-$500

766   Large, colorful and crisply decorated Vellum glaze vase, painted in 1928 by Lenore Asbury with hanging leaves and berries. Marks on the base include the Rookwood logo, the date, shape number 2551, V for Vellum glaze and the artist's initials. Height 14⅛ inches. Minor scratch. Uncrazed. $4500-$5500

767   Rare and unusual Standard glaze tankard, painted in 1897 with cranes flying through a pine forest by Kataro Shirayamadani. Marks on the base include the Rookwood logo, the date, shape number 564 B, a small diamond shaped esoteric mark and the artist's cypher. Height 11¼ inches. Small glaze flake from rim and straight craze line in the body which does not show on the inside. $4000-$6000

768   Large and impressive Vellum glaze vase decorated with life size irises by Ed Diers in 1929. Marks on the base include the Rookwood logo, the date, shape number 925 A, V for Vellum glaze and the artist's initials. Height 15½ inches. Glaze discoloration near the rim on one side. Uncrazed. $4000-$5000

769   Large and important Standard glaze pitcher decorated with the portrait of a Native American by Grace Young in 1899. Marks on the base include the Rookwood logo, the date, shape number 838 A, the title, "Sleeping Bear Sioux" and the artist's monogram. Height 14⅜ inches. Minor rough spot on base and on end of handle and minor glaze scratches. $10000-$15000

770   Standard glaze jardiniere decorated with wild roses by M.A. Daly in 1887. Marks on the base include the $700-$900
Rookwood logo, the date, shape number 180 C, L for light Standard glaze, S for sage green clay and the artist's
initials. Height 7½ inches.

771   Early Vellum glaze vase with sprays of fruit blossoms, painted in 1904 by Sara Sax. Marks on the base include the $400-$600
Rookwood logo, the date, shape number 166 Z, V for Vellum glaze body and the artist's monogram. Height 4½
inches. Uncrazed.

772   Unusual Rookwood Architectural Faience tile, decorated with an Arts and Crafts style landscape by Cecil Duell, $1500-$2500
circa 1915. Marks on the back include Rookwood Faience, shape number 1157 and the artist's initials. A small
embossed square appears in the lower right hand front corner of the plaque. Size 4⅜ x 8⅞ inches.

773   Standard glaze vase with lily of the valley decoration, done in 1907 by Laura Lindeman. Marks on the base $300-$400
include the Rookwood logo, the date, shape number 917 D and the artist's initials. Height 6¾ inches.

774   Vellum glaze vase decorated with an Arts and Crafts woodland scene by Lorinda Epply in 1912. Marks on the $1000-$1250
base include the Rookwood logo, the date, shape number 925 D, V for Vellum glaze body, V for Vellum glaze
and the artist's monogram. Height 8½ inches.

775 Unusual Standard glaze vase, carved and painted in 1898 by M.A. Daly with poppies. Marks on the base include the Rookwood logo, the date, shape number 856 C, a faded paper label and the artist's initials. Height 13 inches. $1250-$1750

776 Dull finish potpourri jar with reversible lid having apple blossom decoration, painted in 1887 by M.A. Daly. Marks on the base include the Rookwood logo, the date, shape number 282 C, W 3 for a type of white clay, S for smear (dull) glaze and the artist's initials. Height 7½ inches. $1000-$1500

777 Architectural Faience tile depicting a woodland scene, made at Rookwood circa 1915. Marks on the back include the Rookwood Faience logo, the number 1227 Y 1 and the number 4 in a circle. The number 1 also appears on the lower edge of the tile. Size is 16 x 16 inches. Minor edge and surface chips. $1000-$1500

778 Modern style Commercial vase covered with Vista Blue glaze, made at Rookwood in 1960. Marks on the base include the Rookwood logo, the date, shape number 7073 and the words, "ROOKWOOD CINTI, O.". Height 7⅞ inches. $300-$400

779 Large mat glaze vase with lotus blossom decoration, painted in 1924 by Katherine Jones. Marks on the base include the Rookwood logo, the date, shape number 2372 and the artist's initials. Height 16⅝ inches. Grinding chips on the base. $1250-$1750

780   Standard glaze ewer with wild rose decoration, painted in 1897 by Olga Reed. Marks on the base include the Rookwood logo, the date, shape number 481, a diamond shaped esoteric mark and the artist's initials. Height 9¼ inches. $300-$500

781   Dull finish vase with incised and painted vine and berry decoration, done in 1881 by Harriet (Nettie) Wenderoth. Marks incised in the base include Rookwood Pottery Cincinnati 1881 in script and the artist's initials, N.W. Height 10¼ inches. Tight ¾ inch line descends from the rim. $400-$600

782   Standard glaze pocket vase with floral decoration, painted by an unknown artist in 1896. Marks on the base include the Rookwood logo, the date, shape number 90 C and the partially obscured artist's initials. Height 3⅝ inches. Repaired. $200-$300

783   Vellum glaze plaque decorated with a harbor scene by E.T. Hurley in 1942. The artist's initials appear in the lower left hand corner. Marks on the back include the Rookwood logo, the date and the numbers, 8 x 10. Size 7¼ x 9¼ inches. Uncrazed. $5500-$7500

784   Dull finish potpourri jar with reversible lid, decorated with stylized mums by Artus Van Briggle in 1887. Marks on the base include the Rookwood logo, the date, shape number 326, W 7 for a type of white clay, S for smear (dull) glaze and the artist's initials. Height 6¼ inches. $500-$700

785   Rare Green Vellum glaze vase decorated with several sailing boats by Sallie Coyne in 1909. Marks on the base include the Rookwood logo, the date, shape number 952 C, V for Vellum glaze body, GV for Green Vellum glaze, a wheel ground x and the artist's monogram. Height 10¼ inches. Cracked and repaired. $1000-$1200

786   Experimental Standard glaze vase covered with Goldstone effect. Marks on the base include the Rookwood logo, the date, shape number 538 E, the notation, "Bailey Black", D for dark Standard glaze and Cincinnati Art Museum accession numbers, "135. '00". Height 7 inches. Small bruise inside the rim. Joseph Bailey was Rookwood's superintendent for many years and spent a great deal of his time experimenting with clays and glazes, this piece being the result of one of these experiments. Listed: S.G. Burt's book, "2,292 pieces of early Rookwood Pottery in the Cincinnati Art Museum in 1916", as item 23 on page 191. $1000-$1500

787   Iris glaze vase decorated with trailing flowers by Sallie Coyne in 1910. Marks on the base include the Rookwood logo, the date, shape number 950 D, W for white glaze and the artist's monogram. Height 8½ inches. $800-$1000

788   Vellum glaze plaque decorated in 1914 by C.J. McLaughlin. The artist's monogram appears in the lower right hand corner. Marks on the back include the Rookwood logo, the date and V for Vellum glaze body. Size 5⅛ x 9 inches. $1200-$1500

789   Standard glaze two handled vase with clover decoration, painted in 1893 by Olga Reed. Marks on the base include the Rookwood logo, the date, shape number 459 D, W for white clay and the artist's initials. Height 5⅞ inches. Small base chips, one burst glaze bubble and some glaze discoloration. $200-$300

790   Early high glaze vase done in 1882 in the manner of Maria Longworth Nichols with oriental symbols and designs and a small bird chasing a moth. Marks on the base include Rookwood in block letters and the date. Height 11 inches. This vase is remarkably similar to 674 in this catalog, a work attributed to Mrs. Nichols by the Everson Museum of Art. $1250-$1750

791 Iris glaze vase with clover decoration, painted by Clara Lindeman in 1904. Marks on the base include the Rookwood logo, the date, shape number 808, W for white glaze and the artist's initials. Height 7½ inches. — $900-$1100

792 Large and showy Standard glaze vase with two large loop handles and chrysanthemum decoration, painted in 1891 by M.A. Daly. Marks on the base include the Rookwood logo, the date, shape number 531 E, W for white clay and the artist's initials twice. Height 11 inches. Tight crack in one handle has been repaired. — $1200-$1800

793 Standard glaze mug with corn decoration, painted by Leona Van Briggle in 1899. Marks on the base include the Rookwood logo, the date, shape number 656 and the artist's monogram. Height 4⅞ inches. Glaze scratches. — $250-$300

794 Standard glaze plate decorated with a mouse by an unknown artist in 1888. Marks on the base include the Rookwood logo, the date, shape number 59 P and W for white clay. Diameter is 6½ inches. A small chip in the rim has been repaired. — $150-$250

795 Vellum glaze vase decorated with cactus flowers by Ed Diers in 1912. Marks on the base include the Rookwood logo, the date, shape number 1658 E, V for Vellum glaze body, V for Vellum glaze and the artist's initials. Height 8⅛ inches. — $400-$600

796   Large Standard glaze jardiniere with grape decor, done by Albert Valentien in 1888. Marks on the base include $1200-$1500
the Rookwood logo, the date, shape number 180 A, S for sage green clay, L for light Standard glaze and the
artist's initials. Height 10½ inches.

797   Early dull finish vase with incised decoration of english ivy, done circa 1881 by Harriet Wenderoth. The base is $200-$300
inscribed, Rookwood Pottery N.W. Height 6¼ inches.

798   Mat glaze vase with Arts and Crafts decoration, carved and painted by William Hentschel in 1911. Marks on the $800-$1000
base include the Rookwood logo, the date, shape number 556 C and the artist's initials. Height 12¼ inches.

799   Standard glaze vase with holly decoration, painted in 1899 by Howard Altman. Marks on the base include the $300-$400
Rookwood logo, the date, shape number 735 DD, a wheel ground x and the artist's monogram. Height 7 inches.

800   Unusual Butterfat glaze bowl, decorated in heavy slip with red flowers by Elizabeth Barrett in 1946. Marks on the $600-$800
base include the Rookwood logo, the date, shape number 2813 C and the artist's initials. Diameter is 13¼ inches.
From the collection of John Reichardt, Kilnmaster at Rookwood from 1943 until 1960.

801   Mat glaze flower bowl with nude figures at either end, designed by Louise Abel and Kataro Shirayamadani and $250-$350
cast at Rookwood in 1927. Marks on the base include the Rookwood logo, the date, shape number 2923 and the
cast monogram of Louise Abel. Height 7 inches.

802   Mat glaze Commercial Rook trivet made at Rookwood in 1919. Marks on the base include the Rookwood logo, $200-$300
the date shape number 1794 and P for porcelain body. Size 5⅜ inches square. Tiny chips at the edges.

803   Vellum glaze plaque decorated in 1917 by Ed Diers. The artist's monogram appears in the lower left hand corner. $3000-$4000
Marks on the back include the Rookwood logo and the date. Affixed to the frame is an original paper title, "Grey
Day E. Diers". Size 7 ¼ x 9¼ inches.

804   Mat glaze tankard with stylized thistle decoration, painted and incised by Rose Fechheimer in 1905. Marks on the $400-$600
base include the Rookwood logo, the date, shape number 775, V for Vellum glaze body and the artist's
monogram. Height 7¼ inches. Some glaze peppering.

805   Standard glaze two handled vase decorated with daisies in 1893 by Carrie Steinle. Marks on the base include the $250-$350
Rookwood logo, the date, shape number 459 E, W for white clay, L for light Standard glaze and the artist's
monogram. Height 4 inches. Minor glaze scratches.

806   Standard glaze vase painted in an Art Nouveau manner with poppies by Mary Nourse in 1903. Marks on the base $650-$750
include the Rookwood logo, the date, shape number 907 DD, L for light Standard glaze and the artist's initials.
Height 9¼ inches. Several glaze scratches.

807   Mat glaze vase with stylized floral decoration, painted in 1930 by Lorinda Epply. Marks on the base include the $300-$500
Rookwood logo, the date, shape number 942 B, a small fan shaped esoteric mark and the artist's monogram.
Height 8⅜ inches. Moderate glaze peppering.

808   Vellum glaze vase with rose decoration, painted in 1928 by E.T. Hurley. Marks on the base include the $900-$1100
Rookwood logo, the date, shape number 6013, V for Vellum glaze and the artist's initials. Height 6⅝ inches.
Uncrazed.

809   Vellum glaze scenic plaque painted by Lenore Asbury in 1921. The artist's initials appear in the lower right hand $3000-$4000
corner. Marks on the back include the Rookwood logo and the date. Size is approximately 9 x 12 inches.
Pictured: "Rookwood Its Golden Era of Art Pottery 1880 - 1929" Edwin J. Kircher and Barbara and Joseph
Agranoff, privately published in 1969, Color plate 10, bottom.

810   Standard glaze ewer with cherry blossom decoration, painted in 1900 by Josephine Zettel. Marks on the base $300-$400
include the Rookwood logo, the date, shape number 725 E and the artist's monogram. Height 5¼ inches.

811   Mat glaze two handled vase with apple blossom decoration by Margaret McDonald, done in 1929. Marks on the $700-$900
base include the Rookwood logo, the date, shape number 6114 C and the artist's initials. Height 10¾ inches.
Small unobtrusive glaze skip on rim.

812 Standard glaze vase decorated with yellow flowers by William McDonald in 1893 and overlaid with silver by Gorham. Marks on the base include the Rookwood logo, the date, shape number 496 B, W for white clay and the artist's initials. Marks on the silver include R 1355 and Gorham Mfg. Co.. Height 10½ inches. Part of the lip has been damaged and repaired and a small area of silver near the neck is a bit loose. — $2000-$3000

813 Large Vellum glaze banded scenic vase showing several birds flying through a forest, decorated in 1910 by Kataro Shirayamadani. Marks on the base include the Rookwood logo, the date, shape number 1660 A, V for Vellum glaze body, a wheel ground x and the artist's cypher. Height 16 inches. — $4000-$5000

814 Dull finish vase decorated with incised and painted clover and butterflies, probably by Helen W. Peachey, a member of the Women's Pottery Club, in 1887. Most of the incising is enhanced with fired on gold. Marks on the base include the shape number 95 C, S for sage green clay, the date August 28th 1887 and the artist's monogram which is incised in one place and painted in another. Height 5⅝ inches. Some roughness on the rim and a small area of loose glaze near the base. — $500-$700

815 Handsome high glaze vase with carved and brightly painted tulip decoration, done in 1927 by Kataro Shirayamadani. Marks on the base include the Rookwood logo, the date, shape number 977 and the artist's cypher. Height 10⅝ inches. — $5000-$7000

816 Vellum glaze vase by Mary Grace Denzler, decorated in 1917 with a woodland scene. Marks on the base include the Rookwood logo, the date, shape number 900 D, V for Vellum glaze body and the artist's monogram. Height 7 inches. — $800-$1200

817   Monumental and important Iris glaze vase by Carl Schmidt, decorated in 1908 with lifelike wisteria. Marks on the $20000-$30000
       base include the Rookwood logo, the date, shape number 901 XX, W for white glaze and the artist's monogram.
       Height 20¾ inches. Small burst glaze bubble at rim, ¼ inch scratch in glaze, minor ¼ inch glaze discoloration.
       This piece is from Rookwood Pottery's Museum, descending in the family of one of the last owners of Rookwood
       and has never been offered for sale until now.

818   Dull finish ewer decorated with incised and painted grasses by Harriet Wenderoth in 1882. Marks on the base include Rookwood in block letters, the date and the artist's initials. Height 12 inches. $400-$600

819   Unusual Iris glaze lidded chocolate pot decorated with holly by Ed Diers in 1904. Marks on the base include the Rookwood logo, the date, shape number 772, W for white glaze and the artist's monogram. Height 9¾ inches. $1250-$1750

820   Two Architectural Faience tiles depicting a woodland scene, made at Rookwood circa 1915. Marks on the backs of both tiles include the Rookwood Faience logo, the numbers 1611 1226 Y and the number 4 in a circle. The left hand tile also has the number 1 on the back and on the lower edge while the right hand tile has the number 84 on the back and the number 2 on the lower edge. Size of each tile is 12 x 12 inches. Minor edge and surface chips. $1500-$2500

821   Standard glaze two handled vase with floral decoration by Carrie Steinle, painted in 1905. Marks on the base include the Rookwood logo, the date, shape number 459 E, a wheel ground x and the artist's monogram. Height 3⅞ inches. $250-$350

822   Limoges style glaze vase decorated in 1882 by Albert Valentien with hollyhocks. Marks on the base include Rookwood in block letters, the date, an impressed anchor mark and the artist's initials. Height 10½ inches. Tight spider cracks in base only. $700-$900

823 High glaze potpourri jar with inner lid and cover, decorated with stylized flowers by C.S. Todd in 1921. Marks on the base include the Rookwood logo, the date, shape number 1321 C and the artist's initials. Height 5½ inches. $700-$900

824 Vellum glaze plaque decorated in 1920 by E.T. Hurley. The artist's initials appear in the lower left hand corner. Marks on the back include the Rookwood logo and the date. Affixed to the frame are an original Rookwood paper logo and an original paper label with the title, "Evening, E.T. Hurley". Size 3⅞ x 7¾ inches. $1500-$2500

825 Mat glaze mug with carved floral decoration, done by Cecil Duell in 1909. Marks on the base include the Rookwood logo, the date, shape number 1008 B, a triangular shaped esoteric mark, a wheel ground x and the artist's initials. Height 5⅛ inches. $200-$300

826 Unusual high glaze pitcher decorated by Jens Jensen with stylized flowers and the faces of two women in 1949. Marks on the base include the Rookwood logo, the date, shape number 6757 and the artist's monogram. Height 7¼ inches. $1200-$1800

827 High glaze compote with striated floral decoration in the bowl, done by Sara Sax in 1924. Marks on the base include the Rookwood logo, the date, shape number 2802 and the artist's monogram. Height 4⅛ inches. $300-$400

828 Tall Standard glaze vase with handsome dogwood decoration, painted in 1883 by Amelia Sprague. Marks on the base include the Rookwood logo, the date, shape number 538 C, W for white clay and the artist's monogram. Height 11⅞ inches. There is a small kiln kiss on the rim. $800-$1000

829   Standard glaze vase decorated in 1898 by Sadie Markland with the portrait of a Native American. Marks on the $1500-$2500
base include the Rookwood logo, the date, shape number 814 B, L for light Standard glaze, two impressed V's,
one above the other, the name (Cita'ge) (Hidatsa) and the artist's initials. Height 7⅞ inches. Glaze scratches
mostly on the back and sides.

830   Large Vellum glaze vase decorated by E.T. Hurley in 1916 with a band of fruit blossoms around the shoulder. $600-$800
Marks on the base include the Rookwood logo, the date, shape number 324 A, the number 393, a wheel ground
x and the artist's initials. Height 15⅜ inches. Drilled and glaze peppering.

831   Standard glaze jug with wheat decoration, painted by O.G. Reed in 1893. Marks on the base include the $500-$700
Rookwood logo, the date, shape number 694, W for white clay and the artist's initials. Height 6½ inches.

832   Vellum glaze harbor scene plaque decorated by Sara Sax in 1913. The artist's name appears in the lower right $1500-$2500
hand corner. Marks on the back include the Rookwood logo, the date and V for Vellum glaze body. Size 3⅞ x 7⅞
inches.

833   Standard glaze bowl with leaf and berry decoration, done by Lenore Asbury in 1896. Marks on the base include $250-$350
the Rookwood logo, the date, shape number 708 B and the artist's initials. Height 3⅜ inches.

834   Rare Iris glaze vase decorated in 1905 by Carl Schmidt with two white egrets wading in a grassy swamp. Marks $5000-$7000
on the base include the Rookwood logo, the date, shape number 950 C, W for white glaze and the artist's
monogram. Height 10⅜ inches. Drilled.

835   Very pretty Iris glaze vase decorated with blue irises by Carl Schmidt in 1900. Marks on the base include the $3000-$4000
Rookwood logo, the date, shape number 796 B, W for white glaze and the artist's monogram. Height 9¾ inches.

836   Unusual Sea Green vase decorated with long leaves which were incised, painted and outlined in heavy black slip $1250-$1750
by Artus Van Briggle in 1898. Marks on the base include the Rookwood logo, the date, shape number 735 D, G
for Sea Green glaze, a star shaped esoteric mark, a wheel ground x and the artist's initials. Height 6¾ inches.

837   Standard glaze vase decorated with two ducks flying through tree tops by Albert Valentien in 1885. Marks on the $1200-$1800
base include Rookwood in block letters, the date, shape number 216, R for red clay and the artist's initials.
Height 12 inches. A tight spider crack in the center of the vase runs in several directions but is not easily seen.

838   Beautiful Black Iris glaze vase, decorated in 1911 by Carl Schmidt with Japanese irises. Marks on the base include $5000-$7000
the Rookwood logo, the date, shape number 1655 E, W for white glaze, the number 1 impressed above the logo
and the artist's monogram. Height 7¾ inches. Some damaged at the rim has been repaired.

839   Commercial mat glaze pitcher with molded corn decoration, designed and possibly colored by John Dee $400-$600
Wareham. Marks on the base include the Rookwood logo, the date, shape number 332 Z and the artist's full
name. Height 9⅛ inches.

840   Unusual Limoges style glaze six-sided vase, decorated by Albert Valentien and Albert Humphreys in 1882, $1000-$1500
showing four babies playing in a wooded area with a dragonfly passing overhead. Marks on the base include
Rookwood in block letters, the date, an impressed anchor and both artists' initials. Height 7 inches. Some small
glaze skips and tiny burst bubbles appear near the base.

841   Vellum glaze plaque decorated by Lorinda Epply in 1922. The artist's monogram appears in the lower right hand $2000-$3000
corner. Marks on the back include the Rookwood logo and the date. Affixed to the frame are an original
Rookwood paper logo and an original paper title, "Foggy Morning, L. Epply. Size 7⅞ x 9⅞ inches. Several burst
glaze bubbles on the surface.

842   Standard glaze vase with dogwood decoration, painted by Irene Bishop in 1900. Marks on the base include the $200-$300
Rookwood logo, the date, shape number 667 and the artist's initials. Height 6⅜ inches. Repair to rim and chip at
base.

843   Impressive Standard glaze ewer with large areas of Goldstone effect, showing a large encircling dragon and $3000-$4000
painted by M.A. Daly in 1889. Marks on the base include the Rookwood logo, the date, shape number 468 A, D
for dark Standard glaze and the artist's initials. Height 13½ inches. A small dimple in the spout is under the glaze
and occurred in the making.

844 Tall Standard glaze vase decorated with carnations by Albert Valentien in 1890. Marks on the base include the Rookwood logo, the date, shape number 553 B, L for light Standard glaze and the artist's initials. Height 13 inches. $800-$1200

845 Iris glaze vase decorated with a single Japanese iris by Kataro Shirayamadani in 1894. Marks on the base include the Rookwood logo, the date, shape number 589 F, W for white clay, several partially obscured marks in red, probably accession numbers from the Cincinnati Art Museum and the artist's cypher. Height 7 inches. Some slight underglaze discoloration beneath the rim. Possibly Listed: S.G. Burt's book, "2,292 pieces of early Rookwood Pottery in the Cincinnati Art Museum in 1916" as item 79 on page 111. $1200-$1500

846 Important Standard glaze charger decorated with the portrait of a young Native American boy, painted by Grace Young in 1898. Marks on the back include the Rookwood logo, the date, shape number T 1061 B, the title, <u>Moki Rabbit Hunter</u> and the artist's monogram. Diameter is 12⅝ inches. The charger was broken cleanly in half many years ago and has recently been completely restored. $3500-$5500

847 Standard glaze pitcher decorated with mistletoe by Pauline Peters-Baurer in 1893. Marks on the base include the Rookwood logo, the date, shape number 259 E, W for white clay and the artist's monogram. Height 4 inches. $200-$400

848 High glaze vase with bright floral decoration, thought to be the work of Elizabeth Barrett. Marks on the base include the Rookwood logo, the date and shape number 2970. Height 11¾ inches. $500-$700

849   Vellum glaze vase with floral decoration, painted in 1917 by Patti Conant. Marks on the base include the $500-$700
Rookwood logo, the date, shape number 1658 E, V for Vellum glaze body and the artist's monogram. Height 8
inches.

850   Blue tinted high glaze bowl decorated in 1926 with blue roses and repeating patterns by Sara Sax. Marks on the $800-$1000
base include the Rookwood logo, the date, shape number 2258 and the artist's monogram. Diameter is 13⅛
inches.

851   Mat glaze vase with fruit blossom decoration, painted in 1935 by Margaret McDonald. Marks on the base include $200-$300
the Rookwood logo, the date, shape number 2969 and the artist's monogram. Height 7¼ inches. Moderate glaze
peppering.

852   Vellum glaze scenic plaque painted by Kataro Shirayamadani in 1912. The artist's cypher appears in the lower $2500-$3500
left hand corner. Marks on the back include the Rookwood logo, the date and V for Vellum glaze body. Size is 7⅝
x 3¾ inches.

853   Crisp Standard glaze two handled vase with jonquil decoration, painted by Mary Nourse in 1900. Marks on the $600-$800
base include the Rookwood logo, the date, shape number 614 E, L for light Standard glaze and the artist's initials.
Height 8 inches. Uncrazed. Very minor glaze scratch.

NOTES

THE BOOKSTORE

Cincinnati Art Galleries is the largest Publisher of classic books on Rookwood Pottery in the world. We have reprinted Herbert Peck's, *The Book of Rookwood Pottery* in soft cover and Virginia Raymond Cummins' informative, *Rookwood Pottery Potpourri*. We also offer copies of Peck's *The Second Book of Rookwood Pottery* and our own classic text, *The Glover Collection*. In addition we offer several major works on other potteries and two important books which take an overall view of American Art Pottery.

Author	Title
CAG	**Rookwood II**
	Second only to the Glover Collection in numbers and second to none in quality, Rookwood II features over 800 exciting artist signed pieces of Rookwood with Museum quality examples from several major collections. Over 40 plaques, silver and copper overlays, carved mats, Art Deco and Art Nouveau themes, fabulous Iris and Sea Green glaze items and many other aesthetically and historically important pieces make this an incredibly informative and handsome book. Soft Cover $35.00 + $3.00 Shipping
CAG	**The Glover Collection**
	Destined to become the standard by which Rookwood and pottery auctions are measured for many years. The Glover Collection features over 1,200 items in full color with prices realized at the largest and most important auction of Rookwood ever held. This is the sale that broke all records for Rookwood and American Art Pottery. The most complete compilation of Rookwood ever undertaken, with very accurate descriptions of each piece in the sale. Soft Cover $45.00 + $4.00 Shipping
Peck	**The Book of Rookwood Pottery**
	The first in-depth coverage of Rookwood, written in 1968 and still considered the best place to start your "education". The most extensive historical look at the pottery includes many examples of decorated pieces, both in color and black and white. Aso included are photos of the pottery itself, its decorators and workers, architectural installations in the United States and a listing of marks used over Rookwood's 80 plus years of operation. 185 pages. Soft cover $19.95 + $2.00 Shipping
Peck	**The Second Book of Rookwood Pottery**
	A companion to the original Rookwood book with new findings, marks and photographs. This volume also includes a complete reproduction of Rookwood's Shape Record Book showing the profiles and sizes of over 4,000 different Rookwood production items. 185 pages. Hard cover $19.95 + $2.00 Shipping
Cummins	**Rookwood Pottery Potpourri**
	An extensive and sensitive look at the lives and stories of the artists and craftspersons who made Rookwood internationally famous. Many photos of the artists and 11 pages in full color of important pieces of Rookwood make this a wonderful compliment to any Art Pottery library. 134 pages. Soft cover $26.00 + $2.00 Shipping
Eidelberg	**From Our Native Clay**
	A most lavishly illustrated look at some of the finest examples of American Art Pottery ever assembled. Wonderful examples from private collections of members of the American Ceramic Arts Society grace this stylish full color book. Pieces of Rookwood, Newcomb, Teco, Weller, Van Briggle, Dedham, Fulper, Paul Revere, Pewabic, Marblehead, Walrath, Robineau, Grueby, Roseville and many others are included. 111 pages Hard cover $40.00 + $2.00 Shipping
Evans	**Art Pottery of the United States**
	An Encyclopedia of Producers and their marks together with a directory of Studio Potters working in the United States through 1960. One of the most complete listings of American Art Potteries ever undertaken, covering over 100 companies from Alberhill to Zark and some 1,500 Studio Potters. This 1987 revision is a most thorough look at ceramic art in America from the 1850s until the 1960s. 445 pages. Hard cover $45.00 + $2.00 Shipping Soft cover $25.00 + $2.00 Shipping
Franklin & James	**American Artists at Auction 5/85-5/90**
	A five year review of American Art sold in the United States from May 1985 thru May 1990. Includes works that did not sell or were withdrawn which gives a clearer indication of an artist's success at auction. Listing of unsold lots provide more examples of an artist's works that can then be viewed in sales catalogs. Over 30,000 entries listed. Soft cover $65.00 + $2.00 Shipping
Clark et. al.	**The Mad Patter of Biloxi – The Art & Life of George E. Ohr**
	One of the most beautiful Art Pottery books ever produced and an excellent scholarly work, this text contains over 190 pages of color and black and white photographs and extensive information on America's most unusual and truly gifted potter, George Ohr. Hard cover $65.00 + $3.00 Shipping
Nelson et. al.	**A Collector's Guide to Van Briggle Pottery**
	The most recent and complete guide to Van Briggle Pottery with 12 pages of color photos of rare and early pieces plus many black ad white photos. Also included are explanations of the many marks of Van Briggle and a complete history of the pottery. Included in the book is a price guide by Scott Nelson, updated in 1991 which covers most of the pieces pictured in the text. 178 pages. Soft cover $40.00 + $2.00 Shipping

Check, VISA or MasterCard only please

- -

Please send me the following books:

_____ copies CAG *Rookwood II*
@ $35.00 each softcover + $3 shipping and handling

_____ copies CAG *The Glover Collection*
@ $45.00 each softcover + $4 shipping and handling

_____ copies Peck *The Book of Rookwood Pottery*
@ $19.95 each softcover + $2 shipping and handling

_____ copies Peck *The Second Book of Rookwood Pottery*
@ $19.95 each softcover + $2 shipping and handling

_____ copies Cummins *Rookwood Pottery Potpourri*
@ $26.00 each hardcover + $2 shipping and handling

_____ copies Evans *Art Pottery of the United States*
@ $45.00 each hardcover + $2 shipping and handling

_____ copies Evans *Art Pottery of the United States*
@ $25.00 each softcover + $2 shipping and handling

_____ copies Nelson *Collectors Guide to Van Briggle Pottery*
@ $40.00 each softcover + $2 shipping and handling

_____ copies Franklin and James *American Artists at Auction*
@ $65.00 each softcover + $2 shipping and handling

_____ copies Eidelberg *From Our Native Clay*
@ $40.00 each hardcover + $2 shipping and handling

_____ copies Clark *The Mad Potter of Biloxi George Ohr*
@ $65.00 each hardcover + $3 shipping and handling

ORDER FORM

Name _____

Address_____

City _____

State _____Zip_____

Phone _____

Credit Card Number _____Ex: Date_____

Sub Total _____

Shipping and Handling_____

Ohio Shipments add 5.5%_____

Total _____

ABSENTEE BID ORDER FORM

I wish to place the following bids with Cincinnati Art Galleries to be executed during its Rookwood II auction, May 30th and 31st, 1992.

I understand that Cincinnati Art Galleries will execute my absentee bids as a convenience and will not be held responsible for any errors or failure to execute bids. I also understand that my absentee bids are subject to all parts of the "Conditions of Sale" which appear in this catalog, and that I am responsible for the purchase price and 10% buyer's premium and the 5.5% Ohio State Sales Tax for all items purchased.

I understand that I am responsible for packing and shipping cost of my purchases. Cincinnati Art Galleries will ship my purchases in the best way possible as soon as full payment has been received, and I understand that four to six weeks should be allowed for delivery.

Lot #	Description	Bid Price
_____	_____	_____
_____	_____	_____
_____	_____	_____
_____	_____	_____
_____	_____	_____
_____	_____	_____
_____	_____	_____
_____	_____	_____
_____	_____	_____
_____	_____	_____
_____	_____	_____
_____	_____	_____
_____	_____	_____
_____	_____	_____
_____	_____	_____
_____	_____	_____
_____	_____	_____
_____	_____	_____
_____	_____	_____
_____	_____	_____

Cincinnati Art Galleries will always attempt to purchase designated lots for the lowest possible amount in competition with other bidders, but we cannot be held responsible for errors or failure to bid. All terms of "Conditions of Sale" apply to absentee bidders as well as those present.

Name _____

Address _____

_____

Phone Number _____

Ohio Resale Number _____

Signature _____ Date _____

Cincinnati Art Galleries
635 Main Street
Cincinnati, OH 45202
513-381-2128
FAX 513-381-7527